THE LINES OF
TORRES VEDRAS

THE NAPOLEONIC LIBRARY

Other books in the series include:

www.frontline-books.com/napoleoniclibrary

THE LINES OF
TORRES VEDRAS

THE CORNERSTONE OF WELLINGTON'S STRATEGY IN THE PENINSULAR WAR 1809–1812

John Grehan

Frontline Books

THE LINES OF TORRES VEDRAS

The Cornerstone of Wellington's Strategy in the Peninsular War 1809–1812

First published in 2000 by Spellmount.

This edition published in 2015 by Frontline Books,
an imprint of Pen & Sword Books Ltd,
47 Church Street, Barnsley, S. Yorkshire, S70 2AS

ISBN: 978-1-47385-274-7

CIP data records for this title are available from the British Library

Printed and bound by CPI Group (UK) Ltd, Croydon, CR0 4YY
Typeset in 10.5/12.5 Palatino

For more information on our books, please email: info@frontline-books.com,
write to us at the above address, or visit:
www.frontline-books.com

Contents

List of Maps

Acknowledgements

This book could not have taken its present form without the assistance of many people and I would like to acknowledge the contribution that each of them has made. I must first thank Ian Fletcher for recommending the book for publication and for his accurate and constructive advice. For the translations of Koch's *Memoirs de Masséna* and de L'Ain's *Vie Militaire du General Foy* I am indebted to Jane Craufurd-Hoyle. Her unsolicited assistance and her frank assessment of my work proved to be utterly invaluable.

I must also express my gratitude to Colonel José Manuel Dos Santos Dias de Carvalho for allowing me personal access to the Busaco (or more accurately Buçaco) Museum and to Antonio Manuel Raminhos Cordeiro Grilo for his translations of the Portuguese drill books and his frequent and informative correspondence. Clive Gilbert of the British Historical Society of Portugal granted me permission to quote from Norris and Bremner's booklet on the Lines of Torres Vedras and he supplied me with other BHSP publications.

The Greenhill Books Napoleonic Library has reprinted many of the most important books of the Peninsular War period and I must thank Lionel Leventhal for allowing me to quote from Oman's *History of the Peninsular War,* D'Urban's *Journal,* Grattan's *Adventures* and Simmons' *A British Rifleman.*

No modern study of the Lines of Torres Vedras or Masséna's Portuguese campaign could be written without reference to the published works of Professor Donald Horward. I am extremely grateful, therefore, for his permission to use his translation of Pelet's *French Campaign in Portugal,* as well as to quote from *Napoleon and Iberia* and *The Battle of Bussaco.*

Ray Cusick provided me with much information and advice, particularly with regards to the telegraph systems used by the British and the Portuguese armies. Mary Kelly of the Library of the Queen's

University of Belfast provided me with details of Masséna's Lopez map. Major Smallman, Secretary of the Royal Engineers Headquarters Mess, supplied the portrait of Colonel Fletcher and Caroline Theakstone of the Hulton Getty Picture Library located the Heath sketch of Torres Vedras. Karl Thompson read and amended the penultimate draft of the manuscript, the final version of which was edited by Lorraine McCann.

Dave Ryan and Richard Partridge of Partizan Press have promoted and supported me for many years. It is a fact that without their encouragement this book would not have been written.

Finally I must thank my wife, Lynne, for the many days that she trudged by my side along the steep slopes of the Serra de Montachique and for the many hours she spent checking my work.

John Grehan
Peacehaven, 2000

Introduction
'The sure game'

The importance of the Lines of Torres Vedras, and their pivotal role in Wellington's strategical plans throughout the central years of the Peninsular War, has largely been unappreciated by historians. Though many hundreds of books have been written about the Peninsular War only two slim monographs on the Lines of Torres Vedras have ever been published in English. The first of these, *Memoranda Relative to the Lines thrown up to cover Lisbon in 1810,* was written by Captain, later Major-General, John Jones RE who was the engineer responsible for the construction of the Lines under Wellington's Commanding Engineer, Colonel Fletcher. First published in its entirety in 1829 this pamphlet was later incorporated into the 1846 edition of Jones' *Journal of Sieges carried on by the army under the Duke of Wellington,* forming the final volume of that work. The second, published 134 years later by the British Historical Society of Portugal, is a guidebook to the present-day remains of the Lines, with a "patchwork" of additional information. In the majority of the other Peninsular War books produced over the last two centuries the Lines are only referred to immediately before and during the few weeks in 1810 when the redoubts were actually occupied by the allied troops. Their conception rarely constitutes more than a paragraph or two; their construction even less.

One of the reasons why so few words have been written about the Lines is that they were never assaulted. There was no heroic struggle for possession of the Lines to stir the pens of the Peninsula diarists or to fire the imaginations of later authors. The building of a chain of earthen redoubts has to compete with the great battles and sieges of the Peninsular War, and it inevitably loses.

The other reason is the failure of some historians to grasp the fundamentals of warfare in the Iberian Peninsula in the early nineteenth century. It is clearly believed by many that Wellington achieved his eventual victory primarily by his successes on the battlefield. However, as Basil Liddel Hart – who was a soldier first and an historian second – declared in *The Strategy of the Indirect Approach*, "Wellington's battles and sieges were perhaps the least effective part of his operations".

Wellington committed his army to battle only with the greatest reluctance. "Depend upon it, whatever people may tell you," he once told the Earl of Liverpool, "I am not so desirous as they imagine of fighting desperate battles; if I was, I might fight one any day I please." It was not simply by fighting battles that Wellington succeeded in the Peninsula. In fact only 50,000 French soldiers were killed or captured fighting the British whereas disease, starvation and the actions of the guerrillas and the regular Spanish armies resulted in approximately 180,000 French casualties. The battles that Wellington did fight were the consequence, not the object, of his strategy.

Wellington was quite certain that he would beat the French even before he set foot in the Peninsula. In 1808 he wrote the following: "Bonaparte cannot carry on his operations in Spain, excepting by means of large armies; and I doubt much whether the country will afford subsistence for a large army, or if he will be able to supply his magazines from France with the roads being so bad and communications so difficult." This is Wellington's adaptation of the old, and much quoted, adage that "Beyond the Pyrenees, small armies are beaten and large armies starve". Wellington knew that, because of the low level of agricultural development and the extreme climatic conditions in Spain, the war would eventually become a bitter fight against starvation. The invaders would consume the scarce foodstuff of the inhabitants and the Iberians, in utter desperation, would be forced to fight back or perish. In order to find food the French armies would have to disperse but any offensive operations by a substantial British army in the Peninsula would compel the French to concentrate their forces. Such a concentration could only be temporary, as hunger would soon oblige the French to scatter once again. "My opinion," Wellington explained to the British Minister for War, "is that as long as we remain in a state of activity in Portugal, the contest must continue in Spain." Wellington's policy from 1809 to 1812 was simple in its design, though necessarily complex in its execution. All he had to do was avoid defeat.

The longer the war continued the greater would be the drain upon the Peninsula's resources and greater too would be the destitution of the population. Eventually every Iberian hand would be turned against the invader and the war then "ceases to be carried on by army against army," wrote an historian just eight years after the end of the war, "and becomes a struggle of a nation against its oppressors." Wellington, therefore, had to perpetuate the war until it reached its exhausted conclusion. But the combined French armies hugely outnumbered his own and though he could run he could not hide, and one day Wellington would have to stand and fight. Until that moment came he would play "the sure game" and, as he told his most trusted subordinate, General Hill, "risk nothing".

If Wellington was to maintain his army in the field then the first consideration was obviously that of logistics. He could not take food from the mouths of his allies or allies they would soon cease to be. Wellington had to obtain his provisions from outside Iberia. For this he would need to be close to a deep-sea port where Britain's maritime and commercial supremacy could guarantee adequate and regular logistical support. His next consideration was for the location of a defensive position which, by virtue of its geographical attributes, could be rendered strong enough for his small Anglo-allied force to do battle against the full might of Napoleon's Imperial armies on equal terms.

The port was Lisbon harbour. The defensive position was the Montachique hills of the Lisbon peninsula. Upon these hills Wellington would build the most extensive range of field fortifications the world had seen, creating an impregnable barrier around the Portuguese capital, with wasted countryside to its front and the Royal Navy guarding its flanks and rear. It was, Sir Robert Southey observed, "a conception which had never yet emerged in war".

These fortifications became known as the Lines of Torres Vedras. This was where Wellington would make his stand, on ground of his own choosing that had been carefully prepared and heavily fortified. If the British were driven from these positions they would be forced to evacuate the Peninsula. If the French failed to break through the defences they could never win the war. Here, before the ramparts of Lisbon, the fate of Spain and Portugal would be decided.

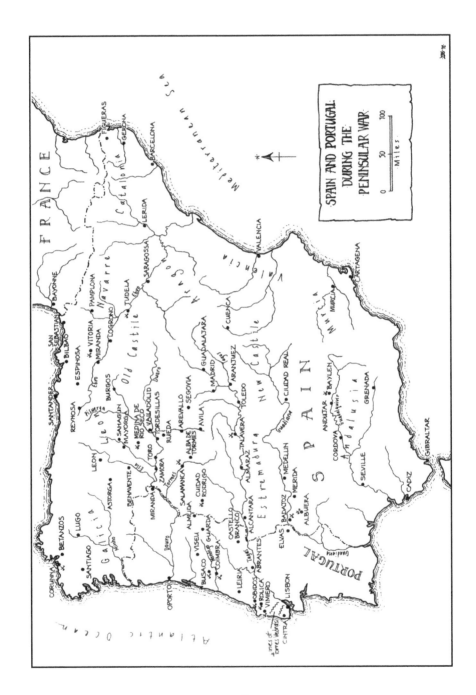

SPAIN AND PORTUGAL DURING THE PENINSULAR WAR

0   50   100
Miles

xii

CHAPTER I

"The Ramparts of Lisbon"

The small boats rode the bar and shot through the rushing surf of the Mondego estuary. English sailors, stripped naked, stood chest-deep in the warm water ready to grapple with the swirling vessels and haul them onto the sand. From the rocking boats red-coated infantry leapt into the surf and trudged up the beach at Figueira da Foz. Out beyond the bar stood the fleet, masts swaying in the heavy Atlantic swell which, one soldier remembered, was "causing the ships to roll so heavily that it was a matter of great difficulty to get on board or leave them". Bringing the cavalry ashore was the most hazardous part of the operation. As Sergeant Landshedlt of the 20th Light Dragoons was to recall, the troopers were directed to stand upright in the boats, bridle in hand, ready to spring into the saddle if the boat capsized. Inevitably, at least one boat was thrown over in the surf but no lives were lost as the horses, sometimes swimming, sometimes wading, carried their riders safely to the shore. It took a whole week for the convoys of ships to disgorge their human cargoes upon the northern shores of French-controlled Portugal. Fortunately there were no French forces in the immediate area, for "had we been opposed from the land", wrote a young English staff officer, William Warre, "I am positive we should never have effected it, so great is the surf on the coast and the bar".[1]

This small British army had dared to trespass upon Napoleon's Europe, where every continental power had been beaten into submission or alliance with the Emperor of the French. Only Britain, sitting remote and secure behind the "wooden walls" of the Royal Navy, remained actively at war with France. But the peoples of Spain and Portugal refused to accept French rule and a savage guerrilla war had broken out throughout the Iberian Peninsula. Britain, always happy to wage its wars on another man's land, was prepared to help the Spaniards and the Portuguese in their fight for independence and so, on 1 August 1808,

1

a British Expeditionary Force under the command of Lieutenant-General Sir Arthur Wellesley began its disembarkation at Figueira da Foz at the mouth of the Mondego river.

Few people in the summer of 1808 could have foreseen that this force – barely 13,000 strong – would help perpetuate the war in Iberia for another six years. When Napoleon first planned to invade Spain he stated that if it was to cost him 80,000 men he would not attempt it "but", he claimed, "it will cost me no more than 12,000". The Peninsular War was to tie down over 300,000 of his troops in a bitter war of attrition that would result in the loss of a quarter of a million French soldiers.[2]

Upon landing Wellesley made contact with the local Portuguese commander, General Freire, who immediately made Wellesley aware of the difficulties of campaigning in the Peninsula. Freire agreed to co-operate with the British army but only if Wellesley undertook to feed his entire force of 6,000 men! As Wellesley was dependent upon the Navy for his own supplies he could not accept such a proposition and when he began his march upon the Portuguese capital he was accompanied by less than 2,000 Portuguese light troops.

The French commander in Portugal, General Junot, Napoleon's former ambassador to Lisbon, sent a corps of 4,000 men under General Laborde to delay Wellesley's advance. Laborde took up a defensive position upon a narrow hill to the south of the old walled town of Obidos adjacent to the main Lisbon highway. Wellesley attempted to encircle Laborde's corps but the French general withdrew in good order to a more extensive range of heights behind the village of Roliça. Wellesley repeated his earlier manoeuvre and again Laborde held his ground until the last possible moment before disengaging.

Laborde had done his job well. By nightfall Wellesley had advanced just seven miles in twenty-four hours, allowing Junot time to march up from Lisbon with the bulk of his army. Britain's decision to support the Portuguese was hardly unexpected and two months earlier Junot's chief engineer, a Colonel Vincent, had recommended the preparation of defensive works at Torres Vedras and around the capital. But rather than taking up defensive positions Junot chose instead to attack the British and drive them back to their ships before more troops could be landed. He was too late. Two brigades of reinforcements had already arrived from England and were preparing to disembark at Maçeira Bay.[3]

Wellesley moved along the coast to cover the disembarkation and he deployed his small force along the semi-circle of hills above the village of Vimeiro that encompasses the bay. Without hesitation Junot attacked the strong British positions only to be repulsed on all fronts. As the French disengaged, Wellesley ordered an immediate advance but with the reinforcements had come a more senior officer, Sir Harry Burrard, who "did not think it advisable to move off the ground in pursuit of the enemy". Junot therefore made good his retreat, occupying the important town of Torres Vedras on the main road to Lisbon. Here, for the first time, Wellesley saw the Serra de Montachique with its narrow and sometimes steep passes that formed an almost continuous line across the centre of the Lisbon peninsula.[4]

The following day Burrard was himself superseded by Sir Hew Dalrymple, with Wellesley being relegated to the role of a divisional commander. A further batch of reinforcements – a strong division under Sir John Moore – had just landed and Wellesley urged his new chief to advance upon Lisbon without delay. Only four roads led to the Portuguese capital beyond Torres Vedras. One ran along the low ground that bordered the River Tagus, the other three crossing the Montachique hills by the passes of Mafra, Montachique and Bucellas (Bucelas)C. Wellesley proposed that Moore's division should occupy the Tagus road whilst the remainder of the army marched along the coast in an attempt to turn the French position at Torres Vedras and seize the pass of Mafra. If this was accomplished Junot would be unable to fall back upon Lisbon. The French general would then have little choice but to try and escape from the Lisbon peninsula by the Tagus road, only to find his route to freedom blocked by Moore.

It was a bold and ambitious plan and Sir Hew, who was as cautious as Sir Harry, would have none of it. When later that same day Junot proposed an armistice in order to negotiate the French evacuation of Portugal, Dalrymple jumped at the chance of liberating the country without further bloodshed. Under the terms of the armistice and evacuation – which became known as the Convention of Cintra (or Sintra) – the French were allowed to retain their weapons and much of the plunder that they had looted from the Portuguese. They were to be repatriated to France in British ships and, upon their return, they were free to take up arms once again. At this point Wellesley, uncomfortable with a subordinate role in an army he had previously commanded and dissatisfied with the armistice arrangements, returned to England. When the details of the Convention of Cintra were published in London there was widespread public outrage. Generals Dalrymple and Burrard were recalled and, along with Wellesley, were asked to explain their conduct to a Board of Inquiry.

With Portugal successfully liberated, the British government urged the new commander of the Expeditionary Force, Sir John Moore, to carry the war into Spain. Napoleon had compelled the King of Spain – Charles IV – to abdicate and the Spanish crown had been presented to

Napoleon's brother Joseph in an attempt to legitimise the French occupation. But the guerrillas and the remnants of the Spanish regular army had met with some success against the over-extended French armies and Joseph had been driven out of his new capital only weeks after arriving in Madrid. Because of the deteriorating situation in Spain Napoleon had decided to deal with the rebels in person and "get the machine working again". Transferring over 100,000 of his most experienced troops from their garrisons in Germany and Italy, Napoleon crossed the Pyrenees and, brushing aside all opposition, reached Madrid on 1 December, reinstating his brother Joseph on the Spanish throne.[5]

Having re-established the French presence in northern and central Spain, Napoleon's next objective was the invasion of Portugal followed by the conquest of Andalusia "which", Napoleon told Joseph, "will make an end of the war". Meanwhile Sir John Moore, having left 10,000 troops in Portugal to safeguard Lisbon, had marched the 250 miles from Lisbon to Ciudad Rodrigo on the Portuguese-Spanish border only to find that the French were once again in control of most of northern Spain and that there were no longer any organised Spanish forces for his army to co-operate with. Yet he was determined to strike a blow at the French and when a captured dispatch informed Moore that the isolated French II Corps was within striking distance he decided to attack. "I was aware that I was risking infinitely too much," wrote Moore, "but something must be risked for the honour of the Service, and to make it apparent that we stuck to the Spaniards long after they themselves had given up the cause as lost." But Napoleon had learnt of Moore's audacious move and the Emperor turned his troops around and rushed northwards hoping to cut the British off from the sea and their only avenue of escape.[6]

A desperate race for the coast then began, with the French cavalry hard on the heels of Moore's rearguard. In sub-zero temperatures the troops were driven on through the snow-bound Galician mountains at a punishing pace. All wheeled transport was abandoned for the sake of speed – even the gold of the military chest was thrown into a ravine – as Moore tried to save his army from encirclement. Hundreds of men died from exposure, or collapsed exhausted into the snow to be trampled under the hooves of the pursuing French dragoons.

When it became evident that the British would reach the sea ahead of the French, Napoleon handed over pursuit to Marshal Soult and the Emperor returned to France, spurred on by the news that Austria was arming for war. Moore's army eventually reached the port of Corunna in northern Spain where, on 14 January 1809, the British transport ships arrived to carry the troops back to England. Soult, however, was not going to let Moore escape without a fight. Two days later, as the first units moved off to embark, Soult launched his attack.

Moore was not caught unprepared. The French attacks were beaten back and the British troops were finally able to embark unmolested. Moore had saved the army (albeit at an enormous cost in men and materiel) and severely dislocated Napoleon's plans for the conquest of Portugal and southern Spain. But Moore was mortally wounded during the battle and he was buried "alone with his glory" in the land he had tried to set free.[7]

With the main British army back in England, Napoleon believed that the war in Spain was "done with" and in those weeks following the evacuation of Moore's army it certainly appeared to most observers that the French force of arms was irresistible. It is quite remarkable that at this stage Britain did not recall its troops from Lisbon and abandon its involvement in the Peninsula. Moore had told the Secretary at State for War only a few months earlier, in November 1808, that: "If the French succeed in Spain it will be vain to attempt to resist them in Portugal . . . The British must in that event, I conceive, immediately take steps to evacuate the country … We might check the progress of the enemy while the stores are embarking, and arrangements are being made for taking off the army. Beyond this the defence of Lisbon or of Portugal should not be thought of." Sir John Craddock, who commanded the rump of the British army in Lisbon, was equally dismissive of Britain's prospects of successfully defending Portugal: "We must not be misled by the supposed idea of a frontier of Portugal. It is at present only a name. The rivers running east and west present no line of defence except Almeida and Elvas, which are one hundred and fifty miles apart. There is no other defence." Yet the Government listened instead to the words of another of its generals. Sir Arthur Wellesley, having been completely exonerated by the Cintra Board of Inquiry, insisted that Portugal could be defended even if the Spaniards were defeated. In a "Memorandum on the Defence of Portugal" written in London on 7 March 1809, and addressed to Lord Castlereagh, Wellesley set out his views on what would eventually become British Government policy. "My notion was," ran the memorandum, "that the Portuguese military establishments, upon the footing of 40,000 militia and 30,000 regular troops, ought to be revived; and that, in addition to these troops, His Majesty ought to employ an army in Portugal amounting to about 20,000 British troops, including about 4,000 cavalry." Wellesley considered that the Portuguese should be offered all the financial and political support necessary to enable them to re-build their army, and in order to effect this the whole of the Portuguese armed force, both regular and irregular, should be placed under the command of British officers. "My opinion was", Wellesley continued, "that even if Spain should have been conquered, the French would not have been able to overrun Portugal with a smaller force than 100,000 men; and that as long as the contest should continue in Spain this force, if it could be put in a state of activity, would be highly useful to the Spaniards, and might eventually have decided the contest." The Government desperately wanted to believe Wellesley and so, on 22 April, in the wake of the first shipment of reinforcements, he returned to Lisbon as commander-in-chief of the Anglo-Portuguese army with the defence of Portugal as "the first and most immediate object" of his attention.[8]

Following the Battle of Corunna, Soult had reorganised his corps and had invaded northern Portugal, capturing the country's second city, Oporto. A second French army – the I Corps under Marshal Victor – also threatened Portugal from the east. Wellesley saw that if the two French armies were allowed to combine his small force of barely 20,000 men would be overwhelmed. His only chance lay in attack.

Wellesley struck first at Soult, driving him out of Oporto and forcing him back over the border into Spain. Wellesley was then able to turn his attention to Victor, who had initially advanced into eastern Portugal almost as far as Castello Branco (Castelo Branco), but who had also returned to Spain. With Portugal liberated once more Wellesley was given permission to continue his operations beyond the frontier. In conjunction with the Spanish army of General Cuesta he arranged to advance into Spain to attack Victor's corps at Talavera whilst another Spanish force under Venegas marched towards Madrid to prevent the French troops in the neighbourhood of the capital from reinforcing the I Corps.

On 16 July, the British army moved forward from its new operational base at Plasencia and six days later the armies of Wellesley and Cuesta reached Talavera. Victor was taken completely by surprise but Cuesta refused to attack and Victor made good his escape towards Madrid. Cuesta, encouraged by the French retreat, then embarked upon a reckless pursuit. Wellesley, without the food and transport that the Spanish authorities had promised to supply, would not be drawn any further into Spain and he took up defensive positions around Talavera to await Cuesta's inevitable return.

Wellesley did not have long to wait. Three days after they had chased off down the highway to Madrid the Spaniards came running back with the combined forces of the I Corps, Sebastiani's IV Corps and the bulk of the Madrid garrison at their heels. Wellesley urged Cuesta to bring his troops into line with the British army but the perverse old general refused to co-operate until the British commander, fearing impending disaster, went down on his knees and begged Cuesta to move his troops before the French attacked. On the night of 27 July, and throughout the following day, Victor assaulted Wellesley's thin red line but without success and on the 29th, with the slothful Venegas at last threatening Madrid, the French withdrew leaving behind seventeen guns and 7,000 dead and wounded.

Wellesley's troubles, however, were far from over. Whilst still awaiting the logistical support from the Spaniards that would enable him to pursue Victor, Sir Arthur learnt that Soult, reinforced with troops from the French V Corps, had broken through the pass of Baños and was moving upon Plasencia. Wellesley had no option but to leave his 4,000 sick and wounded to the care of the Spaniards and retire as quickly as possible over the River Tagus before he was cut off from Portugal.

The British army withdrew across the Tagus unopposed but it was so desperately short of food that Wellesley was forced to abandon his offensive adventure in Spain. "I must either move into Portugal where I know I shall be supplied", he informed his Spanish allies, "or I must make up my mind to lose my army." On 21 August 1809, the British army marched back to Portugal with Wellesley determined "not to have anything to do with Spanish warfare, on any ground whatever, in the existing state of things". The experience of the last two months, Wellington explained to Lord Castlereagh, "has opened my eyes respecting the state of the war in the Peninsula". His "plan", he told General Beresford a week later, "now is to remain on the defensive ... I must be satisfied with maintaining myself in Portugal".[9]

Though their British allies had withdrawn, the Spanish people fought on. From tiny village groups to well-armed units numbering in their hundreds, guerrilla bands continued to capture French couriers, attack foraging parties, trap convoys and hunt down stragglers. The provincial Spanish armies, frequently beaten but never destroyed, likewise displayed an irrepressible resilience. Sometimes totalling only a few thousand and always short of food and equipment, their willingness to re-form and fight again, even after the severest of reverses on the battlefield, kept alive the spirit of resistance throughout the country.

In order to police this vast and hostile land the French generals had to disperse their battalions ever more widely but in doing so they risked exposing a part of their forces to an attack by the British army which was lurking menacingly just inside the Portuguese border. Wellesley understood this quite clearly. "I believe," he declared to the Portuguese Regency Council, "that if we are able to maintain ourselves in Portugal, the war will not end in the Peninsula".[10]

The invasion of Portugal was therefore a matter of the highest priority to the French and Napoleon ordered that the conquest of Andalusia and southern Spain should be postponed until Portugal had been subdued. "It was at Lisbon that the fate of the Peninsula was to be decided and perhaps the destiny of the world," a French staff officer noted in his diary, "if the British were forced to abandon the capital they would lose all their influence in Spain. Portugal would submit and Spain, exhausted and discouraged, would follow its example as soon as it was abandoned". Wellesley, recently created Viscount Wellington in recognition of his victory at Talavera, knew that it would only be a matter of time before the French attacked Portugal once again. "You may depend upon it," he advised Lord Castlereagh as early as August 1809, "their first and great object will be to get the English out". Yet Wellington was convinced that the French did not have enough troops in Spain to mount a serious attack upon Portugal "without abandoning other objects and exposing their whole fabric in Spain to great risk". But following his decisive victory over the Austrians at Wagram in July, Napoleon was now able to turn the full might of his empire's enormous military machine upon the conflict in Iberia. "Within a year, despite all their efforts, the English will be expelled from Portugal", claimed *Le Moniteur* on 27 September, "and the Imperial eagle will float proudly over the ramparts of Lisbon".[11]

Wellington nevertheless believed that, despite its long frontier, Portugal could be successfully defended if the entire Portuguese war effort was controlled by Britain through its ambassador by means of a large subsidy. On 14 November, he re-stated the views that he had earlier expressed to Lord Castlereagh to the recently appointed Secretary of State for War, the Earl of Liverpool: "If in consequence of the peace in Germany the enemy's army in the Peninsula should be largely reinforced, it is obvious that the enemy will acquire the means of attacking Portugal . . . Even in this case, however, I conceive that 'till Spain shall have been conquered, and shall have submitted to the conqueror, the enemy will find it difficult, if not impossible, to obtain possession of Portugal, if His Majesty should continue to employ an army in the defence of this country, and if the improvements in the Portuguese service should be carried to the extent of which they are capable.

"The extent of the army which it would be necessary that his Majesty should employ in Portugal ought to be 30,000 effective men, in aid of the whole military establishment of Portugal, consisting of 3,000 artillery, 3,000 cavalry, 36,000 regular infantry, and 3,000 cacadores and militia".[12]

As well as safeguarding the sovereignty of Portugal, this force "if it could be placed in a state of activity," Wellington reasoned, "would be highly useful to the Spaniards in their contest with the French". Wellington fully appreciated that "the more ground the French hold down, the weaker they will be at any given point", and their occupation of Spain would never be secure whilst a British army stood unbeaten upon their flank. "The French are most desirous that we should withdraw from the country," Wellington explained, "but know that they must employ a very large force indeed in the operations which will render it necessary for us to go away". He calculated that if the Spaniards continued to resist them, the French would never be able to detach a body of troops from their forces in Spain that would be strong enough to conquer Portugal and "if they should be able to invade it, and should not succeed in obliging us to evacuate the country, they will be in a very dangerous position; and the longer we can oppose them, and delay their success, the more likely they are to suffer materially in Spain".[13]

Since its landing on the beach at Figueira da Foz in 1808, the operations of the British army in the Peninsula had been entirely offensive. The experiences of the Talavera campaign (and Moore's Spanish campaign before it) had taught Wellington that he could place no reliance upon the Spaniards. Spain was without an effective government, due as much to the French occupation of many of the major cities and command of the main highways, as to the Supreme Junta's inability to control the actions of its generals. The Spanish armies were weak and scattered and their commanders jealous and divided. (In Wellington's words the Spanish troops "have no discipline, they are not efficient, they are defective even in the spirit of troops; they cannot be depended upon for any operation of any description, and they want means of all kinds"). The land was poor and barely able to support the local population let alone the armies of France and Britain, and the people of the country had shown themselves to be unappreciative of Britain's efforts and unwilling to assist their allies with food and transportation. In Portugal, by contrast, the authority of the Regency Council was unchallenged (at least by any formal body) and its army and its officers were prepared to fight under a British commander. Wellington could ensure that his army was adequately provisioned through the port of Lisbon with a secure supply line from the capital all the way to the Portuguese-Spanish border. He knew that he would have to re-build Portugal's defences and re-arm its people, but Wellington was certain that the Portuguese would stand with him in

9

the defence of their own realm. He would turn Portugal into an armed camp from which the French would never be able to evict him and from where, with the Spaniards, he could eventually mount a combined operation of "a more extended description" with regularly organised magazines and established lines of communication.[14]

All this, though, was going to cost money and the Portuguese would require "very extensive pecuniary assistance". The British Government had already agreed to subsidise the Portuguese Regency at the rate of £600,000 a year but this sum fell far short of what was required, as the country was virtually bankrupt. When Junot invaded Portugal in 1807 the Prince Regent, the rest of the royal family and some 15,000 of the country's wealthiest citizens fled to the Portuguese colony of Brazil, taking with them almost half of all the money in circulation. Prince John, having established his court in Rio de Janeiro, opened up all Brazil's ports for trade with nations friendly to Portugal. Most of this trade was taken up by Britain and the loss of import duties at Lisbon was a ruinous blow to the Portuguese finances, which were already crippled by the war. Though the Portuguese Government did a great deal to raise extra revenue to pay for the war effort by reforming the tax structure, collecting rents from crown and church lands, introducing a stamp tax and even starting a national lottery, only the most pressing debts had been paid and the salaries of the civil servants and the pay of the army were in arrears.[15]

In November Wellington announced a deficit in the Portuguese budget of £900,000, towards the relief of which he proposed that the British Treasury should pay £300,000. The Cabinet refused to be responsible for the budget deficit but offered to raise the Portuguese subsidy to £980,000 per annum. Wellington urged the Portuguese Regency Council to accept this arrangement. "I am positively certain that the Ministers will be unwilling to go to Parliament to ask for more money", he told the British Ambassador on 14 November, "and that Parliament will not grant a larger sum even if Ministers should ask for it". On 2 December 1809, there was a major upheaval in the Government and Wellington had to re-state his arguments to the new administration. In the new Cabinet Wellington was fortunate in having his eldest brother, the Marquis Wellesley, in the position of Foreign Secretary and another brother, William, as Chief Secretary for Ireland. The support of his influential brothers was essential, as few people in either London or Lisbon believed that the small British army would be able to hold the French at bay.[16]

In his opening speech the King told the new Parliament that the Government was determined to defend Portugal and "as long as this great cause could be maintained with a prospect of success, it should be supported". However, when the Government asked Parliament to vote for the increased expenditure for the defence of Portugal, it faced considerable opposition. In the Lords, Marquis Wellesley explained that "Portugal was the most military position that could be occupied for the purpose of assisting Spain" but Lord Grenville replied that "Portugal was the least defensible country in Europe. It has the longest line of frontier compared with its actual extent of any nation". It was their "sacred duty", Grenville insisted, "to see that not one more life was wasted, not one more drop of blood shed unprofitably". General Lord Moira declared that the idea of defending Portugal was "utterly impracticable". In the Commons Sir J. Newport thought the cause "hopeless", and others believed that because of "the overwhelming power of France" nothing was left "but to escape".[17]

The motion in favour of supporting the Portuguese was carried with a Government majority of sixty-two but the general belief in England was that when Napoleon transferred his veteran troops from the Danube into Spain the British army would be overwhelmed and forced to evacuate the Peninsula. This view was shared by Wellington's own troops. From the most junior officers, such as Ensign Aitchison who wrote that "an attempt at defence with an army so reduced and enfeebled as ours will have annihilation as its result", to the most senior of Wellington's generals, Lord Hill, who considered that "the cause is hopeless", the whole army was in daily expectation of being recalled to Britain. These opinions, expressed in the private correspondence of many officers during the spring of 1810, helped to spread the contagion of doubt throughout England. Such views became so widely held that Lord Liverpool had to tell Wellington that "a very considerable degree of alarm exists in this country respecting the safety of the British army in Portugal". Wellington's plans for a safe evacuation, therefore, were a prominent feature of his dispatches during this period and he told Liverpool that if he was provided with "a large fleet of ships of war, and forty-five disposable tons of transports, I shall try, and I think I shall bring them [the British troops] all off".[18]

This did not allay Liverpool's fears: "the chances of a successful defence are considered here by all persons, military as well as civil, so improbable that I could not recommend any attempt at what may be called desperate resistance". He consequently advised Wellington that he would "be excused for bringing away the army a little too soon, than, by remaining in Portugal a little too long, exposing it to those risks from which no military operations can be wholly exempt". To this Wellington replied: "All the preparations for embarking and carrying away the army, and everything belonging to it, are already made, and my intention is to embark it, as soon as I find that a military necessity exists for so doing. I shall delay the embarkation as long as it is in my power, and shall do everything in my power to avert the necessity of embarking at all. If the enemy should invade this country with a force less than I think so superior to ours as to create a necessity of embarking, I shall fight a battle to save the country, for which I have made the preparations; and if the result should not be successful, of which I have no doubt, I shall still be able to retire and embark the army …

"I shall stay as long as I can, going at last, when the enemy shall move into the country with a force which I shall think so superior to that under my command as to oblige me to evacuate … If we do go, I feel a little anxiety to go like gentlemen, out of the hall door (particularly after all the preparations I have made to enable us to do so), and not out of the back door."

He told the minister that he would not be "frightened away by a French force just because it was numerically stronger than his". He might be forced to fight a pitched battle in front of Lisbon but he had no intention or desire to attempt what Liverpool called a "desperate resistance". If the Government did not want Wellington to risk the safety of the army in a major engagement then he would remain in Portugal until the French invaded with a superior force and then he would "embark at an early period" without any attempt at resistance.[19]

The Tory Government, though, was committed to continuing the war against France and the abandonment of Portugal would have been portrayed by the Whig Opposition as a major failure of policy. In fact it is difficult to see how the Tories, under attack from all sides for "year after year of wasteful expenditure" on unsuccessful military operations, could have remained in office if the Portuguese expedition had ended in yet another embarrassing withdrawal. So, despite the doubts and fears at home and in the army, Wellington received the approval of the Cabinet "to persevere in the contest in the Peninsula as long as it can be maintained with a reasonable expectation of success". The subsidy to the Portuguese Government was increased in April 1810 to £1,500,000 and 30,000 Portuguese troops were brought under British pay. Wellington was also provided with the 30,000 British troops he had asked for and Lord Liverpool even promised a reinforcement of a further 8,000 men plus 49,000 tons of shipping.[20]

Having at last received the backing of his own government, Wellington now had to win support for his plans from the Portuguese authorities. When Prince John and the Portuguese court fled to South

America a five-member regency council was left to continue the functions of government. By 1810 only two members remained on the council and three new members were selected. The new Council comprised the Bishop of Oporto (Patriarch elect), the Conde de Redondo, Ricardo Raymundo Nogueira (former professor of Law at Coimbra University), the Principal, Antonio da Sousa (whose brother was Ambassador to the Court of St James) and Dom Miguel Forjaz who was the Secretary of the Council and the member responsible for the management of the war effort. Forjaz was a firm supporter of the alliance with Britain but he was bitterly opposed by the other members of the Council, particularly da Sousa, who was envious of Forjaz's position and who was severely critical of Wellington's defensive plans. Da Sousa was a fierce patriot and he resented the extent to which his country had become dependent upon Britain's financial and military assistance.

Wellington managed to secure the appointment of Sir Charles Stuart, the British Ambassador, to the Council and he promised Stuart that he could depend upon his support for Forjaz "as being the best instrument to cooperate with us to carry on the war". The Sousa faction, however, sent a representative to Brazil and wrote to the Prince of Wales and the Duke of Sussex complaining of Wellington's policies. Eventually Lord Wellesley, in his role as Foreign Secretary, pressurised the Brazilian court into giving Wellington the authority to retain or dismiss da Sousa. Admiral Berkeley, who commanded the British squadron at anchor in the Tagus, was placed in command of the Portuguese navy and was also given a seat on the Council. The subsidies to the Portuguese Government were put under Wellington's and Stuart's control. The Regency Council remained divided throughout the difficult months that followed and the power struggle in Lisbon was to create considerable unrest in the capital. On more than one occasion it prompted Wellington to threaten to "recommend to His Majesty's Government to withdraw the army". As this would also have meant the withdrawal of the British subsidy, however, the Council was compelled to acquiesce to Wellington's demands and continue their grudging acceptance of his plans for the defence of Portugal.[21]

CHAPTER II

"A Design of Terrible Energy"

Wellington had learnt that in the Peninsula "subsistence is the great difficulty always found." Spain is a country of high, open plateaux and extensive mountain ranges. Scorched and in places utterly dry in summer, the plains are flooded by the rains of autumn and the sierras lashed by the driven snows of winter. "All who run and ride through the Peninsula," a nineteenth-century traveller was to discover, "will read thirst in the arid plains, and hunger in the soil-denuded hills." Neither Wellington, nor his allies or his enemies, could maintain a large army in the field for more than a few weeks before it would be compelled to break up or move to another area in search of food. Yet if Wellington was near to a deep-sea port he could keep his army together indefinitely. Though the British army was over 1,000 miles from England, Britain's unrivalled mastery of the seas meant that the most certain and secure supply line of the Peninsula was from the Channel ports to Lisbon harbour.[1]

The French armies had no such sources of supply. War must pay for war and Napoleon's troops were expected to live off the land upon which they fought. In his great campaigns in the rich and fertile plains of northern Italy and the valley of the Danube this policy had enabled Napoleon's armies to manoeuvre with astonishing speed, unencumbered by long supply trains, unrestricted by magazines and unconcerned for their communications. In many areas of Spain and the border regions of Portugal there was scarcely enough food in any year to support the indigenous population and the march of a ravenous army through such districts could prove ruinous to the local economy. Little wonder that, as one French hussar was to observe, "the husbandman guided his plough with one hand, while he held in the other a sword", and the peasantry exacted a terrible revenge upon any French soldiers that they captured.[2]

The two British sorties into Spain had both resulted in ignominious and perilous retreats. Talavera had been dismissed as a Pyrrhic victory by the Whig Opposition and Corunna as a disaster. A repeat of such operations would, at best, lead to a minor success followed by the inevitable withdrawal in the face of superior numbers or, at worst, to a major defeat. There were simply too many French troops in Spain for Wellington's small army to engage. However widely dispersed the French armies might be, in the face of a serious threat from the British they would concentrate, albeit temporarily, in overwhelming force. Wellington therefore intended to remain close to his Lisbon base where he knew that his army would be regularly fed. He would let the French come to him. It would be they who would have to march through almost 200 miles of barren and inhospitable countryside and battle with the Portuguese for the very means of survival. "Hunger and thirst have ever been, and are, the best defenders of the Peninsula against the invader", wrote the traveller Richard Ford, and these were the weapons with which Wellington would fight for the independence of Iberia.[3]

Wellington appreciated the fact that the "line of frontier of Portugal is so long in proportion to the extent and means of the country, and the Tagus and the mountains separate each other, and it is open in many parts, that it would be impossible for an army, acting on the defensive, to carry on its operations upon the frontier without being cut off from the capital". Wellington, consequently, had no intention of trying to stop the invaders on the border. "The scene of operations of the army would, therefore, most probably be considerably within the frontier, whether their attack be made in winter or summer."[4]

The object of the defending forces, Wellington told his Commanding Engineer, "should be to oblige the enemy as much as possible to make his attack with concentrated corps. They should stand in every position which the country could afford such a length of time as would enable the people of the country to evacuate towns and villages, carrying with them or destroying all articles of provisions and carriages." Wellington then intended to "bring matters to extremities, and to contend for the possession and independence of Portugal in one of the strong positions in this part of the country". But he could not risk engaging a superior French force with the small army under his command unless he was able to fortify his defensive positions in advance, and it was upon these fortifications that the whole of Wellington's defensive policy was founded.[5]

His great plan was for the construction of a vast range of fortifications across the entire breadth of the Lisbon peninsula from the Tagus to the sea, through which the French army would not be able to

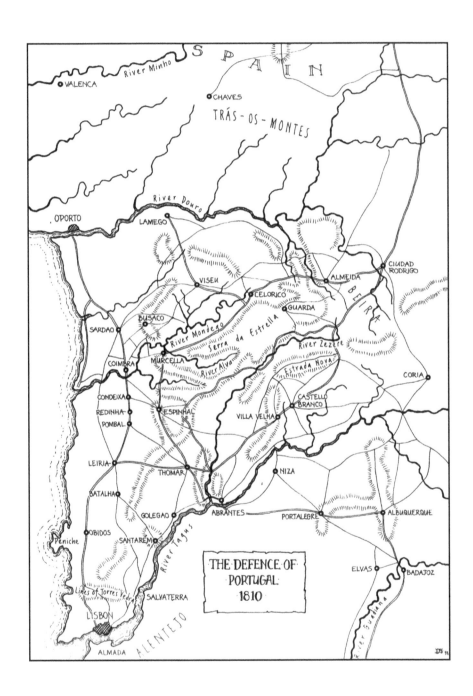

THE·DEFENCE·OF·
PORTUGAL·
1810

penetrate. Wellington intended to order the depopulation and devastation of the countryside in the path of the invaders. The French would be drawn on, ever deeper, through the wasted land until, hundreds of miles from their bases in Spain, they would stumble upon the massive lines of defences behind which would be the serried ranks of the Anglo-Portuguese army. It was, as Colonel Napier saw, "a design of terrible energy" requiring enormous sacrifices to be made by the people of Portugal. Yet, as Wellington was to stress, "it is better that a part of the country should suffer than that the whole should be lost".[6]

For Wellington's plan to work it was obviously essential for him to calculate accurately the precise route that the invaders would take. Portugal "is an open frontier", Sir John Moore had written during his advance into northern Spain, "all equally rugged, but all equally to be penetrated". Whilst this statement was essentially correct, most of the roads in Portugal were made of either heavy sand or were covered with masses of loose stones and there were in fact only a few points on the frontier that were crossed by roads capable of conveying a large army deep into Portuguese territory. There were no such roads along the entire northern frontier from the estuary of the River Minho to the River Douro. This borderline faced the Spanish province of Galicia which, following the Corunna campaign, was once again held by the patriots. The occupation of this part of Portugal, or even its regional capital, Oporto, would not have brought about any significant result. For Lisbon (unlike its counterpart, Madrid) was not only the political but also the moral and economic heart of the country and whilst it remained free Portugal remained unconquered. To reach Lisbon from the north three rivers have to be crossed, the Minho, the Douro and the Mondego. The Minho was bridgeless along its journey through Portugal and only fordable after prolonged dry weather. The Douro and the Mondego are both major rivers and an attempt to force the passage of either of these obstacles in the face of a hostile enemy would be fraught with danger.[7]

The whole of the southern half of Portugal, the regions of the Alentejo and the Algarve, possessed only one major road of military significance. This was the main highway from Madrid to Lisbon. Between 1580 and 1807 Portugal had been invaded twenty-three times and on thirteen occasions the invaders had used this route. It ran through Badajoz and Elvas, the two strongest fortresses on the Portuguese-Spanish frontier, and crossed the River Tagus under the guns of another fortress at Abrantes. Badajoz was still held by the Spaniards and Elvas by the Portuguese and the passage of the Tagus at Abrantes, if the northern bank was held in force by a defending army, would be hazardous in the extreme. Any advance south of the Tagus –

through the Alentejo – would only lead the invader to the heights of Almada, where he would still be separated from the capital by the estuary of the Tagus. As the Royal Navy maintained a strong presence in the Lisbon basin, the invaders would never be able to cross the river at this point. "In fact, neither Lisbon, nor anything else of consequence can be injured by this measure," Wellington assured the British Ambassador. "They cannot prevent our embarking and going out of the Tagus; neither can they prevent our using the river for the communications of the army above Lisbon; nor can they injure the town itself." For a further thirty miles upstream from Lisbon the Tagus remained an impassable barrier to an army of the nineteenth century. It is only near Salvaterra de Magos that the Tagus could be forded. An invader from Spanish Estremadura could cross the river there or at any point upstream, but the only permanent bridge at that time (a bridge of boats) was another sixty miles upstream – at Abrantes.[8]

It was therefore extremely unlikely that the principal French attack would be delivered south of the Tagus but, if used in conjunction with an attack from the north, an approach from the south might prove highly dangerous. "The enemy will make his attack in two principal corps," Wellington told Colonel Fletcher. "His object will be, by means of his corps south of the Tagus, to turn the positions which might be taken up in his front on the north of that river, to cut off from Lisbon the corps opposed to him; and to destroy it by an attack in front and rear at the same time."[9]

This was Wellington's greatest fear. If the Anglo-Portuguese army was drawn away from the Lisbon peninsula to meet a threat from the northern frontier, a subsidiary force from the south could ford or bridge the Tagus and cut Wellington's army off from the capital. Such a strategy was so real a possibility that Wellington decided that if the French had an army in motion anywhere in the vicinity of the frontier around the fortresses of Badajoz or Elvas he must leave a considerable proportion of his own force south of the Tagus. In the winter the corps south of the Tagus would constitute approximately a third of Wellington's entire disposable force. In the summer, when the Tagus might be easily crossed, Wellington considered that he would have to leave half his army in the Alentejo. On 9 January Lieutenant-General Sir Rowland Hill was given command of the corps that was to operate south of the Tagus. It was to be a mixed body consisting of the British 2nd Division, two Portuguese brigades under Major-General Hamilton, Slade's brigade of British cavalry and one of Portuguese cavalry, with two brigades of Portuguese artillery. If the French advanced into Portugal, whether in a single body or with a corps on both sides of the Tagus, the two wings of the allied army would withdraw and form a junction below the point at which the river could be crossed.[10]

The main French effort would, almost certainly, be delivered north of the Tagus somewhere along the ninety or so miles of the Beira frontier. This district, between the Douro and the Tagus, was land that Wellington had gained some knowledge of during the Talavera campaign and he also ordered the entire area to be carefully surveyed. By the winter of 1810 most of central Portugal had been accurately mapped on a scale of four miles to the inch, the information being gathered from a variety of sources but mainly from the reconnaissances made by specifically employed "exploring officers". The Beira frontier is divided into two by the Serra da Estrella or Estrela (the Mountains of the Stars) which cross the border line at right angles, halfway between the Douro and the Tagus. The passes either side of the Estrella were described by Wellington as "the two great entrances into Portugal" and he was certain that the French attack would be made along one, or both, of these natural approaches. Throughout the previous century Portugal had fought its wars upon the frontier and General Doumouriez, in his treatise on the defence of Portugal published in 1766, advocated a defensive stand in the passes of the Serra da Estrella. "What could be done against a force entrenched amongst the mountains," he asked, "where there is no passage for wagons and artillery?" The argument against occupying these passes is that the defending forces would be completely separated from each other by the mass of the serra itself. An invader could concentrate his strength against either one of the passes safe in the knowledge that the defenders would be unable to reinforce the threatened wing. Wellington therefore dismissed any idea of attempting to hold the passes of the Serra da Estrella.[11]

South of the Estrella were two routes, one of which ran across the mountains of the Sobreira Formosa, the other via Castelo Branco, Abrantes and the valley of the Tagus. It was along the first of these routes that Junot invaded Portugal in the winter of 1807-8. This was the worst road between the Estrella and the Tagus that Junot could have chosen, for even though the Portuguese offered no resistance he lost many men along the way and he had to leave behind his artillery. This road was never again used by the French for an advance upon the Portuguese capital.

The second route was a more likely avenue for the invaders to take but it would probably involve the French having to force the passage of the River Zezere in the face of the defending army and would certainly have entailed the besieging of the fortress of Abrantes. There were actually two roads that ran east of the Zezere, the old Castelo Branco road and the new bypass, the Estrada Nova. If the French were to invade in this direction it would be along the Estrada Nova that they would march despite the fact that it ran along a virtually barren and completely deserted mountainside. Even though Wellington doubted that the French would use this road he decided to eliminate it from all consideration by destroying it. He ordered the road to be blasted with gunpowder along several points where the track passed along steep precipices, rendering it absolutely impassable for guns and wagons. Companies of irregular troops were stationed at each of these points to hinder any attempts by the French to repair the road.[12]

North of the Estrella, through Ciudad Rodrigo and Almeida, were three routes; one by the valley of the Douro, and two by the valley of the Mondego. The route by the Douro ran through Pinhel and Lamego and led only to Oporto and northern Portugal and could be of no practical use to an invading army aiming for Lisbon. This left just two roads for the French to take, both of which travelled into Coimbra, one north of the Mondego, the other to the south of that river. So, although Wellington had some 400 miles of frontier to defend, there was no doubt in his mind that the main French advance would be made along either one of these roads.

Although both of these roads crossed some difficult ground they also travelled through areas of cultivated land and a number of towns and villages. But of the two roads the route south of the Mondego, through Celorico and Ponte da Murcela, was far superior to the Celorico-Viseu-Coimbra road and was also considerably shorter. It was this southern route that Wellington firmly believed the French would have to follow. This paved highway, which was one of the few roads in Portugal suitable for the movement of heavy artillery, passed through a narrow defile where it crossed the River Alva at the Ponte da Murcela. At this point Wellington ordered the construction of a line of earthen redoubts for it was here that Wellington calculated that he would "fight a battle to save the country".[13]

Yet Wellington was not simply going to chance everything on a single pitched battle despite the strength of the defences he was building at Ponte da Murcela. "I have fought battles enough," he told Sir Charles Stuart, "to know that even under the best arrangements, the result of any one is not certain." Until the end of May the Tagus is not fordable but from June to September or October the river can be crossed in many places as far downstream as Salvaterra and the position on the Alva could be turned from the south by an enemy army crossing the Tagus above that point. So, even though Wellington would attempt to stop the French at Ponte da Murcela, he had to find further defensive positions below the point where the Tagus could be forded or bridged. He knew that the most important consideration was the defence of Lisbon. "In case the enemy should make a serious attack upon Portugal," Wellington wrote to Admiral Berkeley who commanded the Royal Navy's 'Red' Squadron in the Tagus, "his object, as well as that of the allies, would be the possession of the city of Lisbon". Wellington was quite prepared to give up the rest of the country to the invaders in order to "confine ourselves to the preservation of that which is most important – the capital". Wellington hoped to be able to halt the French at Ponte da Murcela but his last stand would be, in all probability, in front of Lisbon. At Torres Vedras, less than thirty miles north of the capital, would be built the great line of fortifications that would deny the might legions of the Emperor Napoleon.[14]

The Lines of Torres Vedras, though they were the most important and elaborate feature in Wellington's strategical plans, were only part of a completely integrated defensive policy which included the re-organisation of the Portuguese regular army, the mustering of the militia, the revival of the ancient call to arms of the "Ordenanza" and the destruction or removal of every commodity that would be useful to the enemy.

The organisation and implementation of these schemes would, however, require time, and the more time that Wellington had, the more complete would be his arrangements. So it was to the great frontier fortresses that Wellington looked to delay the French until his plans reached fruition.

THE FORTRESSES

Portugal's first line of defence, ironically, would be the border fortresses of Spain. Built to threaten Portugal, the massive walls of Ciudad Rodrigo and Badajoz were now to defend it. Both were still held by the Spaniards and they could be expected to defy the French for a number of weeks.

Ciudad Rodrigo was the smaller of the two. It was only a second-rate fortress with medieval walls yet it occupied a vitally important post astride the main highway from Salamanca and northern Spain. Without question the invaders would have to capture Ciudad Rodrigo if they were to advance upon Lisbon from the north-east. The fortress was unlikely to defy the French for long but, as General Hill observed, "the Spaniards often fight longer than they are expected, when they get behind a wall".[15]

Badajoz, far to the south in Spanish Estremadura, was much larger and stronger than Ciudad Rodrigo. Its fortifications had recently been improved, the approaches were protected by four independent forts and along the entire northern face of the fortress the River Guadiana, which is over 300 yards wide at this point, lapped up to the very foot of the walls. The road from Madrid to Lisbon crossed the Guadiana at this point and passed through Badajoz. The fortress would have to be captured before the French could mount a secondary attack upon Portugal south of the Tagus.

Portugal's second line of defence was its own frontier fortresses of Almeida and Elvas. Both were capable of a prolonged defence and all that Wellington had to do was ensure that they were adequately garrisoned. Almeida was placed under the command of the British colonel, William Cox, with 5,000 men consisting of one regiment of regulars and three regiments of militia. Elvas was held by two regiments of regulars and three of militia – 8,000 men – under the Portuguese general Leite.

Four other Portuguese fortresses, Peniche, Valença, Abrantes and Campo Maior, as well as a number of smaller forts, were also placed in a state of defence. Peniche is a small, fortified peninsula on the Atlantic coast forty miles north of Lisbon. Its many sheltered creeks provided ideal harbours for boats and because of its location it was virtually impregnable. "The Isthmus over which the peninsula of Peniche is approached," a British officer on the Portuguese staff wrote in his diary for December 1809, "is covered with water at High Tides, and from the line of Works describing a sort of arc, very powerful cross-fires may be established upon every part of it. There are nearly 100 guns upon the work, the brass ones especially good." If the French penetrated as far as the Lisbon peninsula Peniche would afford an ideal base for allied raids against the rear of the enemy and act as a sanctuary for refugees and as a rallying point from which stranded troops or partisans could be carried off by the Royal Navy. Its defences were improved under the guidance of British engineers sent from England with the intention of occupying it permanently. The fortress was placed under the command of General Blunt and was the depot of seven Portuguese infantry regiments and one artillery regiment with some 2-3,000 recruits to man its defences.[16]

Valença, on the River Minho in the north of the country above Oporto, was situated, according to Captain Eliot who surveyed the area in 1810, "in a point of no small importance" and its defences, destroyed by Soult in 1809, were fully repaired and armed with fifty cannon. This fortress would only come into play, however, in the unlikely event of the French making their attack from Galicia.

Abrantes (once known as "The Key of the Tagus") is located on a hill above the north bank of the Tagus upstream from Lisbon. It is situated at the point where the road from Spain via Castelo Branco crosses the road that runs from north to south down the Portuguese frontier from Almeida to Elvas. Under the protection of its commanding defences had been laid a boat-bridge across the Tagus which could be taken up if the fortress was in danger of attack. Wellington ordered the fortifications of this strategically important town to be re-built and strengthened with new earthworks and redoubts, under the direction of a British engineer. It was garrisoned with two militia regiments.[17]

The fortifications of Campo Maior, a small, medieval fortress close to the Portuguese-Spanish border a few miles north of Elvas, were also restored and the place garrisoned by a single battalion of militia. Later this fortress was handed over to the Spanish army of Estremadura as a place of arms. The fortress of Marvão, which is situated between Castelo Branco and Elvas, was garrisoned with 400 men of the Portalegre militia and was armed with thirty-seven guns.

The Spanish fort of La Concepción, situated on the border between Ciudad Rodrigo and Almeida, was repaired by a contingent of Portuguese troops from Almeida. It was garrisoned by men of the 9th Portuguese Line Regiment with 120 artillerymen serving twelve cannon and two howitzers.

In the Lisbon area the forts that guarded the estuary of the Tagus, those of Cascais, São Julião and the Bugio, were garrisoned and the old citadel of Lisbon, the Castelo de São Jorge, received a force of 1,000 troops but no improvements were made to its defences.

Wellington also ordered the construction of two ranges of field fortifications. The first of these was a line of earthwork redoubts near Penacova behind the River Alva, a left-bank tributary of the Mondego, where Wellington expected to make his decisive stand against the French. Here an abrupt ridge commanded the important Ponte da Murcela, the only bridge across the Alva, which carried the most direct road from Celorico to Coimbra south of the Mondego valley. The ridge dominating the left bank of the Alva offered an excellent defensive position to dispute the river crossing. The redoubts were armed with British 6-pounder and 9-pounder cannon. The second was a system of redoubts and trenches built on the east bank of the River Zezere to cover the main Castelo Branco to Abrantes road at the point where it crosses the river. Though Wellington doubted that the French would use the route through Castelo Branco he decided to position 5,000 militia (under Colonel Wilson) in the mountains of the Sobriera Formosa and to have a further 3,000 militia and Portuguese regulars with 200 or 300 cavalry on the Zezere under Lecor.[18]

THE DEVASTATION OF THE COUNTRYSIDE

Wellington's next step was to put in hand measures for the depopulation and devastation of the countryside in the regions through which the invaders would be likely to pass. This was nothing new to the Portuguese. In their struggle for independence from Spain past generations had become accustomed to the King's command to "execute the Ordinance". Upon this summons the women and children would abandon their homes and retreat towards the capital whilst their menfolk fell upon the invaders. Wellington intended to develop this vague patriotic call to arms into a well-defined and systematic policy. On 1 March 1810, he sent a confidential memorandum to Lieutenant-General Bacellar who was the Governor of the border province of Beira. Bacellar was told that the province was to be left to its own resources for its defence and Wellington made the following recommendations:

> In case it should be necessary, preparations and arrangements must be made for destroying the bridges over the Coa, between Pinhel and Villa Torpin, and Castelo Bom …
>
> Whenever a bridge or road is destroyed, a party of the Ordenanza must be stationed to prevent the enemy from repairing it; and a party must, in the event of the British army quitting this part of the country, be stationed on this side of the bridge of Almeida …
>
> It will likewise be necessary to have parties of the Ordenanza at the several fords on the Coa, from Castelo Bom to the junction with the Douro …
>
> If the enemy should penetrate by passing the Coa, it does not appear that it will be very easy to prevent him from entering the valley of the Mondego. The bridges on the Mondego, in the whole extent of its course from Celorico to Ponte da Murcela, ought to be broken, and arrangements should be made for that purpose, and for posting a party of the Ordenanza at each bridge.

Wellington also ordered Bacellar to prepare to demolish the bridges over the Alva and the Zezere, as well as every other minor river, but not to actually demolish them until he was certain that the enemy would be likely to use them.[19]

As well as destroying many roads and bridges (and four Portuguese engineers were employed expressly for this purpose) Wellington arranged for the repair or development of a number of lateral routes that would assist the rapid transfer of allied troops from the upper Tagus to the centre of the Lisbon peninsula and to Wellington's concentration point at Ponte da Murcela. The first of these ran from Castelo Branco to Abrantes and then along the main highway to Lisbon through Santarém. This road crossed the Tagus at Vila Velha, where a flying bridge was established. A detachment of militia formed a permanent guard to defend this vital river passage. The second, and most important, was the road from Tomar and Espinhal to Ponte da Murcela. Known as the "military road" or the "Espinhal Communication" this route also had a link with Abrantes and, therefore, indirectly with Castelo Branco. "It is really a most important line of communication," Wellington told Beresford, "without which all our combinations for defence … must be very imperfect." The road from Almeida to Ponte da Murcela – the principle highway from the northern frontier – was also improved. Whilst this was the expected invasion line it was also the route that Wellington would use in his withdrawal to the Alva and he did not want his retreat impeded by poor roads. The improvements on these roads reduced the marching time from Viseu to the Tagus (and therefore the junction of the two wings of the allied army) from nine days to just three.[20]

Wellington followed this by issuing a Proclamation to the People of Portugal ordering them to abandon their property if the French should invade. Wellington fully expected to be forced back by the French. "I shall risk nothing at any great distance from the sea," he explained to Admiral Keats. "I shall withdraw gradually towards Lisbon in proportion as I shall find myself pressed by the enemy." As he retreated he expected the Portuguese to leave their homes and remove or destroy anything that might be of value to the enemy. Wellington calculated that the French would be unable to gather sufficient stocks of food to permit them to form magazines along the invasion route and that they would be able to carry with them provisions for no more than one or two weeks, expecting to supplement their rations from the resources of the land through which they advanced. Wellington intended to deny them these resources and to impede and delay their march so that by the time the French reached the Lines of Torres Vedras the invaders would be exhausted and half-starved. "Resistance, and the determination to render the enemy's advance into their country as difficult as possible by removing out of his way everything that is valuable, or that can contribute to his subsistence, or frustrate his progress," ran the Proclamation, "are the only and certain remedies for the evils with which they are threatened." This appeal was later followed by a more detailed Proclamation:

They should be unremitting in their preparations for decided and steady resistance; those capable of bearing arms should learn the use of them; or those whose age or sex renders them unfit to bear arms should fix upon places of security and concealment, and should make all the arrangements for their easy removal to them when the moment of danger shall approach. Valuable property, which tempts the avarice of the tyrant and his followers, and is the great object of their invasion, should be carefully buried beforehand … or destroy provisions which cannot be removed.[21]

On 11 May 1810, Wellington issued another proclamation which gave a list of punishable war crimes:

Firstly: Refusing to supply carts, boats, or beasts of burthen when required.
　　Secondly: Refusing to remove their articles or animals out of reach of the enemy.
　　Thirdly: Disobedience of the orders of the magistrates, to proceed to and remain at any station, with carriages, boats, etc.
　　Fifthly: Embezzlement of provisions or stores which they may be employed to transport.[22]

Wellington also demanded that all the boats on the major rivers should be registered and placed under the jurisdiction of the local authorities. Each boat was to be numbered and the name of the owner, the village to which he belonged, and the boat's number were to be marked on the side. Because the rivers passed through more than one province it was decided to appoint zones of responsibility to selected officers or officials. Along the Tagus, for instance, the Governor of Abrantes was responsible for the movement and registration of all vessels from Vila Velha to Tancos; the Governor of Santarém was responsible for the stretch of the river from Tancos to Valada; another officer at Vila Franca was in charge of the river from Valada to Alhandra, and the final length from Alhandra to Lisbon was controlled by an officer stationed in the capital who was nominated "officer of the marine". It was intended that when the invasion began the registered vessels in each zone would be collected and formed into divisions under the authority of the appointed official. All the boat-bridges on the Tagus for a distance of 150 miles north of Lisbon (which were under the command of a Bridge Master at Abrantes) were also to be withdrawn and all the ferries and other small craft were to be burnt.[23]

All animals were to be driven away (other than horses suitable as cavalry mounts, which had to be handed over to the military authorities), mills and ovens were to be destroyed and all foodstuffs that could not be carried off were to be spoiled. "The moment that the enemy crosses the frontier," Wellington wrote to William Beresford, "the governor of the province of Estremadura must be told that it is necessary to order all carts, carriages, and other means of conveyance, with all the provisions they can carry away. He ought to have all his arrangements prepared for ordering them off as soon as the French approach." As with the boats, all the carts had to be registered in the village or district where the owner resided.[24]

The Portuguese were also ordered to be prepared to evacuate their homes in the path of the invaders. "I hereby declare," began another Proclamation, of 4 August, "that all magistrates or persons in authority who remain in the towns or villages, after receiving orders from any of the military officers to retire from them; and all persons, of whatever description, who hold any communication with the enemy, and aid or assist them in any manner, will be considered traitors to the state, and shall be tried and punished accordingly."[25]

As Wellington did not believe that the French would be strong enough to leave detachments to protect their lines of communications, he reckoned that in the mountainous regions around the frontier it would be sufficient for the natives to take to the hills for a few days whilst the invaders marched by. Thus the inhabitants near the Mondego valley were to remove to the rugged Serra de Alcoba, those close to the Zezere valley were to find refuge in the villages along the Zezere river, and the people in the vicinity of the Serra da Estrella were to retire into that mountain. The people of the western Beira were instructed to fall back to Oporto and the inhabitants of Estremadura were told to be ready to retire to Lisbon and the protection of the Lines of Torres Vedras. Large stocks of food were shipped into Lisbon and Oporto ready for the mass emigration from the provinces. Wellington asked the Regency Council to strengthen and arm the Lisbon police force in order to ensure that his communications through the Tagus would not be compromised by civil unrest during the period when the population of the capital was swollen by thousands of refugees.

If a secondary attack was delivered south of the Tagus through the Alentejo the inhabitants near the frontier were to seek sanctuary at Elvas and those in the northern parts of the province were to move into the hills around Niza and Portalegre. The inhabitants of the western areas of the Alentejo were to make for Setúbal, and those in the south were to go down to the Algarve.[26]

THE PORTUGUESE ARMED FORCES

"I consider the Portuguese Government and army as the principals in the contest for their own independence," wrote Wellington to Lord Liverpool on 14 November 1809, "and that the success or failure must depend principally upon their own exertions, and the bravery of their army." As well as rebuilding and re-equipping the regular army, Wellington intended to revive the militia and call out the men of the Ordinance – the Ordenanza. "If arms can be supplied for the militia," he advised the Secretary of State for War in January 1810, "there is no doubt that there will be in this country not less than a gross force of 90,000 men, regularly organised, besides the whole armed population of the country and the British army."[27]

The population of Portugal in 1809 was calculated as including 1,250,000 males capable of bearing arms and so there should not have been a problem in recruiting for the armed forces. But military service was unacceptable to most young men and it was found necessary to enforce conscription with very severe penalties meted out to those who attempted to desert. "The officers and soldiers of the militia, absent from their corps, are liable to penalties and punishments," Wellington told Britain's representative on the Regency Council. "First, they are liable to the forfeiture of all their personal property, upon the information that they absent from their corps without leave; secondly, they are liable to be transferred to serve as soldiers in the regiments of the line, upon the same information; and lastly, they are liable to the penalties of desertion, inflicted by the military tribunals."[28]

Recruiting was organised on a local basis by the Captain-Major (Capitão Mor) of the Armed Inhabitants, or Ordenanza, of each district. These officials were either resident manorial noblemen of towns or villages or, in the cities or where the local lord did not reside on his property, the chief magistrate.

Each regiment of the regular army was allocated its own recruiting area and when recruits were required for the regiment the Captain-Major would be instructed to collect together the requisite number of men from his district and send them off under an armed escort of the Ordenanza to the regiment. The militia was recruited in much the same way from those males not selected for the regular army.

All the remaining males between the ages of 16 and 60 in each district were numbered by the Captain-Major (assisted by his executive officer the Sargent Mor, who acted in the same capacity as a major in the regular army) and divided into companies of 250 men. Every captain of a company had his own colours. The combined companies of each district were referred to as a brigade. In April 1810 the following *General Return of the Armed Population of the whole Kingdom of Portugal* was published, arranged by province:[29]

Province	Pikemen	Fusiliers	Cavalry	Unarmed	Total
Algarve	6,364	2,992	1,956	3,123	14,505
Alentejo	19,691	7,545	73	–	27,309
Estremadura	45,649	8,027	1,637	3,313	70,710
Oporto	26,631	21,339	45	22,695	58,626
Minho	22,834	15,531	–	25,626	43,123
Trás-os-Montes	19,160	19,685	–	3,678	66,991
Setúbal peninsula	6,781	533	25	7,339	14,678
Lisbon area	28,550	1,900	–	–	32,894
Totals	219,040	105,012	3,478	76,994	411,838

The militia and the Ordenanza were to play important roles in the defence of the country. They were to "do the enemy all the mischief in their power", Wellington instructed General Leite at Elvas, "not by assembling in large bodies, but by impeding his communications, by firing upon him from the mountains and strong passes, with which the whole country abounds, and by annoying his foraging and other parties that he may send out". In March 1810 he advised General Bacellar in Beira to have his Ordenanza "in the best order and prepared for service. The companies must act independently and separately, each in its own district; unless in cases where two or more companies joining can defend a point interesting to the districts to which both belong." The French would find themselves stranded in a barren, deserted and hostile country. Their communications would be cut and their patrols and posts would be continually under attack. "In short," wrote a British officer on the Portuguese staff, "every strong Post upon his line of march should be made the grave of some of his people".[30]

Wellington demanded the embodiment of every one of the forty-eight militia regiments of the national establishment. In theory this should have mustered some 70,000 men but never more than 45,000 were ever under arms at any one time. Many of the districts were too sparsely populated to raise their full quota of 1,500 men and in other districts the local authorities were unwilling or incapable of enforcing recruitment. The militia began their training on 22 October 1809 (and they started by practising "walking" two days every week!).[31]

Of these forty-eight regiments, eight were from the Alentejo and the Algarve regions south of the Tagus. Three of these were taken to form the garrisons of Elvas and Campo Maior and the other two were employed as a corps of observation on the Lower Guadiana. The regiments from the Lisbon area were engaged in building, and then manning, the Lines of Torres Vedras. Three other regiments were in garrison at Almeida, two at Abrantes and one at Peniche. The remaining regiments from the Beira and the Trás-os-Montes were formed into five independent divisions under the overall command of General Manuel Bacellar, the military governor of Beira, with headquarters at Lamego. The first of these divisions – seven regiments from the coastal districts between the Douro and the Mondego led by Colonel Trant – were to cover Oporto and prey upon the rear of the invaders as they marched upon Lisbon. Six regiments under Silveira were to guard the northern frontier region of the Trás-os-Montes against French raids from the Spanish province of Leon. Eight regiments under Millar were to remain around Oporto as a reserve to support either Silveira or Trant. Lecor, with three regiments, was kept around Castelo Branco and, finally, four regiments under General Miranda were stationed at Tomar from where they could either support Lecor or strengthen the garrison of Abrantes.[32]

As well as the militia and Ordenanza, membership of which was obligatory, there were two other categories of irregular troops, both of which were formed from volunteers. The first of these was the Loyal Lusitanian Legion. Embodied in England with a cadre of emigrant Portuguese officers who had left Portugal when Junot disbanded the army, the Legion was shipped to Portugal in 1808 where it recruited over 3,000 men organised into three battalions of infantry, an incomplete regiment of cavalry and a single brigade of artillery. The Legion operated more or less independently around Oporto and the Beira frontier until 1810 when it was brought under Beresford's direct control. Its separate existence ended in 1811 when it was incorporated into the regular army. Finally, there were the companies of civilian volunteers that were raised and funded by the commercial and academic communities of the larger towns and cities. They were raised for local defence and some units had already seen action in the 1809 campaign against Soult at Oporto.

The real fighting, nevertheless, would have to be done by the Anglo-Portuguese army. The Portuguese Army had been disbanded by Junot when the French occupied the country in 1807. After the evacuation of Portugal by the French the following year, the Portuguese Regency Council ordered the complete restoration of the army. Such a task, however, proved beyond the means of the Portuguese authorities and, in February 1809, they asked for British help. The man that the

Portuguese wanted to take control of the army was, naturally enough, Sir Arthur Wellesley. But Sir Arthur, knowing that the Portuguese command would be subordinate to the British field commander in the Peninsula, declined. Instead the offer was passed on to Major-General William Carr Beresford, who was recommended by Wellesley as being "the best officer we had for the command of an army". Beresford took up the post of commander-in-chief of the Portuguese Army with the local rank of Marechal do Campo in March 1809. He had served as Governor of Madeira, when Britain had occupied the island in the name of Prince John following the royal family's escape to Brazil, and had some knowledge of the Portuguese language. Wellington retained overall command of the Anglo-Portuguese forces with the Portuguese title of Marshal General.

In theory the twenty-four Line Infantry regiments, the six Caçadore (light infantry) battalions, the twelve cavalry regiments and four artillery regiments together should have totalled almost 51,000 men. However, in 1808 only 22,361 infantry, 3,422 cavalry and 4,031 artillery had been mustered. Gradually, as more men were conscripted, the regiments began to reach fighting strength. But the return of the old troops to their regiments and the trickle of new recruits to the depots created further problems. Junot had confiscated and destroyed most of the stores of weapons of the old army and in September 1808 the authorities were able to arm and equip only 13,600 men. Vast quantities of muskets were imported from Britain between August and November and by the beginning of December there were 31,000 troops fully equipped for service in the field, including 2,052 cavalry. There were still some 1,400 cavalry without mounts and the lack of horseflesh in Portugal was a severe handicap to the mobility of the artillery. Portugal was not a horse-breeding country and with the British cavalry and artillery also competing for the limited supply of remounts it was not possible to procure sufficient horses for all the regiments. As a result, four of the twelve cavalry regiments were sent to perform garrison duty in the country's fortresses and their mounts were distributed amongst the remaining eight.[33]

Having mustered and equipped the various regiments they now had to be turned into a fighting force. For this to be accomplished each battalion and squadron had to be furnished with the correct number of efficient and experienced officers. The old officers, like their men, had been recalled and most of them re-occupied their former posts; but few possessed the military knowledge or ability to lead their commands effectively.

The Portuguese officer corps was notoriously unprofessional and

31

many of them were far too old to remain on active service. In theory one-third of all officers were promoted from the non-commissioned ranks of the Line regiments. The other two-thirds were chosen from aristocratic cadets who accompanied the regiments to learn the profession of arms. In practice, however, commissions were sold or given away "by intrigue and corruption" often to men with no military training. Advancement for those officers without money or influence was almost impossible. Beresford therefore decided that the only way to bring the army up to British standards of discipline and training was to draft British officers into every regiment. He had, though, to be careful not to injure Portuguese pride and patriotism, for to simply remove all the senior officers would have appeared a gross insult. His way of solving the problem was by ruling that wherever a Portuguese officer was in command of a regiment or a battalion he should have a British as second-in-command under him and, similarly, if a British officer was the regimental or battalion commander then his second-in-command was to be Portuguese. If a brigade was led by a Portuguese officer then the two colonels of the regiments that formed the brigade were both British and vice versa. Each battalion also received between two to four British captains but no subalterns, which meant that there would still be openings in the junior commissioned ranks for the patriotic young Portuguese.

To encourage ambitious British officers to transfer to the Portuguese service they were offered one step in rank in the British service and another in the Portuguese. Therefore a lieutenant, for example, became a British captain and a Portuguese major and he was permitted to draw the pay from both his British and Portuguese commissions. Many of the old or incompetent Portuguese officers were either dismissed or given relatively unimportant administrative posts to make way for the influx of the British officers. Between 15 March and 4 July 1809, 108 Portuguese officers were retired, most of whom were captains or lieutenants, and in July a further 107 were dismissed from the service. Despite the offer of promotion few British officers were willing to transfer to the Portuguese Army, especially as their date of commission into the Portuguese service usually meant that they were junior to the Portuguese officers of the same rank. Nevertheless, by the end of October eighty-four officers had joined the Portuguese Army and over 359 British officers served with the Portuguese Army during the war.[34]

The Portuguese rankers were found to be "well enough, very obedient, willing and patient", but the Portuguese Army still used the old Prussian system of formation and manoeuvres introduced into the army in the middle of the previous century. For the Portuguese regiments to be able to integrate with the British on the battlefield their entire drill had to be changed to the British pattern. This job was entrusted to Major-General John Hamilton, who was appointed Inspector-General of Infantry. Throughout the winter of 1809-10 training depots were established in every province and each regiment was assigned to a particular depot. Hamilton had the British infantry drill book translated into Portuguese as the *Instrucções para a formatura, exercicio e movimentos dos Regimentos de Infanteria* and issued to each regiment. Both battalions of a Portuguese regiment fought together in the field, giving a ten-company format which allowed exact replication of the manoeuvres of a British ten-company battalion. To help with the training one or two British sergeants were added to each battalion. Some of these NCOs distinguished themselves and received Portuguese commissions; one of them, John Schwalbach, becoming a general and later a baron in the Portuguese nobility. The cavalry, the artillery and the Caçadores likewise adopted the respective British regulations.[35]

By the beginning of 1810 the British and Portuguese units of Wellington's army could be moved in the same formations by the same words of command and, on 4 January 1810, Wellington was able to write enthusiastically to the Earl of Liverpool: "I have had opportunities of seeing fifteen regiments in the Portuguese service and . . . the progress of all these troops in discipline is considerable . . . I have no doubt but that the whole will prove a useful acquisition to the country." By 22 February they had reached a level of competence such that he felt confident he could integrate some of the Portuguese regiments into the British divisions. The 1st and 3rd Caçadores joined the Light Brigade to form the Light Division; John Hamilton's Portuguese Division was attached to the British 2nd Division, and a Portuguese brigade was added to each of the 3rd and 4th Divisions and two to the recently formed 5th Division. In addition, there were four independent Portuguese brigades, each composed of two Line Infantry regiments and one battalion of Caçadores. There were also four regiments of cavalry with the army brigaded together under General Fane and seven brigades of artillery totalling forty-two guns drawn from all four artillery regiments. Almost half of Wellington's 52,274-strong field army was now Portuguese and in the event of the British being forced to evacuate Portugal Wellington intended to take a large proportion of the Portuguese army with him as it was "becoming so good as to be worth the expense of removing them".[36]

Another problem with the re-organisation of the Portuguese Army was with the commissariat. Britain had agreed to pay for 20,000 (later 30,000) Portuguese troops to serve with the British Army but the responsibility for feeding them still lay with the Portuguese authorities. The Portuguese commissariat was divided into two departments, one being responsible for the supply of provisions, the other for transportation. The former, the *junto da direcção geral dos provimentos das munições de boca para o exértio,* had Intendants in every province and storekeepers, or Feitors, in every town. The method of supply was that the Portuguese Government contracted with the junta for the different kinds of provisions and forage at a fixed price and the Feitors were then directed to purchase on the spot what was required at the cheapest possible price. The impecunious farmers could not afford to sell their products at such low prices and consequently they offered as little as they could to the army, hiding the rest. What food the army did manage to acquire, whether by purchase or simply by seizing what it could find, was paid for in government bills which were rarely honoured and were regarded as worthless. As a result, the troops were always half-starved; "the Portuguese army could not be in the distress under which it suffers, from want of provisions," Wellington complained to the British minister in Lisbon, "if only a part of the food it receives from the country were paid for". Although Wellington ordered changes to the commissariat structure, the problem was never satisfactorily addressed and the Portuguese troops were always inadequately supplied. Nevertheless, by the spring of 1810 Wellington was able to inform Lord Liverpool that the Portuguese were ready to take the field. "We have done everything for the regulars that discipline could do … and the regulars have been armed and equipped as far as the country would go … If the Portuguese do their duty, I shall have enough."[37]

THE LINES OF TORRES VEDRAS

It is widely believed that the original idea of building a line of fortifications across the Lisbon peninsula was conceived by a Portuguese major, José Maria das Neves Costa. Towards the end of 1808 Neves Costa examined the hilly districts north of the capital and the following June he submitted a report *(Memória Militar respectiva ao Terreno ao Norte de Lisboa)*, with maps, detailing his ideas to Dom Miguel Forjaz, the Portuguese minister of war. This information was passed on to Wellington in the autumn of 1809. Yet Wellington did not need to be told about the defensive characteristics of the Lisbon peninsula. When he had first landed in Portugal the previous year he had been supplied with "an excellent map and topographical accounts," Wellington had told the Board of Inquiry on the Convention of Cintra," which had been drawn up for the use of the late Sir Charles Stuart". This officer, not to be confused with the British Ambassador to Portugal of the same name, had commanded a mixed force at Lisbon in 1796 and he had perceived "that if the French should ever seriously attempt the conquest of Portugal, here was the vantage ground of defence", and Wellington had seen for himself that it was "very difficult to adopt any line of march in Portugal which will not afford strong positions to an enemy acting on the defensive." Furthermore, the report on the defence of Lisbon written by the French engineer, Colonel Vincent, which suggested the building of fieldworks at Torres Vedras, "the right of which could be extended to the Tagus, the left to the sea", had also come into Wellington's possession.[38]

With this knowledge and experience Wellington was formulating his defensive plans as early as March 1809 (three months before he was in receipt of Neves Costa's report) when he proposed to the British Government that "twenty pieces of brass (12-pounders) ordnance upon travelling carriages should be sent to Portugal, *with a view to the occupation of certain positions in the country*" [author's emphasis]. A few weeks later, in May 1809, he asked General Mackenzie to "urge the completion" of works to defend the passage of the Tagus at Abrantes and to examine the Tagus along its length, particularly between Punhete and Abrantes, in order to locate every point where the river could be forded in the dry season. Defensive works were then to be constructed at any of these points where an important road crossed the river. Later that month Colonel Fletcher was already reporting on the feasibility of erecting batteries for the defence of the upper Tagus. Wellington also asked the Secretary of State for ordnance and military stores which included tools, iron wedges, rope, iron, steel, tarpaulins, sandbags and ballast baskets "in order to get this country in a proper state of defence", having already (on 7 May) sent two engineers "with orders respecting the defence of Lisbon [and] the Tagus". Consequently, when it was suggested by Forjaz that Neves Costa should receive some form of reward for his original proposal to build a defensive barrier north of Lisbon, Wellington replied that he had never seen Major Das Neves Costa in his life and that when he examined the ground recommended by Neves Costa he found that "no reliance" could be placed upon the Major's observations. In fairness to Neves Costa his report must have helped to consolidate Wellington's own developing ideas, though, and even if Neves Costa's maps and plans were flawed, Wellington was being uncharitable in refusing to grant him the recognition that the Portuguese believed, and still believe, was his due.[39]

In October 1809 Wellington undertook a thorough reconnaissance of the countryside to the north of Lisbon. Accompanied by Colonel Fletcher his Commanding Engineer, and the Quartermaster-Generals of both the British and Portuguese armies (and, of course, Neves Costa's maps) Wellington examined the roads, rivers, peaks and passes of the Montachique and Montejunto hills. Immediately following his survey, on 20 October, Wellington issued a formal memorandum to Fletcher detailing his plans for the construction of two successive lines of trenches and redoubts which became known as the Lines of Torres Vedras.

"In whatever season the enemy may enter Portugal, he will probably make his attack by two distinct lines, the one north, the other south of the Tagus; and the system of defence to be adopted must be founded upon this general basis," Wellington explained to Fletcher in his memorandum. "In the winter season the river Tagus will be full, and will be a barrier to the enemy's enterprises with his left attack, not very difficult to be secured. In the summer, it is probable, as I have stated, that the enemy will make his attack in two principal corps, and that he will also push one through the mountains of Castelo Branco and Abrantes. His object will be, by means of his corps south of the Tagus, to turn the positions which might be taken in his front on the north of that river; to cut off from Lisbon the corps opposed to him; and to destroy it by an attack in front and rear at the same time. This can be avoided only by the retreat of the right, centre, and left of the allies, and their junction at a point at which, from the state of the river, they cannot be turned by the passage of the Tagus by the enemy's left." The Tagus could be crossed in no less than twelve places between Abrantes and the sea during dry weather and Fletcher was therefore instructed to plan the defences to run from a point below the lowest ford (at Salvaterra de Magos) across the whole of the Lisbon peninsula to the estuary of the River Sizandro (Zizandre) on the Atlantic coast.[40]

If Wellington was unable to stop the French at Ponte da Murcela then the Anglo-Portuguese army would withdraw towards these defences, the first of which would take the form of a number of independent strong-points designed to block the four main roads into Lisbon. At Torres Vedras, Sobral de Monte Agraço, Arruda (and later Alhandra) large entrenched camps would be built, each capable of holding between 2,000 and 5,000 soldiers and dozens of cannon. If the invaders were to break through these strongpoints the army would withdraw along a selected route to a second, even more substantial, line of fortifications which were built some three to five miles behind the first line between Alhandra on the Tagus to Carvoeira on the coast. The chosen road between the two lines would be commanded by strong works upon which the rearguard could stand to hold back the advancing enemy whilst the Anglo-Portuguese army took up its positions on the main defences. Other roads running southwards which the French might use to outflank the retreating army would be destroyed.

When complete, in 1812, the Lines comprised 152 works which mounted 534 guns, required 34,125 infantry to man their ramparts, and covered fifty-two miles of ground. "The Lines were of such an extraordinary nature that I daresay there was no other position in the world that could be compared to them," wrote a French officer who first saw the Lines in 1810. "In effect, it was not enough to encounter this formidable wall of rocks, supported on one side by the sea and on the other by an immense river. Behind it was a great capital with its arsenals, workshops, magazines to furnish all needs, workers of every description, artillery depots, and numerous batteries where large calibre guns were concentrated." But Wellington's plans did not end there. The object of the allied forces, Wellington had told Colonel Fletcher, was the defence of Lisbon. "There is another also connected with that first object, to which we must attend," Wellington explained to his Commanding Engineer, "viz., the embarkation of the British troops in case of a reverse."[41]

THE EMBARKATION POINT

The British Government had made it quite clear to Wellington that the forces he commanded constituted the only effective field army that Britain possessed and Lord Liverpool repeatedly stressed that "the safety of the army is to be your first object." Even though Wellington fully expected to stop the French at Torres Vedras, arrangements had to be made to establish a secure embarkation point.

Because of the rocky nature of the coast of Portugal there are few spots suitable for such a major operation and only four places were given any serious consideration. Lisbon itself could not be used. It would have been "difficult, if not impossible, to bring the contest for the capital to extremities, and afterwards to embark the British army" because, as Wellington had explained to Viscount Castlereagh, "Lisbon is so high up the Tagus that no army that we could collect would be able at the same time to secure the navigation of the river by the occupation of both banks, and the possession of the capital." One of these, either Lisbon or the southern bank of the Tagus, would have to be given up and the Portuguese would obviously abandon the navigation of the river, and with it the British army's port of embarkation, before they would surrender their capital. Admiral Berkeley, who commanded the British squadron stationed in the Tagus, therefore suggested the little bay of Paco d'Arcos. Wellington rejected Paco d'Arcos as it was within artillery range of the south bank of the Tagus and, as has already been explained, Wellington believed that the French would make a secondary attack south of that river.[42]

The second place to be investigated was Peniche. This small peninsula, some forty miles north of Lisbon, was already strongly fortified and virtually impregnable. In December 1809 Peniche was inspected by Marshal Beresford's Quartermaster-General: "This is the most favourable position that can be conceived for embarking the British army, should it ever be necessary to do so. The circumference abounds with creeks and clefts in the rocks, inside which there is always smooth water, and easy egress for boats. They are out of reach of fire from the mainland: indeed, there is sufficient room to encamp a large force perfectly beyond the enemy." Peniche was favoured by the British Government who saw it as a second Gibraltar that could be held by British troops even if Portugal was overrun and occupied permanently by the French. Wellington knew that he could defend Peniche against attack almost indefinitely. But if the French invasion took place between June and November, when the Tagus is fordable, the allied army might be forced to withdraw eastwards for fear of exposing its flank and a retreat to Peniche would be impossible. Also, the main Lines of Torres Vedras were only twenty-two miles north of Lisbon and Peniche was well outside these defences. So, despite its obvious strengths, Peniche was discounted as the final embarkation point.[43]

The next place to be considered was Setúbal which Wellington visited on 23 October 1810. This town, which became an important commercial and fishing port, lies over twenty miles south-east of Lisbon. Wellington calculated that Setúbal could be held for eight days and would be a practical point for embarking the army. Being on the south side of the Tagus, however, meant that Setúbal could be cut off by a French army operating in the Alentejo. So, though unsuitable as the main embarkation point, Setúbal was not completely ignored: defensive posts were constructed on the approaching road and the ground around the bay was fortified and prepared as a secondary embarkation area.

As none of these places were regarded as entirely satisfactory Wellington instructed Fletcher to investigate the coastline south of Lisbon. Fletcher subsequently reported that the small bay of St Julian (São Julião), though far from ideal because "at intervals, such a sea rolls in for days together that no boat can with safety approach the shore", could be made secure enough to allow an uninterrupted embarkation. Situated just a few miles below the capital, the bay was partially sheltered by a rocky promontory upon which was built the sixteenth-century fort of São Julião da Barra which, "from its extravagantly high scarps and deep ditches", recorded Captain Jones of the Royal Engineers, "can never be successfully assaulted against the slightest opposition". Wellington had found his embarkation point.[44]

The works to cover an embarkation had to embrace an area of land sufficiently large enough to contain the whole army, along with all its artillery and stores, and they had to be strong enough to hold back the enemy for a number of days in case of adverse weather conditions. The outer perimeter at St Julian was composed of a line of detached redoubts (closed, independent forts) and intermediate defences. It extended for over 3,000 yards from the mouth of the Tagus near Fort das Maias to the Atlantic by the old tower of Junquiera. The fortifications embraced the town of Oeiras and the whole promontory of Fort St Julian. Altogether twelve separate works were constructed, which held seventy-four guns with over 4,000 defenders, and the place was provisioned with 100,000 prepared rations. Work began on the defences around St Julian before the first ground was broken at Torres Vedras.

There was a further requirement for a small, fully enclosed post to be built within the principal trace of such a size and strength that it could be held by a limited number of men should a part of the army be left ashore due to the onset of a gale after the bulk of the army had been embarked. This was provided by the construction of a substantial stone redoubt on the summit of the height immediately in front of Fort St Julian. This work was to be garrisoned with 1,340 men and was armed with twenty 24-pounders. These were the heaviest ordnance mounted in any of the works around St Julian or even in the Lines of Torres Vedras. The reason for concentrating all the big guns here was that if the French turned any of the guns captured from the other redoubts upon this last post they would be overmatched by these much heavier pieces.

The final consideration was for a strong and secure position to protect the rearguard during the last moments of the embarkation. This was adequately met by Fort St Julian itself and from the fort a ramp was built through the outer ravelin wall down to the beach. Four jetties were also built on the shore to facilitate boarding the boats.[45]

As the safety of the army might well depend upon the defences at St Julian, these were subject to the tightest possible security. "You will give directions to the officer who will command at St Julian," Wellington wrote to Colonel Peacocke at Lisbon, "to attend to the orders heretofore given respecting the works, and to allow no person whatever to go into or to inspect them, excepting the officers of the engineers or artillery."

Although the lines north of Lisbon were to be manned by native troops and militia, the defences at St Julian were to be garrisoned only by the Royal Marines and regular British infantry. The works remained secret for many years after the war and in Jones' original account of the construction of the Lines of Torres Vedras the plans of the St Julian defences were intentionally omitted. "No plan is given of the positions of Almada, Oeiras (St Julian) or Setúbal," Jones explained, "as it is possible they may, in the course of years, be again occupied." In fact this area continued to be occupied by the Portuguese Army, more military establishments were built, and in the twentieth century the fort at St Julian became a headquarters for NATO.

At Setúbal, the secondary embarkation point south of the Tagus, a short line of seven redoubts was constructed. These defences incorporated eight windmills, each being linked by a communications trench. This line was designed to accommodate a single infantry division whilst the remainder of the army embarked. The town of Palmela on the road to Setúbal was also given "some security" so that it could be held by a rearguard whilst the main allied force retired upon the Setúbal defences.

In the event of the army being forced into an immediate and precipitate withdrawal before the completion of Wellington's defensive lines the Brigade of Guards (one of the few formations that had maintained discipline throughout the retreat to Corunna) was to cover the retreat and embarkation. The combined Light companies of the brigade would be the last troops to embark.[46]

These then were Wellington's plans for the defence of Portugal. The border fortresses would have their fortifications strengthened and their garrisons reinforced. The Portuguese Army would be re-formed and in every province the militia would be re-constituted and armed. As soon as the invaders crossed the borderline the native population would abandon their homes and seek sanctuary in the mountains. Everything they could not take with them was to be destroyed. Crops were to be burnt, wells polluted and the ovens and mills dismantled. All the smaller roads were to be blocked or broken up so that the French would be forced to move in one great mass which would slow their march and exacerbate their logistical difficulties. To further impede their progress the bridges over the major rivers would be mined and all the boats removed or burnt. The flanks and rear of the enemy would be constantly harassed by the Ordenanza and the militia, who would cut off stragglers and attack patrols.

As the enemy advanced, so the Anglo-Portuguese army would withdraw until they reached Ponte da Murcela or, if their flank was threatened by a subsidiary invasion force south of the Tagus, the retreat would continue. The allied army and the inhabitants of the towns and villages below Ponte da Murcela would retire upon Lisbon, which would have been turned into a huge fortress. Behind the forts and entrenchments of the Lines of Torres Vedras the army and the non-combatants would be supplied by the ships of the British merchant marine, whilst the invaders starved in the "scorched earth" around them. Even if the French were to penetrate the Lines and drive the British back to their ships, the defences around St Julian and Setúbal would enable Wellington to evacuate the army in complete safety. There would be no second Corunna.[47]

All this would soon be put to the test and the great contest for the possession of Portugal, which Sir Charles Oman called "the central crisis of the whole war", would commence. It would be a campaign that neither side could afford to lose, for there would be no second chances. If Britain was expelled from Portugal she might continue the war on a smaller scale through the Spanish fortress-port of Cadiz (which the French would never capture if it was adequately garrisoned), but Cadiz is situated on the south-western tip of Spain and its occupation by an allied army would mean little to the people of Castile or Navarre or the abandoned Portuguese. Offensive operations from such a base were also likely to be limited to amphibious raids along the adjacent coastlines. Though some guerrilla bands might still continue to oppose the French occupation forces, the Peninsular War would effectively be over the day that the French marched into Lisbon.[48]

For Napoleon the war was proving to be far more problematical than he had ever imagined; it had been in progress for three years and was becoming an increasing burden upon France's economic and military resources. Napoleon had to win, and win quickly. He therefore planned no other offensive actions anywhere in Europe. Every other Imperial ambition was to be suppressed until Portugal had been conquered. With peace in central Europe, Napoleon had more troops available for the invasion of Portugal than he had at any time in the past or would ever have in future. If he could not conquer Portugal now then it would remain forever beyond his grasp and the war in Spain, which was costing the lives of 50,000 French soldiers each year, would know no end.

CHAPTER III
"Persevering Labour"

It was on 20 October 1809 that Lieutenant-Colonel Richard Fletcher, Royal Engineers, received Wellington's memorandum ordering him to examine the proposed positions for the Lines in front of Lisbon. The first defensible point below which the Tagus was fordable was at the mouth of the Castanheira river. In the event of an attack from the north Wellington intended to place 10,000 men, including all the cavalry, behind the Castanheira between the Tagus and the heights to the west. The highway from Madrid to Lisbon ran alongside the Tagus and, with the exception of three detached corps guarding the other paved roads into Lisbon, the main body of the allied army would be stationed below the position at Castanheira. These detached corps were to consist of 5,000 men at Torres Vedras, 4,000 men at Sobral de Monte Agraço and 2,000 men at Arruda. If the French attack was delivered along the road by the Tagus, and if they succeeded in forcing the Castanheira position, the allied army would fall back to Alhandra. Similarly, if the enemy attacked through either Torres Vedras, Sobral or Arruda the army would withdraw to Mafra, Cabeça de Montachique or Bucelas. Here, across the southern arms of the Montejunto, would be constructed the principle line of the defences and Fletcher was asked to review the following positions:

1. He will examine particularly the effect of damming up the mouth of the Castanheira river, how far it will render the river a barrier, and what extent it will fill.
2. He will calculate the labour required for that work, and the time it will take, as well as the means of destroying the bridge over the river, and of constructing such redoubts as might be necessary on the plain. He will state particularly what means should be prepared for these works. He will also consider the effect which might be produced by scarping the banks of the river.
3. He will make the same calculations for the works to be executed on

the hill in front, and on the right of Cadafões; particularly on the left of that hill, to shut the entry of the valley of Cadafões.

4. He will examine and report upon the means of making a good road of communication from the plain across and hills with the valley of the Cadafões, and to the left of the proposed position, and calculate the time and labour it will take.

5. He will examine the road from Otta Abringola, Labougueira to Merceana, and thence to Torres Vedras; and also from Merceana to Sobral de Monte Agraço. He will also examine and report upon the road from Alenquer to Sobral.

6. He will entrench a post at Torres Vedras for 5,000 men. He will examine the road from Torres Vedras to Cabeça de Montachique, and fix upon the spots at which to break it up might stop or delay the enemy; and if there should be advantageous ground at such spots, will entrench a position for 4,000 men, to cover the retreat of the corps from Torres Vedras.

7. He will examine the position of Cabeça de Montachique, and determine upon its line of defence, and upon the works to be constructed for its defence by a corps of 5,000, of which he will estimate the time and labour.

8. He will entrench a position for 4,000 on the two heights which command the road from Sobral de Monte Agraço to Bucelas.

9. He will entrench a position for 4,000 men on the height of Ajuda, between Sobral and Bucelas, to cover the retreat of the corps from Sobral and Bucelas; and he will calculate the means and the time it will take to destroy the road at that point.

10. He will construct a redoubt for 200 men and three guns at the windmill on the height of Sobral de Monte Agraço, which guns will bear upon the road from Sobral to Arruda.

11. He will ascertain the time and labour required to entrench a position which he will fix upon for 2,000 men, to defend the road coming out of Arruda towards Vila Franca and Alhandra, and he will decide upon the spots at which the road from Arruda to Alhandra can be destroyed with advantage.

12. He will construct a redoubt on the hill which commands the road from Arruda, about one league in front of Alhandra.

13. He will examine the little rivers at Alhandra, and see whether by damming them up at the mouths he could increase the difficulties of a passage by that place.

14. He will fix upon the spots to construct redoubts upon the hill of Alhandra on the right, and prevent the passage of the enemy by the high road, and on the left, and in the rear, to prevent by their fire the occupation of the mountains towards Alverca.

15. He will determine upon the works to be constructed on the right, and prevent the passage of the enemy by the high road, and on the left, and in the rear, to prevent by their fire the occupation of the mountains towards Alverca.

16. He will determine upon the works to be constructed on the right of the position upon the Serra de Serves, as above pointed out, to prevent the enemy from forcing that point; and he will calculate the means and the time required to execute them. He will likewise examine the pass of Bucelas, and fix upon the works to be constructed for its defence.

17. He will calculate the means, time and labour required to construct a work upon the hill upon which a windmill stands, at the southern entrance of the pass of Bucelas.

18. He will fix upon the spots on which signal-posts can be erected upon these hills to communicate from one of these positions to the other.

19. It is desirable to have an accurate plan of the ground.

20. He will examine the island in the river opposite to Alhandra and fix upon the spot, and calculate the means and the time required to construct batteries upon it on the approach to Alhandra.

21. He will examine the effect of damming up the river which runs by Loures, and calculate the time and means required to break up the bridge at Loures.[1]

Throughout military history long defensive lines have rarely succeeded in repelling a strong and determined attacker. It is impossible for a defending army to man every part of such a line, whereas the attacker can concentrate all his strength upon a single point and overwhelm the defenders. Furthermore, when the fortifications of such a line have been breached, the line no longer retains any defensive capability as its flanks and rear are completely exposed to the attacker. Consequently, no attempt was to be made by Fletcher to construct a continuous linear rampart and, as large sections of the Montachique hills are inaccessible to cavalry, artillery and all forms of wheeled transport, no fortifications at all were necessary for many miles of the proposed defensive area. The Lines of Torres Vedras were therefore to be composed of a series of individual forts placed so as to defend roads, passes and low-lying ground and, where possible, grouped close enough together to be mutually supporting. Each fort was also to be rendered capable of an independent defence so that even if the line was pierced at one point the garrisons in the other redoubts could still fight on. These forts were to be manned by second-line troops, allowing the field army to remain massed behind the fortifications ready to move to the support of the defenders at any threatened point.

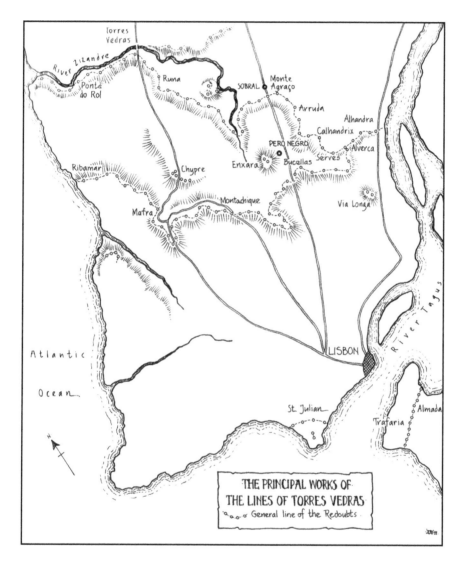

THE PRINCIPAL WORKS OF
THE LINES OF TORRES VEDRAS
o-o-o General line of the Redoubts

The front of the area selected for the Lines was divided by the main range of the Serra de Montejunto, a steep and rugged height that projects fifteen miles north of Sobral de Monte Agraço. Any movement by an assailant across the front from Alhandra to Torres Vedras and the western end of the Lines would involve a two-day march around the Montejunto. No comparable obstacles prevented the transfer of the defending forces to any point along the defensive line which meant that, apart from a corps of observation on each flank, the allied army could remain in a single body. If the enemy were to succeed in penetrating the

45

defensive line then the full force of the field army could fall upon the attackers before they could exploit the breakthrough.

Fletcher was given sole responsibility for the construction of the Lines, with Wellington visiting the area to inspect the work in progress on only one occasion (February 1810) and Wellington arranged for Fletcher to have all the men, money and materials that he would require. "As the works carrying on under Lieutenant-Colonel Fletcher may require the employment of persons in the country, and the use of materials," Wellington wrote to the Commissary-General, "without waiting for the employment of those persons, or the purchase of those materials by an officer of the Commissariat, I have to request that all orders for workmanship, labour or materials, drawn by Colonel Fletcher upon the Deputy Commissary-General at Lisbon, may be paid; Colonel Fletcher being held accountable for the money." Fletcher was assisted by Captain John Jones (the original historian of the Lines), eleven other officers of the Royal Engineers, two from the King's German Legion, and three from the Portuguese army. There were also eighteen men of all ranks from the Royal Military Artificers, the forerunners of the Royal Sappers and Miners.[2]

In June 1810 Fletcher joined the field army on the frontier, leaving Jones in charge of the work in progress. Despite his relatively junior rank, Jones was vested with "plenary control" over all the Portuguese authorities of the towns and districts through which the Lines passed and no one, "of whatsoever rank, civil or military, Portuguese or English", was allowed to interfere in any manner with his arrangements.[3]

Work on the Lines began almost immediately. As it was possible that the French invasion would start within a few months, attention had to be focused upon St Julian and the line of retreat to the embarkation point. Strong, enclosed works to block the passes of the three roads that travelled over the Montachique hills to Lisbon and the main highway that ran along the Tagus, were the works that had to be built before any others. On 31 October Marshal Beresford was therefore asked to send 600 militia to Torres Vedras, 500 to Sobral and 800 to St Julian. Fletcher ordered 19,000 palisades (barriers of wooden stakes) and 10,000 facines (bundles of branches tied together used as inner supports for field fortifications) to be prepared at Torres Vedras and along the banks of the Tagus. Orders were also placed in England for 1,500 pickaxes, 1,500 mattocks and 300 felling axes to be sent to Lisbon. Ground was first broken at St Julian on 3 November under Captain Wedekind of the KGL. at Sobral de Monte Agraço on 4 November under Captain Williams; at Torres Vedras on the 6th under Captain Mulcaster; at Mafra on 17 January 1810 under Captain Ross; at Ericeira on 19 February under

Lieutenant Rice Jones; at Montachique also on the 19th under Mulcaster; at Via Longa on 24 February under Lieutenant Stanway; at Arruda on 17 March under Lieutenant Forster; and at Ponte do Rol under Lieutenant Thompson on 26 March. Fletcher established his headquarters at Lisbon.[4]

The manpower available to Fletcher was considerable. The workforce was composed of both forced labour and volunteer workers. The forced labour came from a conscription of males within a radius of forty miles from the works and the four regiments of the Lisbon militia, the latter being engaged as pioneers. The militia were employed in pairs, marching up from Lisbon to serve alternate tours of duty. On 20 December notices were posted in the towns and villages close to the proposed defensive area asking for volunteer labourers and skilled "mechanics". The militiamen were paid an additional two vintems (a little over one and a half pence) per day for their efforts, the labourers were paid six, and the mechanics twelve vintems. Rations were also provided for the workmen. The workers were paid every week in silver (deductions being made for the rations) and approximately 5,000 to 7,000 workmen could be found employed on the Lines at any one time. Men were also taken from the Line regiments of the regular army to act as artificers. These troops were nominally under the orders of a captain based at Mafra and a subaltern at Alhandra.[5]

The men were employed in gangs of some 1,000 or 1,500 peasants and militiamen, each gang under the command of a single engineer officer with the assistance of just two or three English or Portuguese military artificers, and much reliance was placed upon the skills of the labourers. Though the peasants were compelled to work under a foreign hand for almost twelve months, whilst their own lands lay untended, there was not a single reported case of insubordination. As Captain Jones was later to concede: "The great quantity of work performed should, in justice to the Portuguese, be ascribed more to the regular habit of persevering labour in those employed than to the efficiency exercised over them."[6]

Fletcher was first instructed to examine the possibility of damming up the River Castanheira with a view to flooding the flat land adjoining the Tagus and in so doing obstructing the road which ran alongside the river directly to Lisbon. On 31 December Fletcher submitted his report on the project to Wellington: "I should conceive, from what I have now seen that the Castanheira river at low water, when the Tagus is low, is not, at that point … a serious impediment." Fletcher therefore proposed to build the dam near to the mouth of the river, using the displaced earth to fill in the hollows. He calculated that this would involve the removal of 20,000 "solid" yards of soil, and at the rate of three yards per man per day, would require the labour of 1,000 men for a week. The whole of the area was to be commanded by fortifications on the hill which overlooked the river estuary and other works which would enfilade any approach to the river by the French. Another redoubt was to be placed about 300 yards from the road leading to the principle ford.[7]

A few days after receiving Fletcher's report Wellington gave his chief engineer permission to dam the river and to construct the suggested redoubts. Unfortunately, when Wellington inspected the work at Castanheira in February 1810, he realised that the position could be turned by its western flank. The Castanheira position was immediately abandoned and the entrenchments filled in. The eastern end of the Lines was then withdrawn further south to Alhandra.

The revised defensive line was divided into eight districts, each one under the command of an engineer. District No.1 ran from the Tagus at Alhandra to Arruda; District No.2 was from Arruda to the Monte Agraço, No.3 ran from the Monte Agraço to the pass of Runa and No.4 from the pass of Runa to the sea. These four districts formed the northern or outer line. The southern and principal line was composed of three districts. On the eastern side of the line, from Quintella on the Tagus to the pass of Bucelas, was District No.5. District No.6 ran from Bucelas to Mafra and No.7 was from the Royal Park at Mafra to the Atlantic. District No.8 was the semi-circle of fortifications around the embarkation point at St Julian. For the purpose of identification, the various works were numbered in the order of their completion.[8]

Along the first seven miles of the southern line (District No.7), from Ribamar on the coast to the pass of Mafra, runs the deep and rugged ravine of the São Lourenço river. This ground is so difficult that Jones believed there were scarcely any points along its front which could be surmounted by a formed battalion. Here the destruction of some peasants' paths and the siting of just twenty guns in six small, enclosed works (redoubts Nos.88-94) was regarded as quite sufficient to enable a small corps of observation to hold this section of the line until reinforced. These forts were erected on spurs that projected into the gorge and enabled the guns to enfilade the more accessible parts of the ascent from the foot of the ravine. The works along this sector were under the supervision of Lieutenant Rice Jones and later Major Fras. Rapozo of the Portuguese engineers.

The pass of Mafra, on the other hand, was strengthened with particular care. "The position of Mafra is undoubtedly very important," Fletcher told Wellington on Christmas Day 1809, "and were it possible to approach it only by the road from Torres Vedras, would be exceedingly strong; but this strength will naturally induce an enemy to attempt the flanks, and, including our whole line of defence from the Tagus to the sea, these are, I fear, our most vulnerable points." Captain Ross, the engineer in charge at Mafra, also believed that even though the ground was "rough and difficult" it was perfectly "passable" and that the redoubts would not prevent a French column from "penetrating with impunity". As a result no less than twenty-seven redoubts were built along this sector and, according to Ross, they were made "as strong or rather stronger than field works usually are".[9]

The first defensive positions at Mafra were formed on the roads approaching the town. On either side of the main road from Torres Vedras by the village of Serra de Vila there was a deep ravine which provided good defensive fronts for 3,000 to 4,000 men to enfilade the road with musketry. Further along the road, at Turcifal, the main church and its surrounding buildings were also turned into a strong infantry post. Just after the village of Bandalhoeira the road was carried over a gully by a stone bridge which was prepared for demolition.

Approximately 800 yards beyond the bridge the road was flanked by a range of heights – the Serra de Chypre (Chipre) – upon which Fletcher proposed to build three redoubts, incorporating three windmills that sat on the crest of the hill. This height stretches for about a mile at an oblique angle from the road and it completely dominates the valley through which the road travels. Eventually four redoubts were constructed on the Serra de Chypre. These were Nos.78-81 comprising eight 12-pounders, five 9-pounders and 970 men.

From the Serra de Chypre the road runs up to, and through, the pass of Mafra. There was already in existence a small redoubt placed on a knoll at the foot of the pass and Fletcher decided to support this redoubt by siting two guns in a windmill which was situated on the crest of the hill overlooking the knoll. At the rear of the serra there was an old road which, when repaired, would allow the defenders of the redoubts on the heights to retreat to the main Mafra defences with their guns if they were forced to evacuate the position.

By the right-hand side of the pass two roads run along the boundaries of a large walled park. This is the Royal Park or Tapada. The roads, sheltered by the walls of the park, offered an attacker an ideal avenue around the flank of the main position. To counter the possibility of such a manoeuvre the park was heavily fortified by adding a banquette (a ledge upon which infantry could stand, enabling them to fire over the wall) and by blocking the roads with loopholed entrenchments. Four redoubts (Nos.74-7) were thrown up on the most commanding points within the enclosure of the park and each feature of the ground overlooking the approach to the park was also occupied by a redoubt. Altogether twenty-one pieces of artillery, including eleven 12-pounder cannon with 1,915 infantry, were detailed for this flank alone.

The main ascent to the pass was heavily entrenched with artillery and infantry positions. The town of Mafra itself was formed into a defensive post and covered by a chain of redoubts (Nos. 85-7) that blocked the only lateral approach practicable for artillery.

Fletcher was concerned that the invaders might attempt to turn the Mafra position by following the ravine behind Cadoçal, to the east of Mafra, to reach the Mafra-Montachique road from where they could fall upon the rear of the defenders. To guard against this a cluster of redoubts (Nos.82-4) was built to the left of the village of Murgeira, some three miles to the north of the Mafra pass.[10]

From the pass of Mafra to the pass of Montachique (District No.6) the hills are generally high and steep. But when Fletcher examined this sector in February 1810 he calculated that to be able to block all the minor roads from the north no less than thirteen redoubts would have to be built. "The points on which it would be proper to place these," he informed Wellington on 24 February, "are in general rocky, and extremely unfavourable for removing, and I much fear that we shall not be able to do anything effectual on this important line by works only." Fletcher promised that he would do all that he could in the time that he had available but strong infantry supports would be essential along this sector of the line. By September eleven isolated redoubts had been thrown up on the hills (Nos.62-73) linked together by a lateral road that ran between the two passes. The redoubts overlooked the difficult country in their front, commanding every approach to the lateral road.

The heights forming the immediate flanks to the pass of Montachique were so naturally strong and favourable for defence that very little labour was expended on them. Instead, considerable attention was devoted to blocking the main Torres Vedras-Loures-Lisbon road which ran through the pass. The road was defended with twenty-four pieces of artillery secured in nine redoubts (Nos.52 to 61) situated on advanced features of the ground. These redoubts were built so close to each other that they formed a chain of posts collectively stronger than the steep flanks of the pass. Yet the ground on the most commanding heights in this area was found to be difficult to excavate and the redoubts could not be furnished with deep ditches or high parapets. This meant that they would be vulnerable to infantry assault and Fletcher advised Wellington that strong, mobile reserves would be essential to reinforce any threatened points. Fletcher observed that there were a great many trees on both sides of the road and he recommended that they should be cut down and left to lie where they fell to further impede the French advance. Fletcher also planned to have a battery of six field guns at Montachique, which could be moved to command either the Torres Vedras road or the road to Mafra. At the rear of the pass, on rising ground 700 yards from the junction of the Montachique and Lisbon roads, a redoubt for 300 men and three field pieces was built to cover a retreat if the pass was forced.[11]

The heights from Montachique to the pass of Bucelas were regarded by both Fletcher and Jones to be so inaccessible that no defensive works were required. Only the road over the ridge of Freixal offered an avenue of attack and this was blocked with three retrenchments (Nos.49-51) mounting eight guns. Redoubt No.51 (of 300 men and four 12-pounder cannon) also commanded a road that travelled to Freixal along the rear of the Cabeça de Montachique.

The road that runs through the narrow pass of Bucelas travels between two high and steep mountains and was therefore easily defended. The approach to the pass was guarded by redoubts 43, 44, 46, 47 and 48, with redoubt 45 placed to the rear to cover the retreat of the defenders should they suffer a reverse. The bridge at the entrance to the pass was mined and the road blocked.

From Bucelas to the Tagus (District No.5) the Serra de Serves, a high and extremely difficult ridge, occupies a front of over two miles with scarcely a break before dropping sharply down to the low ground bordering the Tagus. This low ground extends for two and a half miles before reaching the river and it required considerable strengthening. A cluster of redoubts (Nos.34-9) formed the main defensive barrier in front of Via Longa, situated roughly in the centre of this stretch of land. Three more redoubts on the spur of the serra formed the left flank and a redoubt (No.33) situated close to the Tagus was built on the right. A cut was also made across the salt-flats bordering the Tagus by widening and deepening an existing ditch. This cut, which was flooded by the Tagus, obstructed the approach to the main position.

Even though these redoubts mounted forty-seven guns with almost 2,500 men in their garrisons, this section of the line, because of the nature of the ground, was still regarded as being the weakest and much reliance was to be placed upon a chain of strong heights forming an almost isolated feature about five miles to the north at Alhandra. Here, to enfilade the main road and flank the low ground, were established redoubts Nos.1-8 of twenty-one guns, including sixteen 12-pounders. A road was formed along the rear of the Serra de Serves to allow troops to pass from Bucelas, through Via Longa, down to Alverca on the main

Lisbon road below Alhandra. The Alhandra position marked the extreme eastern end of the first line.

The whole line, twenty-four miles long (twenty-two miles if measured in a straight line from end to end) and comprising fifty-nine redoubts with 232 pieces of artillery and requiring 17,500 men to garrison its works, constituted the principal line of defence across the Lisbon peninsula. Some five to nine miles ahead of this line a series of detached works was also constructed. Originally designed simply to block the approaches to the main line and to delay the invaders whilst the Anglo-Portuguese army took up its positions behind the defenders, they developed into a barrier almost as strong as the line in their rear.

The most important of these advanced posts was built at Torres Vedras, from which place the entire defensive system took its name. The Torres Vedras fortifications were built on the heights of São Vicente which overlooked the Coimbra-Lisbon highway. The ground was found to include a large proportion of rock and hard gravel but by 2 January 1810, Captain Mulcaster estimated that he had only "a month's work in store" to finish all the fortifications at Torres Vedras. The defences consisted of five redoubts (Nos.20-4) and held forty guns and 2,200 men. In addition to these linked redoubts the Convent of São Joa and the old Moorish castle, which stands on a small hill in the centre of the town, were also re-fortified and armed with five 12-pounder and three 9-pounder cannon to form redoubts Nos.25 and 27. "I wish you could see my intrenchments," Mulcaster wrote to a fellow engineer who was with the field army. "Unlucky dogs that ever have to attack them."[12]

To the west of Torres Vedras the open countryside offered the enemy a route around the heavily fortified town, the only obstacle being the little river Zizandre. The passage of this river was consequently guarded by three redoubts (Nos.30-2) with a combined firepower of eleven guns and 973 men.

The other major advanced work was situated at Sobral de Monte Agraço. This redoubt (No.14) was built to hold 1,590 men and twenty-five guns, including fourteen 12-pounders. In advance of this fort three independent redoubts were placed at points on the ridge from where they could enfilade the ascent and flank the main work. As with Torres Vedras, the flank of the Sobral position could be turned, in this case by the road through Arruda. Consequently, redoubts Nos.9-13 were thrown up to obstruct the passage of the road where it ran through the Arruda pass.

The last of the original forward posts was the group of redoubts at Alhandra, referred to above. Initially the first fortifications on this eastern extremity of the Lines were to be at Castanheira, with Alhandra forming only part of the second line. When the works at Castanheira were abandoned, Alhandra became not just the principal but the only fortified position on the Tagus apart from the redoubts at Via Longa. The road which ran along the flat land by the Tagus was an easy and obvious route for the French to take, with no naturally strong features to impede their march, and Fletcher fully appreciated that "with respect to the position at Alhandra, of course, nothing more can be expected than that some of the most prominent points should be taken to *assist* the defence". Nevertheless, Fletcher told Jones that "as much as possible should be done there ... whether by scarping or works ... you will cause redoubts to be commenced on such parts as may afford good flanking points ... They should, I conceive, have a ditch not less than 10 feet deep and 15 feet wide ... The bottom of the ditch should be palisaded ... They should not be for less than 200 men, and three or four pieces of artillery each. Should you find parts of the height that are favourable for scarping, you will employ a body of workmen upon them to render these places impracticable".[13]

Following these instructions Jones rode over to Alhandra. Initially 1,500 men were employed in the construction of four redoubts (Nos.122-4) across the accessible ground behind Calhandriz and two months later, on 29 August 1810, Jones submitted a report on the work completed by that date. The Alhandra position, he explained to Fletcher, naturally divided into four sections. The first of these was composed of an isolated range of heights with a deep and difficult valley skirting its front and left. Some 2,000 yards of ground along the summit of these heights had been cut and blasted to form a continuous scarp more than ten feet high. The scarp was flanked throughout its length by musketry and cannon and redoubts had been placed on the crest of the heights.

The second section was from the bottom of the heights to the Tagus, a front of approximately 700 yards, most of which was low and flat. Across this ground a retrenchment had been dug, complete with a ditch and flanked by a redoubt built against the foot of the heights.

The third section was a hill which formed the left flank of the Alhandra position. Parts of this height had also been scarped and two redoubts (one for 400 men and eight 12-pounders, the other for 350 men and six cannon) had been erected on the most commanding points.

The last and most vulnerable part of the Alhandra position was the long, south-facing rear. The ascent to the position from the rear was gentle and very open and almost impossible to defend. The rear would only be attacked if the French were able to march through the hills to the west of Alhandra but Jones was very concerned about this western flank because behind Alhandra were heights which, if occupied by the enemy, would cut off the retreat of the garrisons of the Alhandra redoubts. Jones therefore proposed either to build a large redoubt capable of holding a full battalion on the heights behind Alhandra or to entrench the hills to the west as far as Ajuda.

On the line of retreat, from Torres Vedras on the northern line to Montachique on the southern line, two retrenchments (Nos.28 and 29) were formed at Enxara dos Cavaleiros. Similarly at Ajuda, between Sobral and Bucelas, redoubts Nos.18 and 19 were built. Constructed just a couple of miles ahead of the main Line, these posts would come into play if the allied rearguard was being hard-pressed by the enemy.

The known fords across the Tagus below Abrantes were also to be defended by batteries. To cover the three main fords between Valada and Salveterra – a distance of five miles – ten earthworks were to be formed to accommodate twenty-four guns. As these positions would have to be abandoned if the Anglo-Portuguese army withdrew to Torres Vedras, the armament would be composed entirely of well-mounted mobile field artillery. Unfortunately battery No.19 was situated so close to the river that it was washed away and when Fletcher inspected the batteries on 25 June he found that the wooden gun platforms had been stolen!

Both flanks of the Lines rested on water – Britannia's domain – and, in order to help deter a French advance along the low ground by the Tagus and the flat beaches by the sea, gunboats manned by the Royal Navy were to patrol between Salvaterrra and Alhandra on the Tagus and from Ericeira to Maceira Bay on the coast. Wellington had also proposed the establishment of batteries on the island of Leitia in the Tagus opposite Alhandra (item twenty of his memorandum to Fletcher) but these were not actually erected until the winter of 1810, when the French were encamped before the Lines.[14]

Finally, Lisbon itself was partially re-fortified. The roads leading into the city through the suburbs were narrow and flanked by stone houses which had iron gratings covering their windows and doors. As Jones regarded these to be ideal supports for irregular troops acting on the defensive, it was considered unnecessary to strengthen the perimeter of the city. However, the Portuguese were "encouraged" to erect barriers and traverses at the entrances to the capital, with other strongpoints being formed inside the city. Artillery was also mounted on the walls of the citadel and the Peña Convent.[15]

All the redoubts of the two defensive lines were, in effect, little more than enclosed battery emplacements situated in positions where artillery fire was required to cover some particular point. The redoubts were placed so as to deny access along a road or to delay the repair of a bridge, or sweep the entry of a pass. Most of the redoubts were

THE LINES OF TORRES VEDRAS

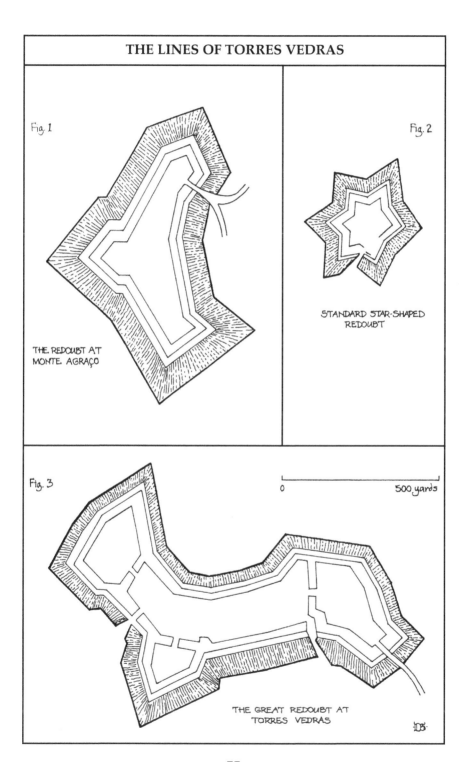

Fig. 1

THE REDOUBT AT
MONTE AGRAÇO

Fig. 2

STANDARD STAR-SHAPED
REDOUBT

Fig. 3

0   500 yards

THE GREAT REDOUBT AT
TORRES VEDRAS

THE LINES OF TORRES VEDRAS

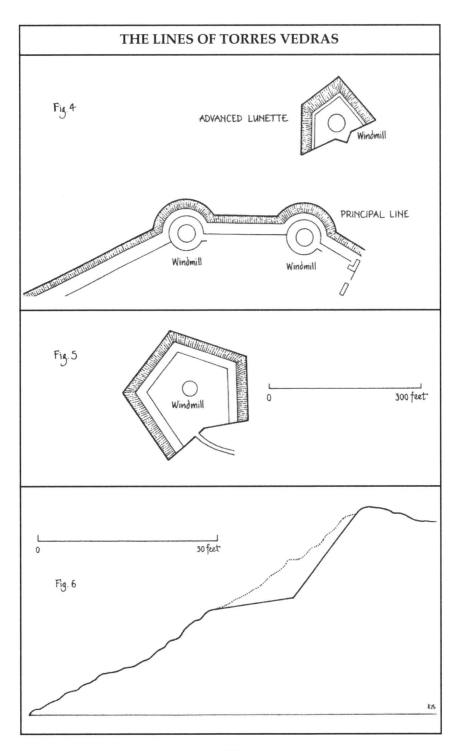

Fig. 4

ADVANCED LUNETTE

Windmill

PRINCIPAL LINE

Windmill

Windmill

Fig. 5

Windmill

0   300 feet

0   30 feet

Fig. 6

THE LINES OF TORRES VEDRAS

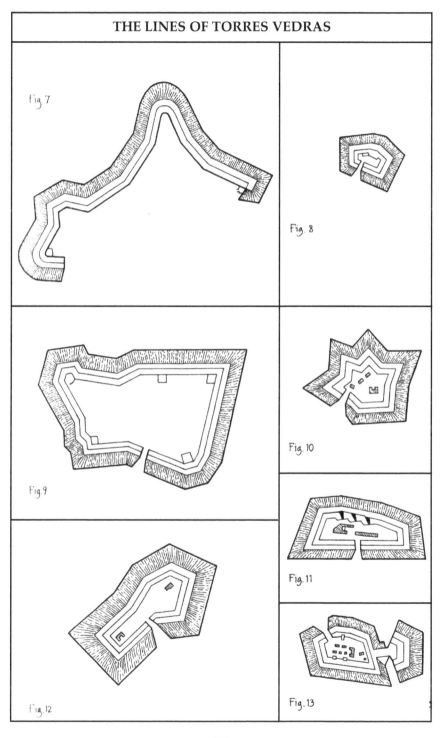

Fig 7

Fig. 8

Fig.9

Fig. 10

Fig. 11

Fig.12

Fig. 13

completely independent of each other and, as Jones explained in his *Memoranda Relative to the Lines thrown up to cover Lisbon,* "were made of a strength of profile to resist an assault, and placed on points where artillery could with great difficulty be brought to cannonade them".

Those redoubts that were built to defend a particular feature of the terrain or point of communication were usually constructed upon the summit of the heights they occupied so that each face of the work would have a full command of the ground in its front or of the point it was intended to protect. These elevated situations also gave the garrison increased protection from direct enemy fire. Many redoubts, though, were placed on top of hills with sides so steep that the effectiveness of the defending artillery was considerably reduced and the muskets of the infantry were unable to scour the whole of the hillside below. Because of this, on some of the very steep hills, particularly on the Monte Agraço, additional small outworks were established in front of the main fortification. Known as flèches, these advanced batteries were made of the same strong profile in their front as the redoubts, and their gorges (or entrances) were equally secured, except that the rear parapets were formed as mere screens so as not to give cover against fire from the main work if they were captured and occupied by the enemy. At these same points, where it was considered likely that the troops of the army would act in conjunction with the redoubts occupying the summits of the very elevated heights, gun emplacements were prepared for field artillery on the best flanking or enfilading positions much lower down on the face of the hill.

With some redoubts, where there was insufficient internal space to permit the mounting of artillery within their walls, the guns were placed on lower, advanced levels which were connected at their flanks with the defences of the main work. Where the purpose of the redoubts was simply to prevent an enemy occupying a certain spot, they were situated on an inclined plane on the reverse slope of the height so that only the front face rose above the crest of the hill, giving the work more protection than if it sat exposed on the summit.

The actual shape and size of each redoubt was determined by the nature and importance of the position which it was to defend and the amount of available ground space. As a result there were a great variety of different constructions. Many of the first redoubts to be built were star-shaped (Figs.2 and 10) so as to permit a flank defence for the surrounding ditch. This design was later rejected, as the angles at which the faces were set were considered so obtuse as to expose the defenders to "friendly fire" from the opposite faces. It was also found that this shape restricted the interior space of the redoubt and did not allow for the concentration of a large number of guns on any single front. The later redoubts were more individual in designs with extensive faces for artillery positions along their fronts (Figs.7, 12 and 13).

Fig.8 is typical of the small redoubts (fifty men and two pieces of ordnance) that were built where ground space was extremely limited. By contrast, Fig.9 (for 500 men and six guns) was built in a situation where there were no space restrictions and the only consideration was the importance of the position it was to defend.

Where a redoubt was erected purely to prevent an enemy establishing himself upon the ground where the fort was placed, the design was kept as simple as possible. Such works (Fig.11) had only a few faces, allowing a powerful defensive fire to be concentrated upon the most probable avenues of attack.

The great works at Torres Vedras and Monte Agraço were by far the largest of all the redoubts and both had secondary defensive positions, or retrenchments, within their walls. Each of the salient angles of the Torres Vedras redoubt (Fig.1) were formed into independent posts, and the Monte Agraço redoubt (Fig.3) had its most salient points cut off by internal earthen traverses. These internal defences were intended to serve as rallying points if the attackers breached or scaled the main wall.

Many of the small, circular stone windmills that were found throughout the region were also frequently incorporated into the defences. Some redoubts were built around the mills, where they were used as observation posts or as secondary strongpoints, and others had the windmills converted into advanced flèches (Figs.4 and 5).

Although the profile of the different redoubts varied on every face and flank, depending on whether it was likely to be stormed by infantry or bombarded by artillery, a number of general principles were commonly adopted. All ditches had to be at least fifteen feet wide at the top and ten feet deep and no parapet was more than ten feet thick unless it was likely to be exposed to heavy bombardment. Jones gives the dimensions of those redoubts open to be "violently cannonaded" as follows:

	Feet	inches
Height of the interior crest of the parapet.	7	0
Height of the parapet above the banquette.	4	3
Thickness of the parapet.	14	0
Berm [a path around the foot of the parapet to allow communication around the work and to stop debris filling the ditch].	2	0
Breadth of the ditch at the top.	16	0
Depth of the ditch below ground level.	12	0

Some redoubts that were built on high knolls, where artillery could never be brought to bear upon them, were made of stone only two feet thick in order to gain more internal space. In many of the very elevated positions the banquettes were raised to within four feet of the crest of the parapet to allow the defending infantry to lean right over when engaging the enemy.

The angle at which the exterior slopes were cut was entirely dependent upon the firmness of the soil. But after the first winter it was found that at any angle greater than forty-five degrees the soil was simply washed away by heavy rain. (Captain Ross, in charge of the works at Mafra, told a friend that the redoubts were more likely to be breached by the weather than by the French!) By 1811 most of the exterior slopes of the redoubts were retained with dry stone walls. The interiors of the parapets were held by facines and sandbags but many of the sandbags rotted and burst after the first winter.

The first line of defence for each redoubt was a row of abattis. These were described by Jones as being formed "solely of the stems and boughs of whole trees, pointed, all the smaller branches being cut off, so that the front of the abattis afforded neither cover nor concealment to an assailant, although it presented a barrier of spears, five, six and seven feet in height". The abattis were usually placed from twenty to thirty yards in front of the redoubt, each stem and large branch being firmly staked into the ground. Behind the abattis were dug trous-de-loup, consisting of between eight and ten rows of pits between two and two and a half feet deep. Each pit was planted with sharpened stakes, as was the intervening ground. Behind the trous-de-loup was the glacis. This was an inclined plain stripped of all cover that led to the top of the defensive ditch. The earth excavated from the trous-de-loup was often used in the construction of the glacis.[16]

The number of troops required to garrison the redoubts and retrenchments was set at a figure of two men per yard of frontage, less the spaces occupied by the artillery. As it was estimated that each man required three feet of room to be able to wield his musket effectively this figure ensured that each parapet was adequately manned and still left a strong reserve in each work to replace those that were killed, or to counter-attack any assailants that broke through the main defences.

Each redoubt was furnished with sixty rounds of ammunition for each artillery piece, eight of which were grapeshot (or canister). The great redoubts at Torres Vedras and Monte Agraço were provided with 160 rounds per gun, including thirty of grape. In addition most redoubts were supplied with twelve to sixteen hand grenades, with the Torres Vedras and Monte Agraço works being issued with 200 grenades. The ammunition was stored in magazines built of splinter-proof timbers, ten inches by eight inches thick, placed at forty-five degree angles against substantial earthen traverses. The floors of the magazines were usually sunk two, three or even four feet into the ground with a drainage ditch dug around the base. The tops of the magazines were set just below the protection of the redoubts' parapets. To keep the ammunition dry the magazines were lined internally with planking and strengthened externally with two feet of earth in sandbags, over which tarpaulins were spread.

The ordnance mounted in the works were Portuguese 12, 9 or 6-pounder cannon, with a small number of 5.5-inch howitzers in some of the larger forts. The guns were mounted on very low carriages and could not be moved over broken ground. There was, therefore, no danger of the guns from a captured redoubt being of any practical use to the invaders. All the guns on carriages were taken from the arsenals at Lisbon but there were insufficient mounted pieces to arm all the works. To make up the numbers Admiral Berkeley was asked to remove the ordnance and ammunition from a squadron of Russian warships that had taken refuge from a storm in Lisbon harbour and had been captured by the Royal Navy at the time of the Convention of Cintra. The weapons and military stores were transported to the Lines by boat along the Tagus. At first the platforms for the artillery pieces were formed from single wooden planks. During wet weather, however, the platforms sank under the weight of the guns and during the summer of 1810 the wooden platforms were replaced with stone.

Secure casks of fresh water were provided for the garrisons at a ratio of one gallon per man, in addition to tubs of water for the use of the artillery crews. A store of entrenching tools was also provided in the following proportions:

		Shovels	*Pickaxes*	*Felling axes*
Works for	400 men	10	6	3
	300	8	4	2
	200	7	4	2
less than	100	6	3	2

The entrance to each redoubt was closed with a barrier-gate and access to the entrance across the ditch was via a wooden bridge of planks and joists which, presumably, could be raised or removed in the event of an attack. In many of the redoubts an earthen banquette was placed behind the entrance, from which the defenders could fire upon any attackers that broke through the gate.

To permit communication between the various clusters of redoubts military roads were traced along the rear of the ranges of heights and therefore concealed from the ground in front. Many miles of roads were completely new, and if they crossed low-lying ground that was susceptible to flooding, were properly paved. Where possible existing country tracks were widened and their surfaces strengthened with small rocks and stones. This network of roads was extended throughout 1811 until it ran along the entire front line from the Atlantic to the Tagus.

Where the ground was suitable for scarping this was done by cutting the front slopes of the heights near their summits as perpendicularly as the soil or rock would permit. Fig.6 depicts a section of scarped hillside nearly two miles in length formed along the summit of the front of the position at Alhandra in August and September of 1810. Much of the upper twenty or thirty feet of that range was found to be a ledge of precipitous rock covered with only a few feet of earth. The rock face was easily made completely insurmountable by blasting with gunpowder.[17]

A system of sending orders and intelligence along the Lines was introduced. It took the form of naval "telegraphs" situated at key points along the line. Various forms of signalling equipment were proposed but the design that was adopted consisted of a mast and a single yard arm. Five drop-balls (inflated pigs' bladders) were suspended from the arm and at the top of the mast a flag or pennant could be flown. Messages were sent in prearranged numerical codes (using Home Popham's *Marine Vocabulary)*, the numbers being formed through various combinations of balls and flags. On the outer line five signal stations were erected:

1. At redoubt No.30 near Ponte do Rol by the Atlantic.
2. On the São Vicente chapel in the great redoubt at Torres Vedras.
3. On the summit of the Monte Socorro above Wellington's headquarters at Pero Negro.
4. At Sobral de Monte Agraço.
5. On the hill above Alhandra on the Tagus.

There was a similar system of telegraphs on the second Line and one at St Julian. As there were no trained signallers with the army, Wellington obtained the services of a party of seamen from Admiral Berkeley's squadron. Each signal station was manned by three sailors who had to remain near to it at all times. By early July, the stations were all completed and manned by sailors. The first trials, however, were not a success. The masts were discovered to be too light for the arms and two of the masts were pulled over by the weight of their yards. The seamen also found that the distance between the signal stations was too great for the messages to be easily read and at Ponte do Rol the signals blended into the background and could not be seen. Stronger masts therefore had to be erected at each station, better quality telescopes were purchased at Lisbon and at Ponte do Rol a pinewood was cut down to give a clearer backdrop. By 3 August, Jones was able to report that he had sent a message from Alhandra to Mafra in clear weather with no difficulty. Eventually it was found that a message could be sent the twenty-nine miles from the Tagus to the sea in just seven minutes and from Monte Socorro to either end of the Line in four minutes. Fletcher also ordered Portuguese-designed "arm" telegraphs to be sent to each signal station. These were simpler to operate and were to constitute a back-up system in case the sailors had to return to their ships.[18]

A network of telegraphs and beacons, which made use of the medieval "atalaias", or watchtowers, along the Portuguese frontier, was also established from Almeida, Abrantes and Elvas to Lisbon to warn of the enemy's approach. Another telegraph at Lisbon maintained communications between the capital and the ships of the Royal Navy anchored in the Tagus estuary.

The land required for the sites of the redoubts and all the associated roads and scarps was taken without any prior reference to its owners or occupiers. Compensation was paid, however, for any crops that were destroyed by the building of the works and for any olive trees that were cut down. More than 50,000 trees were felled to form the magazine platforms, the barrier-gates, the bridges, abattis etc., the majority of which were taken from the Royal parks (especially the park at Mafra) and were provided free of charge, but payments were made for any trees taken from private woods. The owners of the mills which were dismantled and incorporated into the works received a monthly payment equivalent to the average profit normally earned by each mill and a lump sum to cover the cost of restoring the machinery. The total expenditure on the Lines, including payments to the Portuguese labourers, reached £60,000 by 6 July 1810. When the Lines were finally completed in 1812 this figure had risen to £200,000.[19]

Throughout the winter of 1809-10 the great range of defences grew in strength and complexity. Wellington furnished neither his own government nor the Portuguese Regency Council with details of the Lines and all documentation relating to the work was carefully controlled. (One day Fletcher saw a plan of one of the works under construction lying on a table whilst he was having lunch. "Ah! this is nicely drawn, but plans are very dangerous things," he said, as he tore it to pieces!) Though thousands of civilians and soldiers were employed in their construction, and huge tracts of land were requisitioned by the army, only a select band of officers understood the importance of the fortifications that were being erected to the north of Lisbon. Even engineers responsible for the building of the Lines failed to appreciate the significance of the work that they were engaged upon or the process by which the redoubts were to be integrated into a complete defensive system. The supervising engineer at Mafra – one of the key points on the second line – believed that the forts in their "fixed open order" were "useless" and that the only way they might stop a French column would be if they were on wheels! "They might do this and no more," wrote Captain George Ross RE, "they offer good supports to any position our army takes." Ross clearly did not realise that this was exactly, and only, what the redoubts were intended to accomplish.

If relatively senior engineers did not realise that these "useless" works would one day be the last bastion in the defence of Portugal it is understandable that the British Ambassador in Lisbon and the Regency Council did not know where the Lines were until the day the troops marched into Sobral, even though the main defensive line was only a day's ride from the capital. So despite covering fifty-two miles of countryside and involving thousands of workers, Wellington was able to keep the Lines of Torres Vedras a complete secret from an enemy who was already gathering his forces on the frontier for the invasion of Portugal.[20]

CHAPTER IV

'Masséna of the Flashing Eyes'

At 02.00 hours on 12 July 1809, following France's victory at Wagram near Vienna, the Archduke Charles of Austria and Napoleon I, Emperor of the French, signed an armistice that ended the war of 1809. Within a week of the cessation of hostilities Napoleon was re-organising his armies ready for the assault on Portugal. There were to be no half-measures. A new army would be formed, headed by the incomparable Imperial Guard, and led by Napoleon, who was determined to "finish the business" in person.[1]

The Danube and the Tagus, however, are almost two thousand miles, and half a continent, apart. Even the Grande Armée, renowned for its prodigious forced marches, could not cover such distances before winter took the mountains of northern Portugal in its unwelcoming grip. The invasion of Portugal would begin, therefore, in the spring of 1810.

Ahead of his advancing armies Napoleon set his propaganda machine into action: "spread everywhere the news of the arrival of the Emperor with 80,000 men", he ordered his chief of staff, "in order to disquiet the English and prevent them from undertaking operations in the south [of Spain]". But the fact was that despite his success against the Austrians in the east Napoleon was becoming increasingly concerned about the security of the northern frontier of his empire. In St Petersburg the nobles were openly protesting against the ban on trade with Britain, which Napoleon had forced upon Russia, and from Prussia could be heard the faint murmuring of German nationalism. Portugal was on the very edge of Europe; Napoleon had to be at its centre. Consequently, he decided to detach only one of the army corps that had taken part in the war against Austria for the invasion of Portugal. This was a second-line formation originally called the "Corps de Reserve de l'Armée d'Allemagne." It was brought up to a strength of 30,000 men, re-titled the VIII Corps, and ordered to march over the Pyrenees in December 1809.[2]

Further reinforcements followed in the wake of the VIII Corps throughout the spring and summer of 1810. Without weakening his garrisons in Germany and along France's northern borders Napoleon was able to assemble another army corps from the 4th Battalions of those regiments already in Spain. This formation, the IX Corps, numbered almost 21,000 men. From the cavalry depots of the sixteen regiments of dragoons that were serving in the Peninsula, eight provisional regiments of two squadrons each were formed and moved into Spain early in the year. The two divisions of the recently created Young Guard, along with three regiments of Guard cavalry and twenty squadrons of the Gendarmerie, added another 20,000 men to the vast body of French troops occupying northern and central Spain. In addition to these large formations, small draughts of single battalions and squadrons were dispatched to join their parent regiments in Spain as soon as they could be formed into "régiments de marche". Altogether the reinforcements sent into Spain amounted to 138,000 men which, by July 1810, brought the French forces in Spain up to a staggering total of 360,000.[3]

From this vast body of men Napoleon allocated approximately 130,000 for the invasion of Portugal and, on 17 April 1810, an Imperial Decree announced the formation of "l'Armée de Portugal". The invasion force was to consist of the II, VI and VIII corps along with an artillery and cavalry reserve, supported by three unattached divisions under generals Kellermann, Bonnet and Serras. In addition, the IX Corps under Drouet, which was forming in France, was to assemble at Valladolid "to reinforce or sustain the invading army in case of need".[4]

There was to be no further extension of French-held territory until Portugal had been conquered and the invasion was to be made in overwhelming strength, in massed formations, under a single commander-in-chief. Yet it was not Napoleon who was to lead the invasion. In December Napoleon divorced the ageing and now barren Josephine and, on 1 April, Princess Marie Louise of Austria became Empress of the French. As Napoleon's attention would now be concentrated upon the enviable task of producing an heir, command of l'Armée de Portugal was entrusted to one of his marshals, the Prince of Essling, André Masséna.

Masséna was France's most experienced serving marshal. He was fifty-two years old and past his prime but he had a proven record as an independent commander and when confirmation of his arrival in Spain was received at Wellington's headquarters the British commander reminded his staff that they were in the presence of "one of the first soldiers in Europe". Napoleon, with whom Masséna had served since

1796, described him thus: "Dull in conversation, decided and intrepid in action, danger gave his thoughts clearness and force … his dispositions for a battle were always bad, but his temper was pertinacious to the last degree: he was never discouraged". But the rigours of the recent war against Austria had taken its toll on his health. "He is no longer the Masséna of the flashing eyes, the mobile face, and the alert figure whom I knew in 1799," recalled General Foy. "He is only fifty-two, but looks more than sixty." Masséna had hoped that the Wagram campaign would be his last and when he first addressed the staff of l'Armée de Portugal he told them quite frankly, "I am here contrary to my own wishes; I begin to feel myself too old and too weary to go on active service. The Emperor says that I must." The reluctant Masséna took with him his son, Jacques, as an aide-de-camp and his eighteen year-old mistress, Henriette Leberton (dressed as an Hussar with tight-fitting breeches and fur-lined pelisse) and, remarkable though it may seem, Masséna's concern for her welfare was to play an influential part in the long and arduous campaign that was to come.[5]

Masséna did not arrive at Valladolid in north-western Spain until May 1810, by which time the opening moves in the campaign had already taken place. On 19 November 1809, Cuesta's army, now commanded by Areizaga, was routed and dispersed at Ocaña and nine days later a second Spanish army met a similar fate at Alba de Tormes. Apart from the Marquis de La Romana's force near Badajoz, there was no other large body of Spanish regular troops to continue the fight so, despite Napoleon's instructions not to undertake any fresh conquests until the British had been driven out of Portugal, Marshal Soult with Victor's I Corps and Mortier's V Corps invaded Andalusia, capturing Seville at the end of February 1810. The treasures of the South American colonies were no longer being shipped to Spain, the first fruits of plunder had already been consumed by the invaders and Andalusia offered an irresistible "harvest yet untouched" to the hard-pressed French forces. However, a Spanish corps under the Duke of Albuquerque escaped into the fortress-port of Cadiz and the local junta appealed to Wellington for help.[6]

The British Government was now in a dilemma. Cadiz was regarded as one of the strongest places in the world and with a powerful garrison supported by the Royal Navy it could be rendered utterly impregnable. But Britain did not possess the military resources to hold both Cadiz and Portugal in sufficient force to guarantee their security. Every soldier that stood on the ramparts of Cadiz was one less man to defend Lisbon and Wellington had already expressed his views on the subject quite clearly. "If you should take up Cadiz," he told the Secretary of State for War, "you must lay down Portugal". Britain had invested too much in Portugal, both financially and politically, to abandon it without a fight and therefore only limited support could be offered to the Spaniards. Nevertheless, by the end of March 9,000 British and Portuguese troops under Sir Thomas Graham, with 18,000 Spanish regulars, were holding the narrow fortified isthmus that separated Cadiz from the mainland and a large proportion of Soult's force became embroiled in a protracted siege.

The II Corps (which was destined to form part of l'Armée de Portugal) had been stationed on the Tagus near Talavera to protect Soult's rear during the invasion of Andalusia. With this mission largely accomplished the II Corps was ordered to link up with Marshal Mortier's V Corps which was to undertake the siege of Badajoz. But Mortier was compelled, partly by the want of supplies and partly by the movements of La Romana's army, to withdraw from Estremadura and he rejoined Soult in Andalusia. This meant that altogether 70,000 French soldiers – twice the number of the British troops in Portugal under Wellington – were removed from the main theatre of the war at the most critical period of the entire conflict.

The II Corps retired to Merida, where Reynier arrived from the north and took over command. The II Corps remained at Merida throughout the spring, keeping open communications between Madrid and Seville. Mortier's march to the south, however, had created a gap of more than 100 miles on the French western flank, which left Madrid exposed to an attack from Portugal. This was exactly the kind of situation Napoleon had tried to avoid when he had insisted that the area under French control should not be extended until the British army had been destroyed. But Wellington had set his mind so firmly upon defence that he never even contemplated taking advantage of this strategical error.[7]

As long as Reynier lay at Merida, where Mortier might at any moment come up from Seville to join him, Wellington was concerned that an attack might be delivered between the Tagus and the Guadiana. "I have no doubt that he [the enemy] will have a corps on each side of the Tagus," Wellington told the Earl of Liverpool, "and that he will occupy the left bank of that river from Almada to its mouth, at the same time that he will attack us on the right bank. Indeed, his recent operations in La Mancha show that he proposes to complete the conquest of the south of Spain, or at all events to insure it, before he will commence his attack upon Portugal; and in that case it is probable that the principal attack will be made by Alentejo, although probably the operations, which must have for their object the possession of Lisbon, will end on the right bank, a large corps being still kept on the left of the river." As the only allied force south of the Tagus was the 20,000 men of

La Romana's Estremaduran army, Wellington transferred Lieutenant-General Hill's corps to Portalegre near Badajoz. Hill's corps, described earlier, totalled 12,000 men with eighteen cannon and amounted to approximately a quarter of Wellington's disposable force. He was ordered to support La Romana and cover Badajoz if the V Corps should unite with the II Corps and make a serious move westwards. Yet, apart from some seemingly objectless manoeuvring, Reynier did not threaten La Romana or Hill, and Mortier was too involved with keeping the tide of insurgency at bay to assist the II Corps. Nevertheless, Wellington was obliged to keep his army divided and an attack from Spanish Estremadura could not be discounted.[8]

Further north there were other dramatic events taking place. In February Junot (VIII Corps) had been instructed by Napoleon to hand over control of Salamanca and Old Castile to Kellermann's Dragoon division and to then subdue the whole of the Leon plains as a prelude to the invasion of Portugal. Control of the provinces of Leon, Zamora and Salamanca was then to be handed over to another unattached division under General Serras. Bonnet's division had also commenced operations and was already advancing into the Asturias and threatening Galicia from the east.

Ney with the VI Corps (also destined to form part of l'Armée de Portugal) had been instructed by Napoleon to draw near to the frontier of Portugal in the vicinity of Ciudad Rodrigo, "to inundate all the approaches to that kingdom with his cavalry, disquiet the English, and prevent them from dreaming of transferring themselves back to the south". General Loison, who had re-entered Spain at the head of a number of battalions that were ultimately to join the VI Corps, was directed to move on from Valladolid and occupy the country around Benavente and Astorga.

All these regions now fell under Masséna's overall command. His authority extended over a front of 300 miles from Santander on Spain's northern coast, through Leon and Old Castile, to Spanish Estremadura. However, the remainder of the French troops in Spain – some 200,000 men, almost twice the force allocated to the invasion of Portugal – were left to pursue their own local objectives. Napoleon had divided Spain into a number of military governments or governorships all of which acted under instructions only from Paris. As a result, even though Napoleon knew that the British were the "only danger" in the Peninsula Masséna could not call upon the assistance of any of these other troops without prior permission from the Emperor himself.[9]

Loison found that La Romana had recently strengthened and re-armed the old fortress of Astorga and it could now only be taken by a formal siege. Loison had just field guns at his disposal and his only hope was to try and bluff the Governor into surrendering. Astorga had not expected to face a siege as soon as the beginning of February and it was only provisioned for twenty days; in addition, its guns, of which there were only fourteen mounted on the walls, were very short of ammunition. Nevertheless, the Governor, Santocildes, refused Loison's offer of surrender and the French general withdrew to La Baneza.

A few days later the advance units of Junot's Corps (the last of the three principal corps of l'Armée de Portugal) entered the province of Leon, and Loison was directed to move southward and join Ney at Salamanca. His place was taken by Clausel's Division of the VIII Corps. Clausel moved up as far as Astorga and again Santocildes was summoned to surrender but Clausel received the same curt reply as had Loison. It was evident that the fortress would have to be besieged but the large battering train that had been promised to l'Armée de Portugal would not reach the front for some time, so further operations against Astorga had to be temporarily postponed.

At the same time that Loison was summoning Santocildes at Astorga, a similar demonstration was being made in front of Ciudad Rodrigo by the VI Corps. Galicia, Valencia and Murcia were now the only Spanish provinces free of French troops and King Joseph had urged Ney to threaten Ciudad Rodrigo with the VI Corps whilst the news of the French conquest of Andalusia was still fresh. Ney promptly concentrated his corps and marched to the border fortress, arriving on the plain surrounding Ciudad Rodrigo on 11 February. He dutifully summoned the Governor, Lieutenant-General Herrasti, to surrender, to which the proud old Spaniard replied, "I have sworn to defend this place … until the last drop of my blood; this I am determined to do". With the siege train still strung out along the road from Bayonne to Burgos there was nothing that Ney could do other than return his troops to their cantonments around Salamanca and wait for the heavy guns to arrive.[10]

Ney's brief appearance before Ciudad Rodrigo had taken him within sight of the British outposts along the Portuguese frontier. On 12 January Wellington had moved his headquarters to Viseu and had pushed the 2,400 men of Brigadier-General Craufurd's Light Brigade (which on 1 March would become the Light Division with the addition of two battalions of Caçadores) up to the line of the River Agueda on the Spanish border. With the invasion of Portugal now imminent, all the allied forces were under arms, including the militia, except for the Lisbon regiments which were still working on the Lines. The provinces beyond the Douro were occupied by General Bacellar's twenty-one regiments of militia under Silveira and the British colonels Trant and Millar. The country between Penamacor and the Tagus was held by Lecor and Wilson with ten regiments of militia, a regiment of Portuguese cavalry and the Lusitanian Legion. The Alentejo was defended by a further four regiments of militia. The militia also occupied the fieldworks and batteries erected on the east bank of the Zezere and the old castles of Alfayates (Alfaiates) and Monsanto, both of which were already armed. The regular Portuguese brigades commanded by Marshal Beresford (which were soon to be incorporated into the British divisions) were at Tomar and Abrantes. Of the British troops, the 1st Division (6,000 men) was with Wellington at Viseu; Hill's 2nd Division (5,000) was with Hamilton's Portuguese Division at Abrantes; the 3rd Division (3,000) under Picton was at Celorico; Cole's 4th Division (4,000) was at Guarda, and the bulk of the cavalry was stationed in the valley of the Mondego. Both extreme flanks were covered by Spanish forces. The Army of Galicia shielded Wellington's northern flank and to the south, around Badajoz, was the army of the Marquis de La Romana.

Thus the wings of the allied defensive line were composed solely of militia and the provincial Ordenanza, with the whole of the regular force in the centre forming an arc some thirty miles in length. The Portuguese at Thomar and the three British infantry divisions at Viseu, Guarda and Celorico, and the Light Brigade at Pinhel, formed a body of 38,000 men, the whole of which could be brought together in two marches at any point between Guarda and the Douro. Hill and Beresford, with Fane's Portuguese cavalry brigade, could also unite on either side of the Tagus via the boat bridge at Abrantes, forming a mass of 30,000 men. There was also a reserve of twelve regiments of militia stationed around Setúbal.

These dispositions were designed to make the French move in masses, as even on the weakest line of resistance they would encounter more than 20,000 men, and by compelling the French to concentrate in large bodies the allies would be given ample notice of the invaders' intentions. If, against all Wellington's predictions, the French invaded Portugal through Castelo Branco it would be the responsibility of Wilson's militia to delay them. After destroying all the magazines at Castelo Branco Wilson was to "gradually" withdraw, Wellington instructed him on 17 January, "occupying and maintaining every defensible post as long as it may be in your power". This would give Hill time to move his corps to the defences behind the Zezere.[11]

Wellington was determined not to be drawn into any offensive action and neither the threat to Astorga nor the accumulation of stores at

71

Salamanca in preparation for the invasion of Portugal would induce him to "incur the risk and inconvenience" of moving his troops from their positions. If he marched to relieve Astorga or to destroy the magazines at Salamanca he could win, at best, only a "momentary" advantage before being forced to retreat back into Portugal. The detrimental effects of an interruption in the training of the Portuguese troops, which would be the consequence of any forward movement, could not be justified by what Wellington considered to be "an operation of doubtful results". Even if such an action was successful he saw that it "would not accomplish an object of any great importance to the war". He had to preserve his army for "the great object" and nothing would entice him from his positions in the mountainous region near the frontier, which Major Dick-son of the Portuguese artillery considered to be immensely strong: "It has in front the fortresses of Almeida and Ciudad Rodrigo which serve as points of reunion … The rugged and mountainous provinces of Trás-os-Montes and Galicia on its left secure that flank, and the fortresses on the right, Alburquerque, Campo Maior, Elvas, Badajoz, Jurmenha, etc., give it security and force."[12]

To support the field army in these advanced positions Wellington had established magazines containing 1,300,000 rations at Viseu, Celorico, Condeixa, Leiria, Tomar and Almeida. From these points 4,000 bullock carts and approximately 12,000 hired mules, organised into convoys of sixty each, carried the stores and provisions to the regiments. All the magazines were limited in size so that they could be easily removed or destroyed if the French attacked.

The VI Corps's demonstration before Ciudad Rodrigo did not unduly disturb Wellington. "The French threaten us on all points, and are most desirous to get rid of us," he told the Military Secretary, Colonel Torrens, on 31 March. "But they threaten upon too many points at a time to give me much uneasiness … and they shall not induce me to disconnect my army … I am in a situation in which no mischief can be done to the army." Nevertheless, when Wellington rode down to Torres Vedras to inspect the work on the Lines at the beginning of February he provided his divisional commanders with instructions for their withdrawal if the French were suddenly to invade. He told them that, if the French advanced in force, no attempt should be made to hold the line of the Coa or defend Celorico. The army on the frontier was to retire behind the Alva, with the hill in front of the Ponte da Murcela (the heights of Moita) held as an advanced post. The Portuguese troops in cantonments at Coimbra, Thomar and Leiria would move northwards and join the British divisions at Ponte da Murcela. General Bacellar was to ensure that all the boats on the Mondego were collected at the designated points and the bridges over the Mondego, as well as the smaller rivers, were to be broken. The Portuguese general was also responsible for organising the evacuation of the inhabitants of the Mondego valley to Oporto, along with all their carts and carriages. He would then muster the Ordenanza and employ them "in annoying the enemy in every situation which it may be practicable". Hill was directed to withdraw across the Tagus at Villa Velha, destroying the flying bridge behind him. Finally, La Romana's Estremaduran army would remain on the frontier around Badajoz from where it could "hang upon the enemy's rear, his communications and detachments".[13]

Wellington's assessment proved to be accurate, however, and apart from a full-scale attack by Junot against Astorga, no further moves were made against the Portuguese frontier until 25 April when Loison's Division of the VI Corps arrived at Ciudad Rodrigo to prepare for the investment of the fortress. A partial blockade of the town was established that night and by the end of the month Ciudad Rodrigo was fully invested as far as the River Agueda.

General Herrasti, the Governor of Ciudad Rodrigo, made an immediate appeal to Wellington to lift the blockade. But, as one British officer clearly understood, it was "more essential" for Wellington to "maintain his army in the positions it occupied, and to preserve it unbroken for the great contest which, he foresaw, it would soon be called upon", and the British commander refused to be drawn into a fight at such an early stage of the campaign. "If the force near Ciudad Rodrigo (Loison's Division) is only 4,000 men, and the Governor wishes to remove them, he is surely able to effect that operation himself," Wellington complained to Colonel Cox at Almeida. "Why are the English to undertake it? If he is not able to effect that object, I am sure it will answer no purpose for us to relieve him, when [in the future] he shall be more seriously pressed." Wellington, of course, wished to encourage Herrasti to make a prolonged defence of the fortress and on 7 May he wrote to the Governor thus: "I shall always be happy to have it in my power to render your Excellency and the city of Ciudad Rodrigo assistance; and the allied army under my command is at present in a situation from which it can move to the aid of Ciudad Rodrigo, if circumstances permit me to do it."[14]

Mermet's Division of the VI Corps was given responsibility for undertaking the siege operations and the French general moved his infantry brigades to within three miles of the fortress. Mermet hoped to avoid a protracted formal siege and on 12 May he sent an officer into Ciudad Rodrigo to offer Herrasti terms of surrender. The old general refused even to read Mermet's letter, and he told the officer that he would not allow any further French representatives into the town. "Now," he declared, "we have to talk only with guns."[15]

The southern walls of the fortress rest on the northern bank of the Agueda, and although the town was blockaded to the north the garrison was still able to communicate with Wellington's army which was only six miles away to the south. The presence of the 30,000-strong Anglo-Portuguese force posed a constant threat to the security of the besieging forces and at any moment the VI Corps might find itself attacked from the rear by Wellington and in front by the Spaniards. Ney therefore suggested to Masséna that a single division with some field artillery should contain the garrison of Ciudad Rodrigo whilst the remainder of the VI Corps, accompanied by the VIII Corps, marched upon Wellington and drove the Anglo-Portuguese back from the frontier. The French would then be able to continue with the sieges of Ciudad Rodrigo and Almeida in safety. Masséna, who only arrived at Salamanca to assume command of l'Armée de Portugal in the second week of May, agreed with Ney that such an attack might benefit the siege operations. However, his senior aide-decamp, Colonel Pelet, persuaded Masséna that he need not attack Wellington, as the allied commander would never risk an engagement in the open plains around the frontier. Consequently, on 20 May, Masséna instructed Ney to begin the siege.[16]

Ney's first task was to gather together sufficient stocks of food and materials to start, and sustain, the siege. The village of Pedrotoro was prepared as a depot for the siege train, another village (Sancti Spiritus) was taken over by the engineers of the VI Corps and converted into a large workshop, and requisitions for food were made upon the other local Spanish villages.

The first convoy of munitions, comprising thirty-four wagons loaded with ammunition, left Salamanca on 18 May. Ten days later the forty-three guns of the siege train, along with fifty-four wagons of biscuit, set off for the front. A further convoy of 100 wagons carrying entrenching tools, sandbags, shot and shell, followed on 30 May. Ney also departed from his base at Salamanca on the 29th to take personal direction of the siege.[17]

Ney arrived at Ciudad Rodrigo on the 30th and he established his headquarters in the monastery of Nuestra Señora de la Caridad, three miles from the fortress. The following morning he inspected the city's defences in the company of Couche of the Engineers and Ruty who commanded the artillery of the VI Corps. Ciudad Rodrigo was only a second-rate fortress. Its main defensive barrier was a medieval wall some thirty-two feet high, with narrow parapets, weak ramparts and old flank-ing towers that were scarcely able to accommodate more than two cannon each. Around this principal enciente was a more recent secondary wall, or fausse-braie, which was built to protect the base of the main wall from artillery fire. But this was situated so far down the slope of the hill upon which the fortress stands that it afforded little protection for the interior wall. Along the western side of the hill the ground falls sharply down to the Agueda river. The works under the main wall along this sector were less formidable than at any other point, as there was neither a fausse-braie nor a ditch. But, due to the nature of the terrain, the wall could not be seen fully to its base and it was unlikely that a practicable breach could ever be made from this side. To the north is a small hill called the Little Teson (or Teso) which is less than 300 yards from the fortress and about the same height as the walls. Behind the Little Teson are a valley and watercourse from which rises a more extensive height – the Teson (Grand Teso). This hill is only 600 yards from the walls and is higher than both the main wall and the fausse-braie.[18]

The Teson clearly provided an ideal platform for the breaching batteries and was the obvious point from which the French attack would be delivered. There was, however, one complicating factor. Immediately to the east of these two hills was an area of suburbs that ran for some two hundred yards from the foot of the Teson. Herrasti had devoted much labour to the fortification of the suburbs. A ditch had been dug around the suburbs of San Francisco and the displaced earth used to form a parapet six or seven feet high. The convent of Santa Clara had been turned into an infantry post and screened with breastworks, while the main road from Salamanca, which ran through the suburbs, had been barricaded and palisades erected all the way from the exposed flanks to the foot of the main glacis. On the other side of the city the Santa Maria suburb and the Santa Cruz convent had also been fortified.

The defences of the fortress itself had also received some improvement. The main wall and fausse-braie were strengthened and bomb-proof shelters were built to store the ammunition and to protect the defenders and inhabitants.

The garrison consisted of almost 2,000 regular infantry, three battalions of locally raised troops, nearly 400 artillerymen, and a little over 200 cavalry of the guerrilla leader Julian Sánchez, making a total of not less than 6,000 men. Around the walls of the fortress were ranged over 100 guns, howitzers and mortars, and the city was packed with ammunition and food.[19]

The besieging force comprised the three divisions of Ney's Corps (Loison, Mermet and Marchand) which numbered around 26,000 men plus 4,000 Dragoons of Montbrun's cavalry division. A further 17,000 men of Junot's VIII Corps were spread in detachments from the Agueda to Felices and Ledesma forty miles from Ciudad Rodrigo.[20]

Whilst the supplies streamed in from Salamanca the French engineers at Sancti Spiritus were assembling trestles for the bridge that would be laid across the Agueda to complete the investment. The trestles were taken to a point (La Carida) three miles upstream from Ciudad Rodrigo and, on 1 June, 300 men crossed the river to secure the bridge-head. A second bridge was put down near a ford at Loro a mile downstream from the fortress. Cavalry pickets were established on the western bank of the Agueda and substantial bridge-heads, capable of holding several artillery pieces as well as 300 to 600 infantry, were thrown up to cover both bridges.

The French had now been in the vicinity of Ciudad Rodrigo for over a month and not a shot had been fired against its walls. Wellington could not be certain that Masséna would actually lay siege to Ciudad Rodrigo, and reports from French deserters indicated that he would merely mask the fortress and make a dash at the allied army. As Masséna's intentions remained unclear, and as the fortress still was not under attack, Wellington could not risk his army in any offensive operations. "The army under my command is … in readiness to move to your assistance, if I should find it practicable to afford it to you," he wrote to Herrasti on 6 June. "I do not propose to move till … the enemy shall have brought forward the whole of his means, and that my movement may be of the utmost possible benefit to you. I assure you that I am sincerely interested in the fate of Ciudad Rodrigo … I hope you will believe, that if I should not be able to attempt your relief, it will be owing to the superior strength of the enemy, and to the necessity of my attending to other important objects."[21]

With the far bank of the Agueda now under French control Ney tightened his grip around the fortress and on 2 June Masséna rode to the front to see how far the VI Corps had progressed. As the two marshals inspected the fortifications of the city together Ney again took the opportunity to repeat his suggestion that the combined forces of the VI and VIII Corps should attack the Anglo-Portuguese army. Masséna was under strict instructions from Napoleon to "besiege first Ciudad Rodrigo, and then Almeida, and then prepare to march methodically into Portugal, which I do not wish to invade until September, after the hot weather and in particular after the harvest". He was therefore obliged to proceed with the siege and he dismissed Ney's proposal. Yet when he left Ciudad Rodrigo for Salamanca two days later he was far from happy. Heavy rains had swollen the Agueda, which threatened to wash away the trestle bridges, and the incessant downpour had turned the siege trenches into muddy streams. Even more alarming was the desperate lack of provisions for the troops. The area around Ciudad Rodrigo, which had supported the VI Corps since April, was now utterly exhausted and all supplies had to be brought in from other regions. The rain had rendered the roads all but impassable, which, coupled with a severe shortage of draught animals to transport the provisions (an impediment to all Massena's movements throughout the entire campaign) meant that the besiegers were often reduced to half rations.[22]

That same day, 4 June, a detachment from Loison's Division secured possession of the Teson and the houses at the foot of the heights, despite two sorties by the garrison. During the night the French engineers gained further ground, their advanced line being drawn within 400 yards of the fausse-braie. Ney also ordered a reconnaissance of Wellington's position and on 5 June Loison sent three strong columns along the western banks of the Agueda. Pushing back the British cavalry, the reconnaissance parties marched for some two miles towards the Portuguese frontier but failed to make contact with any major allied units. Despite this Ney posted all of Marchand's Division, a brigade of Mermet's Division and Lamotte's cavalry brigade on the west bank of the Agueda to guarantee the security of the besieging troops.

Ney need not have worried about the allied army, though, for Pelet's assessment – that Wellington would not attack the besiegers – was entirely accurate. Through a captured dispatch sent to Masséna from Napoleon, Wellington was aware of the strength of the forces opposing him. This knowledge was supported by reports from General Craufurd's Light Division, which formed Wellington's front line on the Agueda. Wellington knew that his army, including the 3,000 men of Carrera's Spanish division which was active in the area, numbered less than the combined strength of the VI and VIII Corps. "To relieve Ciudad Rodrigo," Wellington told his brother Henry, "I must leave the mountains and cross the plains, as well as two rivers, to raise the siege. To do this I have about 33,000 men, of which 3,000 are cavalry. Included are 15,000 Spaniards and Portuguese, which troops (to say the best of them) are of a doubtful quality. Is it right, under these circumstances, to risk a general action to raise the siege of Ciudad Rodrigo? I should think not." Wellington knew that most of Junot's Corps was within two days' march of the fortress and that Ney, with 5,000 cavalry at his disposal, would be alerted the moment the allies made any offensive movement. Nevertheless, Ney's outposts were kept in a constant state of alert and his pickets were engaged every day in skirmishes with the troops of the Light Division and the 1st Hussars of the King's German Legion.[23]

Herrasti continued his vigorous defence with another sortie from the southern gate of Ciudad Rodrigo against the Teson, and Loison was forced to place three companies of grenadiers in the ravine at the foot of the heights. Over the next two days sorties by the garrison kept the besiegers on their guard and, on 7 June, the allies achieved a significant success when a convoy of 100 mules carrying grain slipped through the French cordon and into the fortress. Yet Wellington seriously doubted the ability and determination of the Spaniards to resist the French. On 15 June he expressed these doubts to General Hill: "I do not feel very confident in the capabilities or inclination of the people of Ciudad Rodrigo to hold out, notwithstanding all their boasting." He also revealed the same concerns to Sir Charles Stuart: "The French have not yet fired a shot at the place, nor have they brought up the heavy ordnance; but the people begin to cry out. I fear that after boasting, they will not hold out."[24]

In the first week of June, Ney's chief engineer, Chef de Bataillon Couche, established the location of the first parallel on the Teson. The routes of the communications trenches that were to run up the rear of the height to the parallel, were also determined. Couche noted that fire from the fortified convent of Santa Cruz would impede the trenching operations and so, on the night of 9 June, the convent was silenced by 100 men who smashed down the door and took the Spanish defenders by surprise. Four days later, on the night of the 13th, all the remaining Spanish-held posts at the foot of the Teson were captured in preparation for the opening of the first trench on the 15th. The trench was to be dug by 2,300 men drawn from all three of Ney's divisions and they were to be protected by a guard of nine companies of grenadiers placed fifty paces ahead of the works and five companies of fusiliers to the rear.[25]

Under the cover of diversionary raids against the suburbs of San Francisco and Santa Marina, the first ground was broken on the Teson at 22.00 hours on the night of the 15th. By 03.30 in the morning, when the workers stood down, 1,400 feet of trenches had been dug.

All this was revealed to the defenders when dawn broke on the 16th and the Spaniards immediately turned their guns upon the Teson. The grenadiers were withdrawn from their forward positions and a fresh shift of workers took over duties in the trenches. The work continued virtually uninterrupted and at noon the workers and guards in the rear of the trenches were relieved, both groups then working a twelve-hour shift, before being replaced at midnight by the night shift. The siege guns, however, were still struggling to reach the front. "The roads are completely impassable," Masséna wrote to Napoleon on 5 June. "It is true that as far as anyone can remember, we have not seen rains so heavy and continual as in this season." The weather was also to hamper the workers as they attempted to deepen the trenches and, despite the fabrication of gutters to channel the water away from the works, the right communication trench had to be abandoned. Meanwhile General Elbé, who commanded the artillery of l'Armée de Portugal, supervised the construction of the first six breaching batteries. Five of these were to be sited on the Teson and one to the right of the heights by the Bishop of Ciudad Rodrigo's palace.[26]

For the next seven days the work on the trenches, parallels, batteries and approaches continued under a constant and effective bombardment from the Spanish guns. In an attempt to restrict the Spanish artillery, a battalion of "Chasseurs de siège" was assembled from selected sharp-shooters and placed in foxholes 100 paces in front of the works to pick off any Spanish gunners that might expose themselves on the ramparts.

With the VI Corps's stranglehold tightening around Ciudad Rodrigo Herrasti allowed Julian Sánchez and his lancers to try and break out of the city. At two o'clock on the morning of the 23rd, Sánchez, with around 100 men, cut his way through the French pickets, losing about a quarter of his force in the process. The following night the defenders were able to claim another success when an attack upon the convent of Santa Cruz was repulsed, the French suffering sixty-eight casualties in the assault.[27]

Wellington was puzzled with the slow progress of the siege operations. "This *bicoque* has been in part invested for nearly two months; and a fortnight has elapsed since the guns moved from Salamanca; and the French are not yet in possession of the ground they must have for the siege," he wrote on 11 June. "This is not the way in which they have conquered Europe!" Yet the day when the bombardment of the city would commence was drawing ever closer. The date selected was 27 June but Ney apparently wished to begin the attack whilst Masséna was still at Salamanca in order to gain all the credit for the capture of Ciudad Rodrigo. But then Masséna arrived at the front earlier than expected and was furious with Ney's haste. In the end, though, the batteries were armed and ready by the 24th and Masséna allowed the bombardment to begin at 04.00 the following morning.[28]

"At dawn every battery opened fire at the same time with all forty-six of their guns," observed Pelet. "At first the city appeared disconcerted. Initially it replied with rather sporadic and uncertain fire; later there was a more intense fire from a number of guns which were superior to ours and of a larger calibre. Soon guns were firing vigorously from both sides and the noise was terrible." A powder magazine was hit, demolishing part of the rampart and dismounting one of the guns, and over 600 inhabitants of the city were killed or wounded on the first day of the bombardment. In reply the Spaniards also destroyed a magazine and the guns in No.6 Battery were put out of action. Fire from the ramparts and from the convent of Santa Cruz took a heavy toll on the men in the trenches and their guard, and it was decided that the convent should be seized as soon as possible. Some of the breaching guns were turned upon the convent and, at 23.00 hours on the 25th, 300 grenadiers stormed and captured the convent, the Spanish defenders retiring into the fortress after offering little resistance.[29]

As the bombardment continued the French sappers pushed their saps (covered trenches) closer to the walls of the city. In doing so, however, they became exposed to enfilade fire from the convent and suburbs of San Francisco. Ney therefore ordered San Francisco to be attacked on the evening of the 26th, but the assault was easily repulsed by combined fire from the suburbs and the fortress.

Throughout the day and night of the 26th and 27th the guns continued to pound the stricken fortress. Much of the city had been demolished, a number of guns had been disabled and a widening breach was forming in both the fausse-braie and the main wall. By the morning of the 28th the breach was declared practicable and Ney made a final bid to induce the garrison to surrender. He sent his aide, Captain Esmenard, with a summons to Herrasti: "I am pleased to render justice to you for the fine defence, and the courage your soldiers have shown ... but all these efforts will destroy you if you continue your defence much longer." The proud old Governor would have none of it: "After forty-nine years of service, I know the military law of war and my military duty. I will know ... when the circumstances are such as to request capitulation after taking care to protect my honour, which is more dear to me than life itself."[30]

Herrasti must have still hoped that Wellington would make a belated attempt to relieve the fortress but the British commander would not be drawn away from the safety of the mountains to aid the beleaguered garrison. "They had provisions for forty days for the whole population when invested," Wellington told Craufurd. "Under these circumstances, and at this period of the operations, I do not think it would be proper to make an attempt to give them relief . . . It would be much more justifiable to incur a risk to make the attempt, after the garrison shall have shown their determination to resist, by standing a serious attack." Wellington was coming under increasing pressure from both the

Spanish authorities and his own officers to take some action to save the fortress: "Why it is thus deserted to its fate, after solemn promises being given to relieve it, appears extraordinary," wrote a British engineer. "The National Honour requires us to do something," commented another British officer, "for t'will be bearing an absolute insult to have the Town taken under our noses without an attempt to save it." Publicly Wellington still maintained the impression that he had not abandoned the place: "My object is to be able to continue in our present situation as long as possible, both to encourage a continued resistance at Ciudad Rodrigo, and to be able to relieve the place, if it should be advisable to attempt it." Yet to Liverpool he admitted that, "It would be impossible to relieve, much less raise the siege of Ciudad Rodrigo." The fortress would ultimately fall to the French, whatever action Wellington might take, and he could not afford the losses to his army that a relief attempt would inevitably incur. As Sir William Napier accurately observed, "if Wellington lost 5,000 men his government would abandon the contest [in the Peninsula]; if he lost 15,000 he must abandon it himself".[31]

After Herrasti's bold reply it was obvious to Masséna that the fortress would have to be taken by storm. In order to mount such an attack the approaches would have to be pushed all the way to the counterscarp so as to minimise the distance over which the attackers would have to run the gauntlet of the enemy fire. Before the saps could be advanced towards the glacis it was clear that the San Francisco area would have to be in French hands. Consequently, in the afternoon of 1 July, the four 12-pounders and two howitzers of No.6 Battery opened fire upon the suburbs and convent. At 21.14 hours General Simon led three columns, each of 200 men, and a party of 150 workers equipped with entrenching equipment and explosives, against San Francisco. Although the garrison offered some resistance, the convent and suburbs were captured and secured against counter-attack at a cost of just two men wounded. On 3 July Herrasti pulled all his remaining outposts back inside the city.

The sappers were now able to extend their trenches down to the Little Teson, where a new breaching battery (No.10) was to be erected. Because of the rocky terrain on the Little Teson earth for the parapets of this battery had to be dragged from the rear. The work, therefore, progressed slowly until, on the morning of 4 July, Captain Treussart of the Engineers noticed that because of the lie of the ground the advanced trench could not be seen by the defenders on the ramparts. He ordered his men to drive a sap straight up the glacis, and the workers had dug to within eighteen feet of the counterscarp to the left of the breach before the Spaniards realised what was happening. The defenders immediately trained their guns upon the sap and the work came to a standstill until nightfall, when the sap was pushed even closer to the walls of the doomed fortress.

No.10 Battery on the Little Teson was completed and armed on 8 July and the sappers reached the crest of the glacis where they began a mine gallery along the wall of the counterscarp. A second approach had also been made up the glacis to the right of the first sap, which would be used in the assault upon the breach. The battery opened fire with its eight 24-pounders at 04.00 hours on 9 July and its effects were immediate, with large pieces of masonry being blown away with every shot that hit the walls.[32]

At three o'clock the following morning the mine in the gallery adjoining the counterscarp was successfully detonated, the debris filling the ditch to form a ramp to the breach. An hour later all the French guns opened fire. "All the batteries were firing simultaneously on the poor city, especially against the breach," wrote Pelet. "Bombs were falling down with great rapidity and excellent marksmanship. On every side arose thick clouds of dust and smoke, pierced by the flames of the fires. The wreckage of buildings and walls was tumbling down with great noise, and several of the small magazines exploded periodically with tremendous detonations. The city seemed overwhelmed by so much firing." Earlier Herrasti had made a final, desperate plea for help. "Oh! come now! now! now! to the succour of this place," he had begged Wellington. Even the Marquis de La Romana had ridden over from Badajoz to urge the British commander to bring off the garrison. But Wellington's plans for the depopulation of the Portuguese countryside had not yet been effected, the militia were deserting in their thousands to bring in the harvest, and the Lines of Torres Vedras were still under construction. Wellington could not risk a defeat that would expose Portugal to invasion before the arrangements for the defence of the country were complete. "If we attempt to relieve the place," wrote General Picton in a letter to a friend, "the French will drive us out of Portugal: while if they get possession of it, they will lose time, which is more important to them than Ciudad Rodrigo. But they have yet to find this out."[33]

For the garrison of Ciudad Rodrigo, time had already run out. By late afternoon of 10 July the guns on the ramparts had been silenced and the breach was a gaping hole 120 feet across. In the French camp preparations for the attack upon the breach were well advanced. The attack was to be made in two columns. The first column, which was to consist of three companies of grenadiers, was to be preceded by an advanced party of fifty sappers plus the Chasseurs de siège and 100 workers with entrenching tools. Its objective was to capture and secure the breach and occupy the adjacent buildings. The second column, composed of six companies of voltigeurs, was to follow up the first column and advance along the ramparts to the left of the breach to the Gate of Conde. They were then to blow out the gate to allow a battalion of the trench guard, which would be waiting in the San Francisco suburbs, to enter the city. The battalion would then be followed by Mermet's entire division, which would deploy in line as far as the Gate of San Pelayo, through which entrance Marchand's Division would enter. The final move would be made by Loison's Division, which would join the other two divisions through the Gate of Conde.

Before the storming parties were released Ney asked for volunteers from the Chasseurs de siège to climb up and inspect the breach. Of the hundred men that stepped forward three were selected. Accompanied by Pelet, as well as Ruty of the artillery and Couche the engineer, the three volunteers slipped out of the forward trench and arrived at the counterscarp. Leaving the officers at the foot of the breach, they climbed over the rubble to the summit and opened fire upon the defenders. This was too much for the Spaniards. At the sight of the three Frenchmen the soldiers of the garrison abandoned the breach and fled into the town![34]

Seeing that there was to be no resistance from the garrison, Ney ordered the red flag to be flown and the storming parties clambered out of the trenches and charged towards the breach. As the attackers crossed the ditch, a Spanish officer appeared on the breach waving a white flag. Herrasti was at last prepared to capitulate.

Herrasti met Ney at the foot of the breach. The Marshal congratulated the Governor on his stout defence and promised Herrasti that his men would receive all the honours of war. The defenders had suffered 1,400 casualties and a further 400 civilians had either been killed or wounded. The city had endured a terrible bombardment. Pelet went into the fortress through the breach and described what he saw: "Everything adjoining it had been crushed, pounded and destroyed. The ruins and devastation extended to the centre of the city. At every step one could see collapsed or burned houses." The following morning the garrison marched out of the city and laid down their arms. The inhabitants were allowed to remain free.[35]

The siege had cost l'Armée de Portugal 182 men killed and 1,043 wounded. It had also consumed 30,000 rounds of precious ammunition and, more significantly, it had occupied seventy-six irreplaceable days. Herrasti loudly condemned Wellington for making no effort on behalf of the city. "The valour, the fortitude, and the sacrifices of the garrison deserved a better fate," he wrote in his report on the siege. "They have had the misfortune of not being supported by the armies of our allies." Certainly Wellington's relationship with the Spaniards was damaged, albeit temporarily, as he indicated in his dispatch to Lord Liverpool on 25 July: "The fall of Ciudad Rodrigo was felt as a great misfortune by the people of Castile in general; and they are not satisfied with the British nation, as an effort was not made to raise the siege of the place. This dissatisfaction … has probably been the cause of their discontinuing all correspondence with us." But Herrasti knew perfectly well what his protracted defence had meant to the outcome of the war: "Although we did not succeed in holding the fortress because this was impossible without aid, we did succeed in the principal objective in the interest of the national cause, by engaging the considerable forces of the enemy for such a long time so that they could not be employed elsewhere …We gave all of Portugal time to prepare for the invasion with which it was next threatened, to remove the subsistence from the necessary points, and to arrange all of the means that later caused the destruction and collapse of the French."[36]

Above: A painting of the fording of the River Mondego by the Allied Army on 21 September 1810. (Author)

Below: A view of the Battle of Buçaco, showing Reynier's II Corps attacking San Antonio de Cantaro. (Author)

General Craufurd's command post at Buçaco. These small circular windmills were found throughout Portugal and many were incorporated into the Lines as secondary strongpoints or as observation posts. (Author)

A view along the Allied line on the ridge of the Serra do Buçaco. (Author)

The Porta da Sula of the walled enclosure of the Convent of Buçaco. Guns were placed in the entrance and the front covered with abattis. Staging was erected above the gate to allow troops to fire over the top of the wall. (Author)

The great redoubt at Torres Vedras. This work actually comprised three forts, Nos. 20, 21 and 22, surrounded by a perimeter wall approximately 1,500 metres long, with another independent work, Fort 23, a short distance away to the northwest. (Author)

Above: Earth traverses were built within many of the larger redoubts to serve as rallying points or secondary defensive positions if the enemy were to enter the work. In the background can be seen two stone-built powder stores. (Author)

Below: Revetted banquettes were placed immediately the entrances of the works. The entrance is visible on the left of the picture. (Author)

Above: Revetted gun emplacements typical of the redoubts of the Lines. (Author)

Below: Part of the defences on the Alhandra heights. Situated on the top of a steep and difficult range of hills, this work could never be bombarded by artillery and was therefore built with high, exposed stone walls quite unlike the low earthen ramparts that formed most of the redoubts of the Lines. (Author)

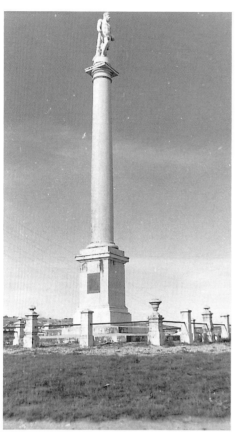

Left: The monument erected by the engineers of the Portuguese Army to commemorate the Lines of Torres Vedras. Erected on the site of No.2 Redoubt overlooking the River Tagus, on one face of the plinth, carved in bold letters are the defiant words of the Portuguese 'NON ULTRA' – no further! (Author)

Below: The embarkation point at St Julian. The fort is still a military headquarters. (Author)

Masséna's retreat from Portugal begins. (Author)

The march of the baggage train following the Anglo-Portuguese army over the Serra de Estrella, 16 May 1811. (Author)

The village of Pombal in flames, as evacuated by the French Army, on the morning of 11 March 1811. (Author)

'Torres Vedras with part of the celebrated lines', by Heath after a painting by Landseer. The great redoubt overlooks Torres Vedras from the hill to the north of the town. (Author)

CHAPTER V

"Bursting of a Volcano"

The fall of Ciudad Rodrigo was seen by the French as a major victory, since it constituted a demoralising blow to the operations of the guerrilla bands in the north-west of Spain to whom the fortress had been considered a secure refuge. To Wellington, its capitulation had always been inevitable and he entertained no regrets at having failed to relieve the garrison. Even the Spanish Cortez at Cadiz eventually had to acknowledge that an attempt to save the fortress might have been "attended by the most disastrous consequences" for the allied army. The real significance of the surrender of Ciudad Rodrigo was that Almeida and northern Portugal were now exposed and certain to be attacked.[1]

Both Masséna and Wellington now pondered on the same question: could the French merely blockade Almeida and starve it into submission whilst l'Armée de Portugal marched upon Lisbon, or was the capture of this fortress an essential pre-requisite to the invasion of Portugal? Masséna had originally been ordered by Napoleon to besiege Almeida but on 29 July he received an instruction from Marshal Berthier which increased his freedom of action: "The Emperor asked me to express his extreme satisfaction with the important capture of Rodrigo. He lets you decide on a battle against the English." Napoleon, however, insisted that the invasion should not take place until the autumn. "I do not wish to enter Lisbon at the moment," he had written at the end of May, "because I could not feed the city, whose immense population is accustomed to live on sea-borne food." So although Masséna could choose his campaign strategy he could not begin his march upon Lisbon for at least another six weeks. With this much time to spare Masséna decided to fulfil his original order and besiege Almeida. The fortress would be the great depot from which the invasion would be launched. Together Ciudad Rodrigo and Almeida would form the secure base which would safeguard Masséna's links with the other French forces in the Peninsula. At Almeida reinforcements and provisions could be gathered before being despatched on the long journey to the front through the rugged and sparsely populated regions of north-eastern Portugal where the roaming bands of Ordenanza and militia would be a constant threat to the army's communications.[2]

The operation against Ciudad Rodrigo had cost the French dear in both munitions and draught animals. Almost all the shot and shell for the heavy siege ordnance had been expended against Rodrigo and 1,500 animals had died during the period of the siege. Before Masséna could begin siege operations against Almeida he had to wait for food and ammunition to be brought from Salamanca and more horses or oxen to be found to drag the siege train across the frontier. "Subsistence was one of our principal concerns," wrote Pelet, "for the meagre supplies found in Rodrigo had been eaten by the VI Corps … Nevertheless, we were most troubled by the lack of artillery horses; those that we had were exhausted and poorly nourished, and dying like flies." These problems threatened to jeopardise the entire campaign and just two days after the fall of Ciudad Rodrigo Masséna returned to Salamanca to supervise the logistical operation.[3]

Whilst the engineers of l'Armée de Portugal set about the rebuilding of the battered defences of Ciudad Rodrigo, the VI Corps continued to probe the allied positions on the éfrontier. The fall of Ciudad Rodrigo had placed the fort of La Concepción in the front line and Wellington decided to abandon this small stronghold if the French attacked. Craufurd, whose Light Division along with the 14th Light Dragoons, the 1st Hussars KGL and Ross' troop of the Royal Horse Artillery still held the allied outpost line, was ordered to "keep his advanced guard in front of Almeida till threatened by an attack by a superior force, and when he retires from Fort Concepción, he will blow up that fort". Mines were laid beneath the main fortifications and, on the morning of 21 July, the mines were ignited in the face of an advance by almost 5,000 men of Loison's Division.[4]

With the ruins of La Concepción occupied by the VI Corps, Craufurd pulled back the Light Division to Almeida where he was determined to hold the line of the River Coa for as long as he was able. For four months Craufurd's Division had controlled a front of approximately thirty miles from the Agueda to the Coa against a French army corps five times its number. Much has been made of this operation yet the French had not delivered an attack in any real strength beyond the Agueda during that period. Now, with Masséna showing "a serious intention of invading Portugal", Wellington was anxious to avoid an action on the eastern bank of the Coa. On 10 July he had told Craufurd that he did not want "to risk anything beyond the Coa", and twelve days later, on the evening of the 22nd, Wellington sent Craufurd the following note: "I have ordered two battalions to support your flanks; but I am not desirous of engaging an affair beyond the Coa. Under these circumstances … would it not be better that you should come to this side with your infantry at least?" Even though the whole of the VI Corps lay about Val de Mula, only three or four miles beyond Almeida, Craufurd remained encamped on the glacis of the fortress two miles away from the only bridge over the river.[5]

The River Coa flows through a deep ravine and the road that leads from Almeida to the bridge twists and turns its way down a steep and rocky slope. The bridge was out of sight and beyond the protective range of the guns of the fortress and the Coa itself was an impassable torrent. Despite the obvious difficulties of his only line of retreat, and with complete disregard for Wellington's advice, Craufurd remained at Almeida throughout the 22nd and the 23rd. On the 24th the French attacked.

At 06.00 hours Loison's Division, with Lamotte's and Gardanne's cavalry brigades in the van, marched in two huge columns from Fort Concepción directly upon Almeida. Behind Loison's thirteen battalions came Mermet's eleven battalions, with Marchand's eleven battalions forming the reserve. During the night the plateau around Almeida had been swept by a torrential storm. "We experienced a storm that for violence, while it lasted, exceeded anything I had ever before beheld," recalled a British officer. "The lightning, thunder, wind, and rain were absolutely awful." Some of the men from the five battalions of the Light Division were still drying off their weapons after the terrible weather of the previous night when the sound of gunfire rolled across the plateau.[6]

Pushing back Craufurd's outlying pickets, Lamotte's cavalry, with the battalion of the Chasseurs de siège in support, advanced to within a mile of the fortress before halting to allow the rest of Loison's Division to join them. By this time the Light Division was under arms and ready for the French assault. Craufurd deployed his battalions in an irregular line extending southwards and westwards from the glacis of the fortress down to the rocky terrain above the gorge of the Coa. The ground was broken with stone walls, enclosures and vineyards and ideally suited to the skirmishing tactics of Craufurd's light infantry, which had beaten off every French patrol sent against them. But this was no mere patrol.

For more than an hour the Light Division waited as Loison's Division formed up for the attack. This delay allowed Craufurd the opportunity to transfer his cavalry and his cumbersome artillery and baggage across the river – an opportunity he chose to ignore. He had miscalculated both the size of the enemy body in front of him and its intention, and when the attack came it was made with overwhelming force.

"The whole plain in our front was covered with horse and foot advancing towards us", wrote Simmons of the 95th. "The enemy's infantry formed line and, with an innumerable multitude of skirmishers, attacked us fiercely." The rolling volleys of the British infantry caused the front ranks of Percy's brigade to falter, but only for a moment; "they came on again", continued Simmons, "yelling, with drums beating, frequently the drummers leading, often in front of the line, French officers like montebanks running forward and placing their hats upon their swords, and capering about like madmen, saying, as they turned to their men, 'Come on, children of our country. The first that advances, Napoleon will recompense him.'"[7]

The French 3rd Hussars had seen that there was a gap between Craufurd's left and the walls of the fortress and the horsemen made a dash for this space. Running the gauntlet of fire from the guns on the ramparts, the 3rd Hussars "trampled down and sabred" a company of the 95th and swung round the flank of the Light Division. With the 15th and 25th Dragoons following up behind the Hussars, the Light Division was now cut off from Almeida. Craufurd's right flank was also being threatened by the 15th Chasseurs a cheval and the full weight of Loison's infantry was being felt in his front.

At last realising that the Light Division was in danger of being trapped with its back to the river, Craufurd ordered his three British regiments to hold their ground until he could move the rest of the division over the bridge. The cavalry and artillery galloped for the bridge followed by the 1st Caçadores in full-bloodied retreat and then, to add to the growing disorder, a gun caisson crashed onto its side on one of the sharp bends and blocked the road. Above the bridge the British infantry was falling back in a state of confusion. There was no ordered withdrawal and it was evident that Craufurd had misjudged the situation. "The fire was hot and the ground very difficult," remembered Charles Napier of the 43rd, as each battalion tried to withdraw from "the murderous position which kept us in fear of being cut off from the bridge".[8]

The speed of the withdrawal of the left and centre of Craufurd's line left a wing of the 52nd Regiment isolated on the right, almost half a mile from the bridge. As these men made a run for the bridge the French seized a hillock which blocked the 52nd's line of retreat and they were only saved by the prompt response of the regimental officers as, by this stage, Craufurd had lost control of the battle. Colonel Beckwith ordered the 95th to halt their retreat and Major Mcleod "turned his horse round, called the troops to follow, and taking off his cap, rode with a shout towards the enemy". Mcleod cleared the French from the hill and the 95th, supported by a wing of the 43rd, held the knoll long enough for the 52nd to scramble down the ravine and across the river.[9]

On the left bank of the river Charles Napier organised the defence of the bridge, placing men of the 43rd and 52nd around its battlements whilst the Caçadores and the 95th posted themselves behind the walls and rocks on the slope above. From the eastern bank of the Coa the leading battalions of Ferey's brigade and some light artillery fired across the river and two companies of the 66th Line and the Chasseurs de siège tried to storm the bridge but were repelled with heavy losses. Ney had by this time reached the bridge and he ordered the 66th and 82nd Line to make another attempt to cross the river. Four times the French tried to capture the crossing in the face of the concentrated fire of the entire Light Division until the bridge "was literally piled with their dead and they made breastworks of the bodies".[10]

The troops continued to exchange shots across the river until around 16.00 hours when a heavy downpour put an end to the fighting. Casualties were high on both sides, particularly in Ferey's brigade which had led the initial attack and the unsuccessful assaults upon the bridge.

Both commanders had acted irresponsibly. Craufurd had actually disregarded written instructions and Ney had recklessly thrown away the lives of his men at the bridge. But there is no doubt that this was a French victory and Wellington was justifiably furious with Craufurd. "I had positively desired him not to engage in any affair on the right of the river," he complained to his brother William. "After all this he remained above two hours on his ground after the enemy appeared in his front before they attacked him, during which time he might have retired across the Coa twice over." Yet, despite his anger, Wellington played down the affair in his official dispatch to the Earl of Liverpool: "For various reasons it had been desirable to keep open communications with Almeida and the right of the Coa as long as was possible; but it was not intended to risk an affair or any loss for that object. The enemy had approached too near, however, before the retreat across the river was effected." Massena's report on the action was, of course, written in the extravagant language of the First Empire: "the Imperial troops have shown once again this day that there is no position which can resist their intrepidity". The Prince d'Essling made no mention of the futile attempts upon the bridge.[11]

Possibly the most remarkable incident of the entire day occurred just after the Light Division had crossed the river and was preparing to resist the attacks upon the bridge. General Picton, having heard the sounds of the battle from his headquarters at Pinhel, had ridden up to the Coa to find out what was happening. Craufurd asked for the support of the 3rd Division but Picton replied that he would do "no such thing" and he rode back to Pinhel leaving the Light Division to face the VI Corps alone. Picton had been instructed by Wellington to "support Brigadier General Craufurd upon the Coa, in case the enemy should collect in force upon the Agueda or on this side of the river". So, in the first serious engagement of the campaign not one, but two, of Wellington's senior officers had disobeyed direct orders.[12]

On the night of the 24th the Light Division withdrew from the Coa and retired upon Celorico. Craufurd established his pickets at Freixedas and Vendala on the main road from Almeida to Coimbra, with the light cavalry forming the outpost line. The rest of the Anglo-Portuguese forces moved back to Guarda. "In this position," Wellington informed Sir Charles Stuart, "I am equally prepared for any operation that it might be in my power to undertake for the relief of Almeida, if it should be attacked; and better prepared for our retreat, if that should be necessary." Wellington was only one day's march away from Almeida but the banks of the Coa are steep and rocky and the only two bridges, at Almeida and Castelo Bom, were now held by the VI Corps. Ney knew that he could concentrate his efforts against the fortress without fear of interruption.[13]

Wellington, on the other hand, was far less certain of Ney's movements. "There is not the smallest appearance of the enemy's intention to attack Almeida;" he wrote in a letter to Hill on 27 July, "and I conclude that, as soon as they shall have got together their force, they will make a dash at us, and endeavour to make our retreat as difficult as possible … Accordingly, I shall leave the cavalry in their present situations, observing all the routes, etc. on which they are at present; and shall move all the infantry of the army, with the exception of the 4th division, which will remain at Guarda . . . The heavy cavalry will be in the plain between this and Celorico, and the light cavalry in front."[14]

Whilst Wellington was preparing to cover his retreat, the VI Corps consolidated its blockade of Almeida. Junot's VIII Corps was moved from the Agueda and placed in the villages to the east and north of the fortress in close support of the besieging forces. General Serras, whose unattached division had been left to hold down the province of Leon and protect Masséna's communications with Salamanca, was also ordered to create a diversion by moving against the Trás-os-Montes frontier. In compliance with these instructions, Serras captured the small walled town of Puebla da Sanabria towards the end of July. The town sits on the edge of the Leon plain a few miles north of Bragança (Braganza) on the Portuguese border and the Spanish garrison had fled into Portugal, leaving behind twenty cannon and considerable quantities of food and ammunition. Serras garrisoned the town with a battalion of the 2nd Swiss Regiment and a squadron of dragoons, and then returned to Zamora.

The Spaniards from Sanabria rallied at Bragança where they joined forces with Silveira's militia brigade. Together with the Portuguese, the Spaniards returned to Sanabria and just four days after occupying the town the Swiss garrison found itself under siege.

The following morning the garrison's cavalry force tried to disperse the besiegers but the dragoons were overwhelmed by the Portuguese horse and the French were chased back into the town. The attackers burnt down the gates of the town but the Swiss bricked up the gateway and the old artillery pieces that were dragged all the way from Braganza were found to have been "long left to rust" and could not be used. The besiegers then tried to mine under the walls of the town and managed to throw down the face of the curtain wall. At this point the Swiss commandant offered to surrender on terms. By pleading that he and his men were not French, the Swiss officer was able to persuade Silveira to allow the garrison to be repatriated and they were marched off to Corunna. The Spaniards re-occupied Sanabria and Silveira took as his spoil the Eagle of the 2nd Swiss. The Eagle was deposited at Lisbon cathedral amid "proper triumph" as the first trophy of the regenerated Portuguese.[15]

The fortress of Almeida is formed as an irregular hexagon situated on a low, granite knoll which in every direction dominates a wide, bare, undulating plateau. Months of hard work had left the fortress in a good state of repair. Its main defences were composed of six bastions and six demi-lunes, or outworks, protecting the short intervening curtain walls. These walls still stand some thirty-five to forty feet above the broad, dry ditch which had been cut from the solid granite of the knoll. The bastions on the north, south and east (those of Santa Barbara, São Francisco and São Pedro) were dominated by massive towers and inside the fortress, close to the north-western front, arose an immense but very old castle which was itself built with four enormous towers.

Inside this medieval castle, which was considered bombproof, was situated the main powder magazine and the central barracks of the garrison. This body consisted of one regiment of Portuguese regular infantry (the 24th Line Regiment), a squadron of the 11th Portuguese

Dragoons and 222 men of the 4th Artillery Regiment. There were also the three militia regiments of Arganil, Trancoso and Guarda, making a total of approximately 3,500 men, a force which the Governor, Colonel William Cox, regarded as "insufficient for its defence, particularly when I look at the description of troops it is principally composed".[16]

Cox promised to hold Almeida for fifty days providing that one of the militia regiments was replaced by another regiment of Line Infantry. "I think that the place is worth saving," he wrote to Marshal Beresford, "and that its defence should not be entrusted to an inadequate garrison, chiefly composed of peasants who are taken from their homes and families." But the fortress was well stocked with food and ammunition and around its walls were ranged over 100 guns, forty of which were 18-pounders or heavier. It was inevitable that Almeida would be captured and its garrison fall into the hands of the French. Another regiment placed within its walls would only be another regiment lost – a loss that the small Anglo-Portuguese army could not afford.[17]

At nightfall on 15 August (Napoleon's birthday) the VI Corps broke ground in front of Almeida. The working parties were composed of 2,500 men from Marchand's Division who, under the bright moonlight, opened two communications trenches and dug the first parallel, some 3,000 yards long, only 360 yards from the fortress. Work in the trenches continued during the day but the granite of the plateau was covered with only two or three feet of soil and the French sappers had to blast through the rock.

Progress was inevitably reduced and appeals were made for more workers to form two shifts of 3,000 men each. This posed a problem for Ney, as large numbers of his troops were away from their regiments collecting food. To help solve his supply problems, Masséna had allowed the soldiers to gather in the harvest and large numbers of men were busy cutting the crops whilst other repaired the dismantled water mills along the local rivers. As a result of these measures, less than 2,000 men paraded for duty in the trenches on the night of the 16th and the work continued slowly in the face of concentrated and accurate gunnery from the ramparts of the fortress.[18]

The attack had been fixed initially on the western front between the bastions of Santa Antonio and São Pedro but eventually it was limited to just the bastion of São Pedro. The fifty-two siege guns were to be placed into eleven batteries, four of which (Nos.1, 2, 3 and 11) were to enfilade the fortress's defences whilst the other seven battered a breach in the bastion. A further thirteen guns were held in reserve to replace any damaged pieces or to form a twelfth battery if required. By 23 August, the ninth night of open trenches, the parallels and batteries had been completed and the first guns were run into No.4 Battery. Two days later all the batteries were armed and fully stocked with shot, shell and powder.

"At last the day arrived for the beginning of the attack against Almeida," wrote Pelet. "We reached the fortress in a thick fog, and the firing started after six o'clock. Although eleven batteries were firing simultaneously, the sight was not very imposing to those accustomed to genuine battles – not too much noise and little effect. On the other hand, the fortress fired considerably and very well." Throughout the day the guns of the opposing forces continued to play, with both sides able to claim some success. A battery platform was damaged on the ramparts, two small expense magazines were destroyed and a number of houses in the town were set on fire. The Portuguese gunners likewise ignited a magazine in No.2 Battery and over twenty men were either killed or wounded.[19]

With the approach of dusk the garrison increased their efforts to replenish the expense magazines on the ramparts from the main magazine before night fell. As the barrels of powder were being loaded from the main magazine onto pack mules, one barrel sprung a leak and left a trail of powder across the castle courtyard and through the open door of the magazine. What occurred next was a disaster that Oman considered to be "unparalleled in magnitude during the whole Peninsular War". A shell from No.4 Battery landed in the courtyard and as it burst it set fire to the trail of powder. The spark ran along the trail, exploded another barrel at the entrance of the magazine and this ignited the entire 150,000 pounds of gunpowder and over a million prepared cartridges. "The earth trembled, and we saw an immense whirlwind of fire and smoke rise from the middle of the place," recalled a French officer. "It was like the bursting of a volcano – one of the things that I can never forget after twenty-six years. Enormous blocks of stone were hurled into the trenches, where they killed and wounded some of our men. Guns of heavy calibre were lifted from the ramparts and hurled down far outside them. When the smoke cleared off, a great part of Almeida had disappeared, and the rest was a heap of debris."[20]

For a few moments after the explosion all the combatants were so stunned that not a single shot was fired and silence hung over the stricken fortress. Cox rushed from his quarters in one of the casemates to determine what had occurred. He found the town "sunk into a shapeless ruin … the devastation was incredible. The ramparts were breached, the guns thrown into the ditch, five hundred people were struck dead on the instant, and only six houses were left standing". As well as the 500 civilians, a further 600 Portuguese soldiers were killed, including the 200 gunners serving the guns on the ramparts on or adjacent to the São Pedro bastion.[21]

Cox's first worry was that the French would take immediate advantage of the explosion to storm through the breached walls and capture the town. He ordered all the men that he could muster of the garrison to defend the walls, where they opened up a heavy fire in an attempt to conceal the extent of the destruction from the enemy. The shocked and demoralised garrison maintained a desultory fire throughout the night until the first light of dawn revealed the terrible truth. The town was in ruins. Not one single building remained undamaged, and dead and mutilated bodies littered the roads and the battlements. The walls of the fortress were found to be damaged but still intact. Virtually all the gunpowder was gone. "We could not see the tower, the church, or the castle", wrote Pelet. "Everything appeared turned upside down."[22]

Almeida could no longer defend itself and its guns fell silent. Only thirty-nine barrels of powder, and a few more barrels in the magazines on the ramparts, had escaped the explosion. This was not enough for even a single day's fighting. There were still some 600,000 rounds of infantry cartridges in the regimental stores (enough for approximately 150 rounds per man) but muskets alone could not save the fortress. Masséna, who had removed himself from Salamanca and established his headquarters in the ruined fort of La Concepción, rode up to the trenches to conduct a close examination of the fortress. At 09.00 hours he ordered his gunners to stand down and shortly afterwards he summoned the garrison to surrender: "The town of Almeida is burning. All of my siege artillery is in its batteries, and it is impossible for your allies to come to your aid. Render yourself to the generosity of the armies of His Imperial Majesty. I offer you honourable conditions."[23]

Cox knew that his situation was hopeless and he agreed to allow Masséna's representative – Pelet – into the town to discuss the surrender. But Cox was determined to resist as long as he was able, to give Wellington time to make an attempt to save the garrison, and all morning the telegraph on the western ramparts of the town was sending urgent signals to Wellington's outposts. Meanwhile Pelet, who was blindfolded so that he could not see the ruined state of the town, was led to a casemate to meet Cox. The Governor's plan was to prolong negotiations until at least noon of the following day and his next move was to send two of his Portuguese officers back with Pelet to arrange the terms of the capitulation. Cox demanded that the men of the garrison be allowed to return to their homes and the few English soldiers in the town be permitted to re-join the allied army. During the negotiations, however, one of the Portuguese representatives, a Major Barreiros who commanded the artillery of the fortress, revealed to Masséna exactly how desperate the situation was inside Almeida. Masséna then suspended the talks and sent Pelet into the town again, demanding an immediate surrender but agreeing to Cox's request that the garrison be allowed to return to their homes.

Cox continued to try and delay the capitulation with further attempts at re-negotiating the terms of surrender but Pelet was not deceived for long. "I realised," Pelet later wrote, "that he wanted to gain one day and give Wellington time to manoeuvre and prepare himself." Pelet left a copy of the surrender document with Cox and returned to the French camp. Masséna, angered with Cox's procrastinations, threatened to renew the bombardment and he gave Cox half an hour to sign the document. He promised to free the entire garrison, including the British, if Cox agreed to an immediate surrender. Cox failed to respond in time and at 20.00 hours the French guns opened fire.

The treacherous Barreiros had remained with Masséna and he aided the French gunners by directing their fire at the remaining magazines in the town. The renewal of the French bombardment soon brought matters to a head inside Almeida and a deputation of Portuguese officers met Cox and told him that unless he capitulated at once they would open the gates of the fortress to the enemy. At 23.00 hours on 27 August 1810, Almeida surrendered.[24]

The following morning the garrison marched out of the fortress and laid down their arms. Arrangements were put in hand to allow the militiamen to return to their homes and for the 24th Line and the British officers to be taken as prisoners to Fort La Concepción. But the Marquis d'Alorna, who had previously been Inspector-General of the Portuguese Army and who had joined the French in 1808, asked permission from Masséna to raise a force for service with the French Army from the prisoners. As there was already a Portuguese Legion serving with the French in Spain, Masséna agreed to d'Alorna's request and rather than face the prospect of an indefinite confinement the prisoners accepted this offer with understandable enthusiasm. Every man of the squadron of the 11th Cavalry, almost the entire regiment of the 24th Line, the surviving members of the 4th Artillery Regiment and almost 200 militiamen took the oath of allegiance to Napoleon. Cox and the other British officers were dispatched to France to await their exchange. Major Barreiros was promoted to the rank of colonel in the French Army.[25]

The Portuguese authorities found Barreiros guilty of high treason and he was sentenced to death, though he was never captured. Da Costa, the Lieutenant-Governor of Almeida who led the deputation of

Portuguese officers that demanded the surrender of the fortress, did not desert to the French but remained with the Portuguese Army only to be arrested and shot for cowardice. Cox was eventually released from French custody and in 1815 he applied for a command in the Portuguese Army. His application was refused.

"The loss of Almeida is a great misfortune," Wellington told his brother Henry on 30 August, and to Hill he confessed that he could not express how disappointed he was "at this fatal event." When they took possession of the fortress the VI Corps seized 172 pieces of artillery, 2,885 small arms, 605,695 cartridges, 39 barrels of gunpowder, 30,000 rations of biscuit, 10,000 rations of salt meat, 24 tons of wheat, 25 tins of rice, 80 tons of maize, 2 tons of beans, 150 tons of straw, 80 tons of barley and 34 barrels of wine. This vast store of food would prove to be of vital importance in the long march to Lisbon – Masséna had been given the means to invade Portugal.[26]

"I am sorry to tell you that the enemy are in possession of Almeida," Wellington informed Hill shortly after receiving news of the disaster. "The manner in which the garrison was supplied with all the necessities for the fort, to the respectable state of the works and to the good spirits which I understood from the Governor that the garrison maintained, I had hoped that the place would hold out to the last extremity … [and] would have detained the enemy till a late period in the season." Of further concern to Wellington was the unexpected desertion of the garrison and a sudden, hostile attack against Wellington's defensive policies by members of the Regency Council in Lisbon, where the loss of Almeida produced "much alarm". The Principal Sousa and the Patriarch criticised Wellington for failing to protect Almeida. They insisted that he should fight the French on the frontier and that the Council should be consulted about the future operations of the army.[27]

Wellington's answer was immediate. "I have already made known to the Government of the kingdom that the fall of Almeida was unexpected by me," he explained to Forjaz, the Secretary of the Council, "and that I deplore its loss and that of my hopes, considering it likely to depress and afflict the people of this kingdom." In reply to the suggestion that he should give battle on the frontier, Wellington was unequivocal: "I should forget my duty to my Sovereign, to the Prince Regent, and to the cause in general, if I should permit public clamour or panic to induce me to change, in the smallest degree, the system and plan of operations which I have adopted, after mature consideration, and which daily experience shows to be the only one likely to produce a good end."

There were also disturbances in the capital and talk of the local militia taking possession of the Lisbon forts to prevent the British troops embarking on the ships in Lisbon harbour. Wellington asked Charles Stuart to demand that the capital be properly policed: "These measures will accustom the mob of Lisbon to the discipline they must undergo, and will keep matters quiet at the critical moment … if I find the Government hesitating upon this subject … I shall forthwith embark the army … and the Portuguese nation will have the satisfaction of losing itself, and the Peninsula, by the folly of the people and the pusillanimity of the Government." With such language Wellington was able to moderate da Sousa's hostility, though he remained the head of a powerful anti-British party and he continued to foment unrest in the capital. But British troops occupied the more important forts and the rebellious militia regiments were sent to join the army on the frontier.[28]

Wellington's concerns about the disaffection of the Portuguese were somewhat relieved when it was learnt that the seemingly enthusiastic shift of allegiance by the Almeida garrison was only a ploy to avoid imprisonment. After being re-organised and assimilated into the appropriate arms of the French service, the Portuguese troops began to desert in large numbers whenever the opportunity to abscond presented itself. Within a week of the fall of Almeida, seventeen officers and 500 men of the 24th Regiment had returned to the allied lines, followed by the entire squadron of the 11th Cavalry which walked out of camp early one morning. By the second week of September only 300 men of the original 3,000 remained with l'Armée de Portugal and Masséna had these disarmed and sent to France as prisoners of war. At first Wellington was unsure whether or not he should accept the deserters back into the Portuguese service, as they had all taken an oath of fidelity to France. "It was well enough for the private men," Wellington conceded, "but highly disgraceful to the character of the officers." He proposed to have the officers cashiered but the Portuguese Regency defused the situation by issuing a proclamation which condoned their actions and claimed that Masséna had broken the terms of the surrender by incorporating some of the militia into the French army instead of sending them to their homes and this, therefore, released the deserters from their oaths.[29]

During the siege of Almeida Wellington had re-grouped his forces and concentrated them along a front of just fifteen miles midway between the Coa and the Mondego. He had brought forward the remainder of his cavalry to join the squadrons that had been operating with the Light Division and together the six regiments formed a thick screen from Guarda to Lamegal. Behind the cavalry was the Light Division which was stationed with Wellington at Celorico; Picton with the 3rd Division was at Caraciehina whilst Cole's 4th Division remained at Guarda. The Portuguese brigades of Coleman and Campbell were at Pinhanços and Pack's brigade was stationed at Jequa. Further south, on the Tagus and the Guadiana, there were now three large bodies of troops. La Romana's 20,000 Spaniards were still around Badajoz, holding Mortier's V Corps in check. A 5th Division, formed from three recently arrived British battalions with two Portuguese brigades and twelve cannon, was placed under General Leith's orders and moved up to Thomar. Finally, Hill's corps was at Abrantes observing Reynier, whose movements, Wellington warned Hill, "will be the clue to everything else". The VIII Corps had stayed around Almeida throughout the siege in support of the VI Corps, with a strong advanced guard posted at Pinhel.[30]

Around the middle of August a rumour reached Wellington that Junot had been withdrawn to Leon, leaving the VI Corps unsupported at Almeida. Wellington consequently moved his infantry up to Castelo Rodrigo "so as to be able to strike a blow, if the enemy should afford an opportunity; and at all events to oblige the enemy to keep his corps in a more collected state during the siege than it is at present, and thus to render the operation more difficult on account of the want of subsistence". The rumour, as it transpired, proved to be false and the allied position was too far forward to be maintained. Yet to have withdrawn before the French advanced from the frontier would have given his political enemies in Lisbon further encouragement and so Wellington held his position until Almeida fell, but the army was in a constant state of alert, the sick were sent to the rear and a General Order instructed all senior officers to ensure that the line of retreat was not "choked up with baggage or carriages".[31]

On the day that the garrison marched out of the fortress Wellington withdrew his army to its previous line between Celorico and Guarda in readiness for a further retreat if the French should advance in force. This appeared to be the case when, on 2 September, a brigade of infantry and 1,200 cavalry drove in the allied outposts in front of Celorico. Believing that this might be the start of the invasion, beacons were lit to signal the retreat and Wellington sent his infantry off down the highroad south of the Mondego leaving just the cavalry at Celorico and Guarda.

With Guarda no longer held in force by the allies, Hill's position in front of Abrantes had become more isolated. The road through Fundão to Guarda could not now be used and Hill was given a new line of march by Sobreira Formosa and Espinhal if he should be required to join Wellington. Hill was told to "retire gradually" along this route if Reynier moved his entire force north of the Sierra de Gata with the clear intention of joining the main body of l'Armée de Portugal. Masséna's invasion plans remained unclear and Hill had to be careful not to be deceived by Reynier's movements into abandoning his position prematurely, for it was still possible that the II Corps might march south of the Tagus "to turn our right, and to cross the Tagus by some of the numerous fords between Abrantes and Santarém". If this was to prove to be Reynier's intentions, Hill's objective was "to prevent the enemy's passage at a point below you", Wellington told him, "[and] prevent the enemy from annoying the march of this part of the army on the great road from Leiria to Lisbon". Wellington directed Hill to have the boat-bridge at Abrantes taken up and the boats held under the protection of the guns of the fortress. Hill was also told to obstruct the fords at Villa Velha "by stakes and stones in the river; blowing up, or otherwise destroying, the roads leading to the fords on both sides". Yet if the II Corps moved northwards to join Masséna, Hill would have to march without delay for Espinhal and the valley of the Mondego along the Espinhal Communication. The same applied to Leith's 5th Division which had to remain at Thomar in support of Hill and also be ready to march for Ponte da Murcela to join Wellington if Reynier moved north of the Sierra de Gata.[32]

It was a full week after the French advance upon Celorico, and almost a fortnight after the fall of Almeida, before either Masséna or Reynier made any further significant movements. The march into Portugal had been delayed by the usual shortage of transport and supplies. "Pack mules, food, wagons, and all kinds of equipment were lacking, and the country offered no transportation, nor were the funds in our treasury sufficient to accelerate the various preparations," recalled Pelet. "In the first place, shoes were deteriorating rapidly, sometimes after four days of rain, and without them it was impossible for the troops to march; moreover … clothing and accoutrements were used up or lost quickly during the war, as was the equipment necessary for the temporary hospitals and ambulance service. Many were surprised that we were not marching. They should rather have been astonished when we started to move."[33]

Masséna had now also discovered that the countryside ahead of him had been depopulated and already the Ordenanza were attacking French foraging parties. It was obvious to Masséna that he would have to compile a large stock of food before he could march further into Portugal. "Each day demonstrates the necessity of this more clearly," Masséna wrote to Napoleon, "but each day makes it more evident that we are not obtaining as much as our activity deserves. The small amount of transport available, and the destruction by the Spanish brigands of several convoys of corn which were coming up from the province of Valladolid, have occasioned delay in the accumulation of the stores." The attacks by the Ordenanza caused Masséna to issue a proclamation stating that no quarter would be given to combatants without uniforms and that they would be shot as "brigands and highway robbers". The proclamation provoked an immediate response from Wellington who wrote to Masséna pointing out that the Ordenanza formed part of the military force of Portugal. Nevertheless, the French continued to shoot the Ordenanza and the Ordenanza replied by torturing and hanging French prisoners.[34]

It was the lack of draught animals, though, that caused Masséna the most trouble. To his regret he had to reduce the artillery of each division from twelve to eight guns for the want of horses and yet he was still unable to find enough animals to carry even the fifteen days rations that the marshal considered to be the minimum that he could afford to take with him. He had also hoped to provide each infantryman with sixty cartridges and to keep a reserve of twelve million rounds but when they marched into Portugal the infantry carried only fifty rounds per man and the reserve was less than four million rounds.

Logistical problems were not Masséna's only worries. The losses in the two sieges and the necessity of providing garrisons for Almeida and Ciudad Rodrigo had reduced the forces under his immediate command to less than 45,000 men. This meant that he had little choice but to incorporate the II Corps into the main body of l'Armée de Portugal in order to have a sufficient force concentrated for the invasion. By doing this, Masséna would leave himself with no troops to protect his lines of communications, as Kellermann and Serras both had their hands full maintaining order in their respective districts. Masséna made these points known to Napoleon and at the same time he begged for a division of the IX Corps (the assistance of which he had been promised back in April) to be transferred to Salamanca.[35]

Masséna appreciated the difficulties that lay ahead and his campaign strategy was realistic and uncomplicated. "The nature of the terrain between the frontier and Lisbon would only permit very simple lines of operation through its narrow passages," recorded Pelet. "Considering the obstacles separating the border and the capital, opposite an alert and superior enemy, we could attempt none of the great strategic manoeuvres which were so brilliant and advantageous. Everything was reduced to choosing the most direct line, the terrain where the English would be least able to resist, where we would have the greatest latitude to manoeuvre in case of a main attack, where the roads would prevent the fewest obstacles, and, finally, where we could hope to find some trace of food." There was to be no secondary attack upon Oporto or south of the Tagus. "Double lines were rejected because of the size of the army as well as the nature of the country. The enemy would be able to throw himself on either line or between them as we approached Lisbon, where the ground became less difficult … A secondary line of operation on the other side of the Tagus would not have been without difficulty because of the numerous forts located there. In addition, such a line would have been completely separated from the main body … The two secondary lines, on Oporto or on the left bank of the Tagus, would subsequently have become accidental lines at best … In this case Lisbon was everything."[36]

Reynier was accordingly summoned to join Masséna. He began his march on 10 September and five days later he had linked up with the rest of l'Armée de Portugal. On the 16th Junot was ordered to concentrate at Pinhel, Ney and the reserve cavalry at Macal de Chão, and Reynier at Guarda. With these dispositions the three major roads to Lisbon – through Belmonte, Celorico and Viseu – were all menaced and the intended line of attack concealed a little longer. Masséna hoped to be able to rush down the right of the Mondego in one mass and reach Coimbra before Hill could join Wellington. Hill's scouts, however, informed him of the II Corps's movements almost as soon as they had taken place and on the 12th he departed from the Castelo Branco region leaving just Lecor's Portuguese at Fundão. Leith likewise broke camp on the 15th and, by 20 September, the two divisions were moving in behind Wellington's rear in the valley of the Mondego.

Masséna had now brought together 65,000 men, a force which Napoleon regarded as adequate for the task he had set his marshal. "Lord Wellington has only eighteen thousand men, Lord Hill has only six thousand," the Emperor wrote in September, completely ignoring the presence of the Portuguese, "it would be ridiculous to suppose that twenty-five thousand English can balance sixty thousand French, if the latter do not trifle, but fall boldly on after having well observed where the blow may be given. You have twelve thousand cavalry, and four times as much artillery as is necessary for Portugal. Leave six thousand cavalry and a proportion of guns between Ciudad Rodrigo, Alcantara and Salamanca, and with the rest commence operations."[37]

Masséna consequently left behind a regiment of Dragoons and four battalions of infantry to garrison Ciudad Rodrigo and Almeida. The siege train and its accompanying artillery crews were placed into Ciudad Rodrigo and communications between the two fortresses were to be maintained by five squadrons of Dragoons. These numbers were scarcely adequate to garrison both places. There would be no spare troops for counter-insurgency work and shortly after the departure of l'Armée de Portugal the local partisans closed in upon the fortresses and cut their links with the other French forces in the Peninsula. Yet this was of no immediate concern to Masséna, for the expedition into Portugal was not going to be conducted as a regular campaign. He would be unable to establish bases along his line of march, as he could not afford the men to guard such establishments nor to keep open communications with Spain. The French advance would simply be a dash to Lisbon through the hostile countryside, the troops being expected to gather what food they could *en route* to supplement the thirteen days rations that they would carry with them.

Although Masséna's intentions remained unclear, the Portuguese were "taking to fly to the mountains from the French". Sadly they were "unaware of the distance to which French rapacity can extend itself", wrote one experienced officer, "or the desolation that awaits their homes and their fields". Wellington was still convinced that the French would make their advance along the main road which ran across the Ponte da Murcela, to where the 6 and 9-pounder cannon of the British reserve artillery were being shipped to be placed in the prepared line of redoubts along the River Alva. Wellington also ordered all the divisions of his army to continue their withdrawal southwards and to concentrate behind the Alva. But on 15 September, Wellington observed that Masséna's headquarters had been moved to Trancoso and concluded that the French would "move a considerable column by Viseu, which would turn any position we might take upon the Alva". Two days later it became clear that the entire Armée de Portugal was set to move north of the Mondego. "The 11th and VI Corps came to Celorico yesterday, and a part of them crossed the Mondego to Fornos," Wellington told Leith on the evening of the 17th. "More have crossed the Mondego this day, and no part of the enemy's army has moved this way. It is generally understood that the whole army is between the Douro and the Mondego, and are about to march upon Coimbra." Wellington correspondingly ordered his infantry to cross the Mondego so as to cover Coimbra. The cavalry were left around Gouvea to monitor the French advance and to ensure that all of Reynier's corps followed the rest of l'Armée de Portugal over the Mondego, as it was still possible that part of the II Corps might move along the main highway south of the river.[38]

Masséna's decision to leave the highway and take the poor roads north of the Mondego was quite unexpected by Wellington. It was not just that the roads were worse but the route was far longer, adding two days to the march and giving Wellington time to concentrate all his forces. However, Masséna had been informed of the defences at Ponte da Murcela and the only apparent alternative route was through Pinhel and Viseu to re-join the main highway at Coimbra. The renegade Portuguese officers on Masséna's staff had led him to believe that "some good roads extended on the right bank of the Mondego through open, easy, flat country up to Coimbra, and that by this means we could turn the position of Ponte da Murcela".[39]

Masséna was unable to verify this information by reconnaissance or by interrogation of local inhabitants, for the Ordenanza were attacking French patrols and in the deserted villages of the Beira scarcely a single person could be found. Likewise, the maps with which Masséna had been supplied were of little help. "We were in effect without maps," complained Masséna's aide-de-camp, "so that we had, as it were, to feel our way along." The principal map that Masséna had to use was the *Atlas Geografico de Espana* by Thomas Lopez. Originally published in 1779 (Masséna's copy was dated 1804) it makes no distinction between roads, and the route through Trancoso and Viseu appears, if anything, to be drawn with greater prominence than the main Celorico-Coimbra highway. Masséna also had an even older map – the 1762 map by the English engraver Thomas Jeffery – and several even more defective ones which had been copied from the Lopez and Jeffery maps. Apart from this inadequate collection, Masséna had been given a few private drawings and a number of incomplete geographical surveys of Portugal. That Masséna had to base his strategy upon such sources of information is quite remarkable when one considers that this was the third invasion of Portugal by French armies in as many years and marching with him he had generals, staff officers, engineers and an entire army corps (the II Corps) that had taken part in the first invasion in 1807. In addition to this he had thirty Portuguese officers on his staff, two of whom were generals.[40]

As soon as the first regiments of l'Armée de Portugal left the main Coimbra highway it became evident that Masséna had been misinformed. The poor roads did not seriously restrict the march of the infantry but the artillery and the wagon train soon began to fall behind. Many horses were lost and vehicle after vehicle broke down and had to be abandoned. Colonel Noel, who was with the artillery of the VIII Corps, has left us a description of the journey to Viseu: "There is no road, only a stony, narrow, dangerous track, which the artillery had all the pains in the world to follow without meeting accidents. It is all steep ups and downs. I had to march with a party of gunners ahead of me, with picks and crowbars to enlarge the track. As each arm only looked out for itself, the artillery soon got left to the rear, and deserted by the infantry and the cavalry. We only arrived at our halting-places late at night, utterly done up. The guns were almost always abandoned to themselves; we did not know what road to follow, having no one to give us information … At noon on the 18th I halted with my two batteries after two hours of incessant uphill, to find myself at the crest of a mountain, with a precipitous descent before me, and beyond that another ascent winding upwards, as far as the eye could reach. We were so exhausted that it was useless to go further that day, but on the 19th, with a party of gunners always working in front to enlarge the road, we moved over hill and vale, completely out of touch with the army."[41]

It was not only the terrain that caused problems for the French. Ahead of the retreating allied divisions the Portuguese were evacuating the countryside as ordered. "They are removing their women and properties out of the enemy's way, and are taking arms in their defence," Wellington told Henry Wellesley. "The country is made a desert, and behind almost every stone wall the French will meet an enemy." The companies of the Ordenanza, which normally remained high in the hills during the hours of daylight, descended into the valleys at night to slit the throats of sentries, ambush patrols and capture stragglers. As well as attacks by the Ordenanza, the militia were now closing in upon the rear of the French column. In fact the campaign was very nearly decided before the French reached Viseu, as l'Armée de Portugal's reserve artillery, ammunition and provisions were almost captured by Trant's militia brigade. The convoy was intercepted by Trant with some 3,000 militia infantry and two squadrons of Portuguese regular cavalry. The convoy was escorted by only a company of Grenadiers at its head and a single battalion of the Irish Legion at the rear. Trant immediately attacked but his cavalry was repulsed by the Grenadiers and his infantry was able to achieve little before the Irish troops hurried up to the front. Suspecting that the Irish battalion was the advance guard of a far greater body of infantry, Trant withdrew after destroying a number of ammunition caissons and taking eighty prisoners.[42]

Wellington was delighted with Masséna's choice of route. "I imagine that Marshal Masséna has been misinformed, and has experienced greater difficulties in making his movements than he expected. He has certainly selected one of the worst roads in Portugal for his march," Wellington informed Lord Liverpool on the 20th, having earlier announced that his enemy's "difficulties" had enabled the British commander to "call in all the detached corps of this army, and we shall have them collected immediately".[43]

Leith's 5th Division was the first of these detachments to arrive, reaching San Miguel de Payares behind the Alva on the 20th, with Hill's 2nd Division and Hamilton's and Lecor's Portuguese only a day behind. The 1st Division and Campbell's and Coleman's Independent Portuguese brigades were already at Coimbra and the 3rd and 4th Divisions were at Ponte da Murcela with the Light Division in front of the Alva at Venda do Poro. The cavalry was pushed out towards Tondella to observe the movements of the French and to patrol the fords of the River Criz. Trant's militia had also been called in to secure the left flank of the allied army and was ordered to march southwards to occupy the road which runs over the Serra do Caramulo. The rest of the militia was directed to move upon Trancoso and Celorico to press upon the rear of the invaders.

On 21 September the cavalry withdrew across the Ponte da Murcela which, along with the bridges on the Criz, was destroyed. Wellington moved his headquarters to a range of steep hills approximately ten miles north of Coimbra. "We have an excellent position here," Wellington wrote that evening to Sir Stapleton Cotton (who was in command of the cavalry), "in which I am strongly tempted to give battle." He was writing from the convent of Buçaco.[44]

CHAPTER VI
'The Glittering of Steel'

L'Armee de Portugal remained at Viseu until 21 September to rest its horses, repair the many damaged vehicles and, it was rumoured, to allow Madame Leberton to recover from the long and uncomfortable ride from Almeida. Whilst he waited for his army to regroup (and his mistress to recuperate), Masséna explained the situation to Napoleon: "It is impossible to find worse roads than these; they bristle with rocks, the guns and train have suffered severely, and I must wait for them. I must leave two days at Viseu when they come in, to rest themselves, while I resume my march upon Coimbra, where (as I am informed) I shall find the Anglo-Portuguese concentrated. Sire, all our marches are across a desert; not a soul to be seen anywhere; everything is abandoned … the women, the children, the aged, have all decamped. We cannot find a guide anywhere. The soldiers discover a few potatoes and other vegetables; they are satisfied, and burn for the moment when they shall meet the enemy." The army had already consumed seven of the thirteen days' provisions with which it had commenced the advance from Almeida and the "few potatoes and other vegetables" gleaned from the fields (along with, according to Baron Marbot, some lemons and grapes) did little to improve the situation. Masséna had hoped to procure much more food at Viseu and to find a town of such size completely abandoned was a considerable disappointment to the French commander. It was because of concerns about the army's dwindling reserves of food that Masséna decided to push on as quickly as possible for Coimbra rather than take the longer, but easier, route to Aveiro and then along the main Oporto-Lisbon coastal highway.[1]

On the 21st the first regiments of the VI Corps marched out of Viseu but it was another three days before the reserve artillery was able to leave the town. On that day, the 24th, the leading units of the II Corps, which now headed the French advance, came up against the allied rearguard in front of Mortágua, some fourteen miles from Buçaco. Reynier pushed the British cavalry back upon Craufurd's and Pack's lines of infantry but the French halted when they came under fire from Ross' Horse Artillery troop. The next morning Reynier mounted a strong attack upon Craufurd's position with two full divisions and the British general withdrew to the village of Moura at the foot of the Serra do Buçaco.

Ney, with the VI Corps, joined Reynier and followed up Craufurd's retreat. He attacked Moura with Loison's Division and tried to turn Craufurd's flank. Wellington had no wish to become embroiled in an attack below the mountain and he assumed personal command of the Light Division, drawing it back to join the main allied force on the steep slopes of the serra. There was only a few hours of daylight remaining and Ney had no intention of pursuing the Light Division any further. Reynier moved away to the east to form camp on the undulating ground around the hamlet of San Antonio de Cantaro, leaving the village of Moura to the VI Corps.

The British 3rd and 4th Divisions had been at Buçaco since the 21st and on the evening of the 25th they were joined by Leith's 5th Division. The 1st and 2nd Divisions and the Independent Portuguese brigades would not arrive until the following day, but then Wellington would have 52,000 men in battle order upon the heights.[2]

Early on the morning of the 26th, the pickets of the II Corps notified Reynier of the movement of large numbers of enemy troops along the crest of the ridge above them. Five battalions of blue-coated Portuguese infantry had been seen marching across the mountain followed by a battery of artillery and some British infantry. They also reported the presence of strong lines of skirmishers posted on the hillside below the crest. "It appears to be a rearguard," Reynier wrote in a dispatch to Ney, "but the position is strong, and it will be necessary to make deployments in order to attack with any success … If you judge that this is a rearguard and you attack, I will also attack. If you decide it is necessary to wait for the orders of the Prince d'Essling. I will also wait." Ney, from his position near Moura, could see several artillery brigades placed amongst the rocks and it was evident that the houses on the side of the mountain had been fortified. A few deserters and stragglers that had been captured by the advance guard of the VI Corps were interrogated and they revealed that a large concentration of allied troops had been drawn up behind the crest of the ridge. "I think a great part of the Anglo-Portuguese army spent the night on the crest of the mountain that dominates the entire Moura valley," Ney replied to

Reynier at 10.30. "This morning the enemy has marched to the left and seems to direct his columns toward the main road of Oporto … I have sent one of my aides-de-camp to the Prince d'Essling to tell him they are in our presence, and that it will be necessary for him to come and observe them. If I commanded, I would attack without hesitating a moment."[3]

Although Ney had guessed incorrectly that he was confronted only by a part of the allied army, it is possible that if he and Reynier would have attacked immediately he could have found the allies still taking up their positions. The movement to the left that he mentioned to Reynier was not a march towards the main Oporto road but in fact was Spencer's 1st Division moving to occupy the position previously held by the 4th Division. Hill's 2nd Division did not reach its allotted post on the right of Wellington's line until 10.30, with the attached artillery still many hours behind. If Ney had attacked early on the 26th he would have encountered no more than 34,000 men, 14,000 of whom were still in the process of taking up new positions.

Ney's aide-de-camp, Captain D'Esmenard, arrived at Masséna's headquarters at Tondella, twenty-two miles to the rear, at about 10.00 hours. Masséna was still in bed with Madame Leberton but upon receipt of Ney's letter he set off for the front. In the meantime, a Portuguese deserter had been taken by the pickets of the II Corps and he was able to furnish Reynier with a reasonably accurate description of the disposition of the allied forces on the mountain. It was evident that the bulk of Wellington's army lay before them and Masséna's presence had now become essential. Masséna arrived at Moura in the late afternoon. Together he and Ney made a reconnaissance of the allied positions. From the base of the serra little could be seen of Wellington's dispositions in the fading light of evening, but this did not appear to worry Masséna. "I cannot persuade myself that Lord Wellington will risk the loss of a reputation by giving battle," he is reported to have said later that night, "but if he does, I have him! Tomorrow we shall effect the conquest of Portugal."[4]

The Serra do Buçaco (or in Portuguese, Buçaco) is a range of steep-sided heights that extends nine miles north-westwards from the Mondego to the main chain of the Serra do Alcoba. Described by a British staff officer as "a damned long hill", it varies in height along its length, the highest point being some 1,864 feet above sea-level and almost 1,000 feet above the surrounding countryside. Three roads ran over the mountain. The most southerly of these roads, which ran from San Paulo to Palmases, crossed the ridge three miles north of the Mondego. The middle road,

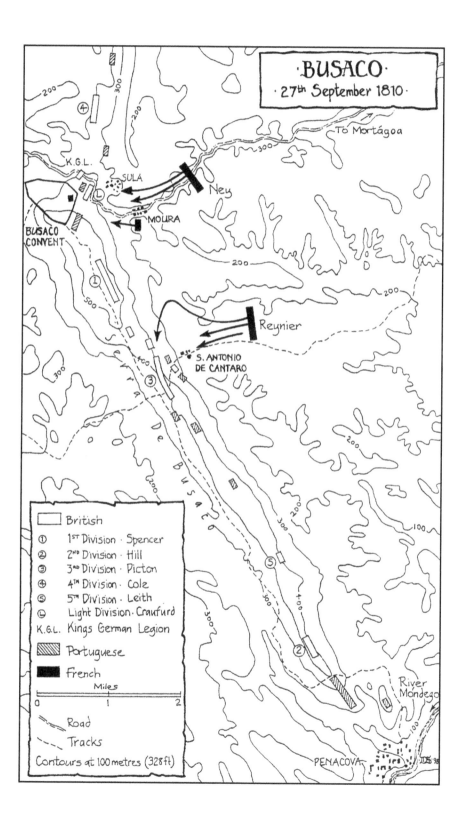

·BUSACO·
27th September 1810·

To Mortágoa

K.G.L.

SULA

Ney

MOURA

BUSACO
CONVENT

Reynier

S. ANTONIO
DE CANTARO

PENACOVA

River
Mondego

☐ British
① 1ST Division · Spencer
② 2ND Division · Hill
③ 3RD Division · Picton
④ 4TH Division · Cole
⑤ 5TH Division · Leith
Ⓛ Light Division · Craufurd
K.G.L. Kings German Legion
▨ Portuguese
■ French

Miles
0   1   2

Road
Tracks
Contours at 100 metres (328ft)

from San Antonio de Cantaro to Palheiros, was a further three miles to the north. The northernmost road, which was the only main paved road, wound its way from the village of Moura along the northern wall of the convent and descended the ridge south-westwards to Coimbra. The wooded grounds of the convent were enclosed by a ten feet high wall inside which was a small chapel surrounded by a low quadrangle. The rest of the eastern hillside was bare heath which, in the opinion of an officer of the 16th Light Dragoons, was in places "so steep and great, that a person alone cannot, without holding and choosing his ground, get down". The slopes were broken by large boulders, steep ravines and outcrops of granite, and the dwarf brushwood and heather which covered the hillside made climbing difficult and tiring. "We are in an excellent position, indeed one which cannot easily be attacked in front," wrote Wellington on the 24th, "and if [the French] wait another day or two, they will be unable to turn it on the only vulnerable point. I shall do everything in my power to stop the enemy here."[5]

On the extreme right of the allied position Wellington had placed the three British brigades of the 2nd Division and Hamilton's two Portuguese brigades. Hill was instructed to hold his position if attacked or, if he was not engaged by the French, to march northwards to the aid of Leith's 5th Division which was situated next in line almost a mile distant.

Leith occupied an extended line from the San Paulo-Palmases road to the south of the San Antonio de Cantaro pass. There was then a gap of nearly a mile to where the Lusitanian Legion was stationed, and a similar empty stretch of ground to where Spry's Portuguese Brigade was posted. On Spry's right, next to the San Antonio pass, were the two battalions of the 8th Portuguese from Barnes' Brigade. Like Hill, Leith was ordered to move to his left to support the 3rd Division if he was not attacked.

Picton, with the 3rd Division, was stationed around the pass on the San Antonio de Cantaro to Palheiros road. North of Picton's line the ridge rises sharply to its highest point (the Cruz Alta). Here, dominating the whole of the Buçaco position, was Spencer's 1st Division. From this high ground the ridge drops abruptly along the eastern wall of the convent enclosure. At this point Pack's Portuguese brigade was posted, with the wall at its back and a steep slope in its front.

Opposite the northern wall of the convent runs the Mortágua-Moura-Coimbra highway. This vital post was held by the 43rd and 52nd Regiments. The remainder of the Light Division was placed in, or on, the slopes above the village of Sula, which was situated halfway down the hillside overlooking Moura.

110

To the rear of the Light Division, on the Monte Nova summit adjacent to the convent enclosure, stood the battalions of the King's German Legion and 200 yards to the north-west was Campbell's Portuguese brigade. These two brigades constituted the general reserve of the army. North of Campbell, and marking the north-eastern limit of Wellington's position, was Cole's 4th Division.

Wellington wanted to conceal these dispositions from Masséna and Wellington's Quartermaster-General, George Murray, issued the following instructions to the army on the 25th: "When upon the Sierra [sic], the troops are to be kept a little behind the ridge, so that they may not be seen by the enemy until it becomes necessary to move up on the ridge to repel an attack."

The wall of the convent enclosure was an integral part of Wellington's defences. An opening was made near Pakenham's Brigade of the 1st Division through which troops could pass into the enclosure and in the entrance of the Porta da Sula a battery was formed, its front covered with abattis. Staging was erected on either side of the entrance to allow troops to fire over the top of the wall. A large part of the eastern wall was knocked down to about shoulder height and loopholes formed at points around the enclosure.[6]

Seventy-six guns were distributed along the mountain. Ross' Horse Artillery was with Craufurd on the Mortágua-Coimbra highway and the other troop of the RHA, commanded by Captain Bull, was posted with the 4th Division. Two Portuguese brigades (twelve guns) under Colonel Dickson were with the 2nd Division and another two Portuguese brigades were with the 5th Division. At the San Antonio pass were twelve guns under Major Arentschildt. With the 1st Division were Lawson's and Rettberg's brigades and Thompson's six guns were with Lightbourne. Along the south-western wall of the convent were the brigades of Cleeves and Passos. These twelve pieces overlooked the slope above Moura and enfiladed the Coimbra highway.

Wellington also had two squadrons of the 4th Dragoons on the wide central top of the mountain "in case of anything forcing its way through the Brigade of Pack, will fall upon it in flank – for the Ground is so favourable that a charge executed here will probably destroy whatever is in its way". This was the only cavalry unit in the battle line. General Fane, with four regiments of Portuguese dragoons and the 13th Light Dragoons, was stationed to the east of Buçaco "to observe and check the movements of the enemy's cavalry on the Mondego". The remainder of the British cavalry was in the plain south of Buçaco around Mealhada on the Oporto-Coimbra road. Lecor's Portuguese infantry division remained at Ponte da Murcella to guard the passage of the Alva.[7]

The centre of the serra has a broad, flat top, some 300 to 400 yards wide, along which large bodies of all arms could move laterally with ease to support any threatened point. The southern half of the position is narrow and rocky, with steep slopes on both eastern and western faces, and the rapid transfer of troops along this sector was not possible. However, some 200 yards down the western side of the ridge there was a rough country track which Wellington's engineers, with the assistance of some local labour, had widened and straightened so that both infantry and artillery could be moved entirely out of sight of the enemy. The only part of the line that Wellington could not easily reinforce was the extreme left, where Cole's 4th Division was placed. But this sector was the least likely to be attacked and Wellington's reserves (Campbell's Portuguese and the KGL) were only a mile away. As well as widening the track at the rear of the mountain, the Royal Engineers had broken up the roads approaching the mountain so as to restrict the movement of the French artillery. They had also barricaded the San Antonio de Cantaro road with abattis and littered it with large boulders.

The only flaw in Wellington's position was some twelve and a half miles to the north where a road passed through the Serra do Caramulo. The road ran from Mortágua, through Boialvo and the Caramulo pass, to Sardão on the main Oporto-Coimbra-Lisbon highway, and effectively turned the allied left flank. This road had been the subject of a special reconnaissance conducted by Major Dundas of the Royal Staff Corps at the beginning of the year and Wellington was well aware of the danger which it posed to his flank. As soon as Wellington decided to occupy Buçaco (on 19 September) he instructed General Bacellar to order the militia brigade of Colonel Trant to "proceed as expeditiously as possible to Águeda and Sardão ... When at Sardão he [Trant] will be on the left flank of the army, and he will cover the road over the Serra leading to Oporto". Although Trant commanded little more than 1,500 men, Wellington apparently believed that this small force could successfully defend the pass as "there were parts of it so extremely difficult", it had been noted, "that if this corps of militia had had the necessary time to destroy the bridges, and to avail itself of the positions afforded by the ravines, which intersect the road, it might have opposed a most decisive resistance to the advance of the enemy." But instead of allowing Trant to march directly southwards from his base at Lamego, Bacellar told him to take a longer route along the Douro and then down the main Oporto-Lisbon highway to Sardão. By the 26th there was still no sign of Trant and as l'Armée de Portugal gathered at the foot of Buçaco Wellington's flank lay unguarded.[8]

On the evening of the 26th the advance formations of the II and VI

112

Corps pushed forwards to the lower slopes of the mountain. An officer of the 2nd Division described the approach of the French army from his position on the summit: "Far as the eye could stretch, the glittering of steel, and clouds of dust raised by cavalry and artillery, proclaimed the march of a countless army; while below me, at the feet of the precipitous heights on which I stood, their pickets were already posted; thousands of them were already halted in their bivouacs, and column after column, arriving in quick succession, reposed upon the ground allotted to them, and swelled the black and enormous masses. The numbers of the enemy were, at the lowest calculation, seventy-five thousand … At a more considerable distance, you might see a large encampment of their cavalry, and the whole country behind them seemed covered with their train, their ambulance, and commissariat." Reynier's voltigeurs and tirailleurs drove the light company of the 88th Regiment from the hillocks at the foot of the heights opposite San Antonio de Cantaro. At the same time, Ney's infantry attacked Pack's 4th Caçadores and the 95th Rifles but these regiments held their ground. There was no further fighting that night and the opposing armies settled down to spend a cold night on the open heath.[9]

The Anglo-Portuguese army slept in battle order, "each man with his firelock in his grasp at his post", wrote one of Picton's young officers. "There were no fires and the death-like stillness that reigned throughout the line was only interrupted by the occasional challenge of an advanced sentry, or a random shot fired at some imaginary foe." By refusing to allow his troops to light any fires Wellington gave his enemy no indication of the strength or positioning of his forces. The French, by contrast, were well supplied with firewood and their camp was "crowned with innumerable fires".[10]

The II Corps was still situated around the village of San Antonio de Cantaro in the direction of Carvalho. Reynier's artillery, commanded by General Tirlet, was also stationed behind San Antonio near the cavalry. Tirlet took fourteen of his twenty-five guns and placed them on several small hills opposite the allied batteries at the San Antonio pass.

The VI Corps was positioned below the Buçaco convent around the Mortágua-Coimbra highway, with the brigades of Loison's Division on the high ground above the village of Moura and Marchand's Division south of the highway. Ney's cavalry was deployed near Marchand's Division, whilst the artillery was placed adjacent to Mermet's Division, which formed the reserve.

The Corps commanders received their battle orders from Masséna late in the evening of the 26th:

II Corps will attack the enemy's right; it will endeavour to break through the enemy's line, after scaling the most accessible point of the mountain. It will reach its objective in one or two columns preceded by skirmishers. Once it has reached the crest at the point selected for attack, it will form up in close column and cross the mountain ridge to the Coimbra road and beyond. It will halt at the Buçaco monastery.

VI Corps will attack by the two tracks leading to the Coimbra road; one of its divisions will be held in reserve, and its artillery will be distributed so as to give support as needed. Marshal Ney will dispose his two assault columns so as to launch them as soon as General Reynier has captured the ridge, and he will then advance on the Buçaco monastery. It will be Marshal Ney's duty to press home his attack if he sees the enemy either trying to counter General Reynier or retiring ... His attack will be preceded by skirmishers. On reaching the crest he will reorganise his troops in order to conform to the further movements of the army.

Junot's VIII Corps was to be held in reserve and the Reserve Cavalry was to be stationed on the Coimbra road behind the VIII Corps. The artillery reserve was positioned either side of the road behind Junot's centre.[11]

There was to be no general advance along the line. The attacks of Ney and Reynier were not to be simultaneous and they would be separated from each other by a distance of over two miles, thus they would not be mutually supporting unless Reynier succeeded with the initial assault. The Buçaco position was certainly very extended for Wellington's army of 52,000 men and Massena expected that the weight and impetus of the heavy French columns would be able to pierce the thin allied line. But by attacking the mountain Masséna was denying himself the use of two of his most effective weapons – his cavalry and artillery. His cavalry was to be kept in reserve to repel any counter-attacks and although Tirlet's fourteen guns were to be brought into action behind the II Corps it would be impossible for them to provide any effective support. From the foot of the serra they would not have been able to fire straight up the ridge 1,000 feet above them. The position eventually chosen by the French gunners was further back beyond San Antonio, some 1,800 yards from the crest of the ridge. This lowered the angle of elevation but at such extreme range the guns would have been ineffective.

Before daylight on the morning of 27 September, Reynier assembled his two divisions at the foot of the serra. He had chosen for his objective the lowest point of the hillside opposite him, which was the dip in the ridge where the road from San Antonio crossed the mountain. Hudelet's

Division was on the left, straddling the road with instructions to seize the San Antonio pass. Merle's Division was on the right near the village of Pendura and was to attack north of the road. All the French battalions were in column with a frontage of just one company and in each regiment the battalions were drawn up one behind the other. In advance of the columns was a dense line of skirmishers.

Merle's Division was the first to move. At approximately 05.00 hours Merle concentrated his two brigades near Pendura and an hour later his advance began. A reconnaissance during the night had revealed that the slope leading up from Pendura was relatively gentle and that no allied troops could be detected north of the road. The French reconnaissance, however, had been defective – north of the road was posted the British 88th Regiment. "All was now ready on our part," wrote Lieutenant Grattan of the 88th, "the men stood to their arms; and as each soldier took his place in the line, his quiet demeanour, and orderly, but determined appearance, was a strong contrast to the bustle and noise which prevailed amongst our opposite neighbours; but these preparations were of short continuance, and some straggling shots along the brow of the mountain gave warning that we were about to commence the Battle of Buçaco."[12]

With his light troops leading the way through the misty dawn, Merle pushed back the light companies of the 5th and 83rd Regiments of Lightbourne's brigade and pressed rapidly up the hill. "The fog cleared away, and a bright sun enabled us to see what was passing before us," continued Grattan. "A vast crowd of tirailleurs were pressing onward with great ardour, and their fire, as well as their numbers, was so superior to that of our advance."[13]

Wellington, watching the progress of Merle's column, ordered two guns from Thompson's battery, under Captain Lane, to move down the hillside where they occupied a small knoll below the southern edge of the plateau. "The French voltigeurs came close to the guns and one was killed only eight paces off," recorded Captain Lane. "An immense column shows itself in the ravine – we with three cheers gave them a few rounds of case and roundshot together at about seventy paces." The Colonel of the 5th Regiment, who was unable to engage the French skirmishers without disturbing the formation of his battalion, withdrew his men beyond the range of the advancing skirmishers but Lieutenant-Colonel Wallace of the 88th took a file from each company of his regiment and sent them down to assist the allied light infantry. The remaining four guns of Thompson's battery, posted near Lightbourne's brigade, also joined in the fight. "Our artillery still continued to discharge showers of grape and canister, at half range," remembered

Grattan, "but the French light troops, fighting at open distance, heeded it not, and continued to multiply in great force."[14]

Ahead of the French was the main body of the 88th (Connaught Rangers) which Picton had reinforced with four companies of the 45th Regiment under Major Gwynne as soon as it became apparent that an attack in the direction of the 88th was imminent. Instead of marching directly upon the 88th, Merle's column swerved sharply to its left, presumably to avoid the fire from Lane's and Thompson's artillery. Passing across the front of the 88th, Merle pushed on towards an unoccupied part of the crest between the 88th and the 21st Portuguese Regiment, which was one of the regiments defending the San Antonio pass.

Hudelet's Division, meanwhile, was already making progress up the road towards the pass. The attack was to be delivered up the road from San Antonio and was to be led by the 1,700 men of the 31st Léger from Arnoud's Brigade, with the two regiments of Foy's Brigade – the 70th Line and the 17th Léger – in support and the 47th Line in reserve. As Meunier approached Picton's line Arentschildt's twelve Portuguese guns opened fire with a heavy salvo of canister. The 31st Léger pressed on but as it came within musket range of the 21st Portuguese and three companies of the British 74th Regiment it found the road blocked with abattis. Despite being unable to use the road, Meunier continued up the rocky terrain in the direction of the pass under an increasing concentration of fire. As he neared the summit of the mountain Meunier halted his depleted, and now disorganised, column and tried to deploy his battalions in line for the final assault.

By this time the head of Merle's Division was nearing the crest of the heights and a detachment of the 4th Léger was sent to occupy an extensive rock formation at the top of the ridge to protect the flank of the main body. The swerve to the left by Merle's column had taken it out of visual contact with the 88th. Wallace, although concerned for the safety of the four companies of the 45th who were situated on his right, was unwilling to leave his position without orders but he despatched one of his officers – Captain Dunne – to the right to assess the situation. A few moments later Dunne returned. He told Wallace that the French had already occupied the rocks and that the four companies of the 45th were about to be attacked by a heavy French column. Wellington was nowhere in sight and so Wallace decided to take the initiative and march to the assistance of the 45th.[15]

Wallace threw the battalion from line into column and advanced rapidly towards Gwynne's position. As it approached the outcrop, the 88th was met with raking fire from the detachment of the 4th Léger ensconced amongst the rocks. Wallace decided to attack immediately before the French could consolidate their position. He took the Grenadier Company and the 1st Battalion Company out of the column and ordered them to assault one side of the outcrop whilst the 5th Battalion Company attacked the rear. Wallace then placed himself at the head of the remainder of his battalion and charged the rocks.

At this moment the four companies of the 45th, which were a little to the left and in front of the 88th, opened fire upon Heudelet's column but the French did not even falter. The ground near the summit at this point is not steep and the French looked certain to reach the crest from where they could roll up the allied flank. Wallace leapt from his horse and together with the 45th he turned the 88th against the head of Sarrut's brigade, which led the French column. He "ran forward at a charging pace into the midst of the terrible flame in his front," recalled Grattan. "All was now confusion and uproar, smoke, fire and bullets, officers and soldiers, French drummers and French drums knocked down in every direction."[16]

Colonel Mackinnon, seeing how desperate Wallace's situation had become, rode over to the San Antonio pass to inform Picton. That general, having satisfied himself that the troops at the pass were no longer under threat, handed over command of the pass to Mackinnon and rode across to see what was happening to the north. "I found the light companies of the 74th and 88th Regiments retiring in disorder,' wrote Picton in his report to Wellington, "and the head of the enemy's column already in possession of the strong rocky point, deliberately firing down on us, and the remainder of a large column pushing upon the hill with great rapidity." Under heavy fire from the 4th Léger, Picton rallied the detached companies of the 88th and 74th regiments and attacked the rocks once again. "The enemy were numerous, well disciplined, and full of ardour," Grattan was later to write, "and besides, from the nature of their position, they had but the alternative of driving our men down, or being themselves flung from the crags amongst which they fought."[17]

Picton's charge drove the 4th Léger from the rocks but the French reformed and tried to retake the position. Picton had ordered the 8th Portuguese Regiment to support his attack and this regiment's 2nd Battalion was now brought into the battle. "A terrific contest took place," wrote an excited young subaltern, "the French fought well, but they had no chance with our men when we grappled close with them, and they were overthrown, leaving half their column on the heather with which the hill was covered." Picton now directed the 8th Portuguese against the main column: "I personally led and directed their attack in the flank of the enemy's column, and we completely succeeded in driving them in great confusion and disorder down the hill." The allies continued the pursuit all the way down the hillside until they were stopped by the fire of the II Corps's divisional artillery. Wallace then formed his men into line facing the enemy to await further orders, or to repel a renewed attack.[18]

Down by the village of San Antonio, Reynier, having seen the repulse of the 31st Léger and the defeat of Merle's Division, rode up to General Foy and angrily called out to him: "Why didn't you start on the climb? You could get troops forward if you choose, but you choose not to." Foy had been ordered to support the 31st Léger but he had understood Reynier's orders to mean that he was to follow up the 31st only when it began to made headway and he was hurt and insulted by his superior's words. Riding at the head of his brigade, he "climbed the mountain seeking more for death, than glory". Ahead of Foy the 31st Léger was falling back whilst over to his right, and within view, Merle's Division was being chased down the hillside. Foy chose as his objective the first, and lowest, hilltop on the right of the pass, steering wide of Arentschildt's batteries.[19]

With the 17th Léger in the van and the 70th Line echeloned behind, Foy directed his brigade to the point where the right wing of the 45th under Colonel Mede was situated with a battalion of the Thomar militia, the 9th Portuguese Regiment and the 1st Battalion of the 8th Portuguese, which had not been involved in the encounter with Merle's Division. This force, composed almost entirely of Portuguese, was all that stood between Foy's seven battalions and the summit. "The right flank of the army would infallibly be turned, and the great road to Coimbra unmasked," observed Lieutenant-Colonel Walker, Assistant Quartermaster-General of the 2nd Division. It was at this moment that Wellington's careful planning was rewarded. He had instructed Leith to move across to join Picton if the 5th Division was not attacked. As it was clear that Reynier had no reserves or flanking detachments to the south of the road, Leith could now move northwards without fear of compromising the line. Similarly, Hill had been ordered to occupy the ground that would be vacated by the 5th Division. So, although Wellington's position stretched for nine miles, as French intentions were revealed the front contracted, concentrating the defending forces upon the threatened points.

Walker galloped off to bring over the 5th Division but found Leith's men were already on their way, marching "by the road of communication in the rear of and nearly parallel to the ridge of the Serra", wrote Leith in his report, "till it should appear their support might be most necessary".

Walker met the leading brigade of the 5th Division and directed them to the pass. "Not one moment is to be lost," shouted Walker, "the enemy in great force are already in possession of the right of the Serra." With the 5th Division was one of Dickson's 6-pounder Portuguese batteries, which Leith dropped off at the pass to help Arentschildt whose guns were running out of ammunition. He also left Spry's Portuguese brigade and his two battalions of the Lusitanian Legion to support Mackinnon. Leith continued with his British brigade to help Picton, who "directed the leading regiment of the brigade to proceed without loss of time to the left".[20]

When Leith arrived he saw that "heavy fire of musketry was being kept up upon the heights, the smoke of which prevented a clear view of the state of things. But when the rock forming the high point of the Serra became visible, the enemy appeared to be in full possession of it". Foy had managed to force his way almost to the summit. The Thomar militia had broken and fled at the first volley but the other Portuguese regiments stood their ground and forced Foy to swerve to his right, where the crest was unoccupied. "We had not moved fifty paces before we found ourselves engaged with a French column moving up the hill," reported Colonel Douglas of the 8th Portuguese, "who finding themselves opposed in front and seeking an unoccupied interval on our left, discontinued their attack on us and by a flank movement gained the crest of the position on the left."[21]

Leith deployed his leading battalion, the 9th British Regiment, across the summit of the plateau and sent his second battalion, the 38th Regiment, to the reverse side of the mountain so that Foy's column could be met head-on. The 38th found that the western slope of the ridge was so densely covered with large boulders that they were unable to climb it. Nevertheless, Leith had led the 9th British diagonally across the plateau so as to place it along the flank of Foy's leading battalions. The 9th, supported by the 74th and some of the 8th and 9th Portuguese which had rallied and re-formed, opened with a volley at 100 yards and advanced firing against the exposed flank of the 17th Léger. The 38th returned from their unsuccessful attempt on the western slope and took up a position on the right of the 9th, with Arentschildt's guns adding their weight to the onslaught. "The ground was covered with dead and dying," remembered one soldier, "not new levies or mercenaries but the elite of the French army." Foy's horse was shot from under him but he was unhurt and he quickly mounted the horse of an aide-de-camp and, now hatless, he cheered his men on up the slope. "My heroic column, much diminished during the ascent, reached the summit of the plateau, which was covered with hostile troops," wrote Foy. "Those on

119

our left made a flank movement and smashed us up by their battalion volleys; meanwhile those on our front, covered by some rocks, were murdering us with impunity. The head of my column fell back to its right, despite my efforts; I could not get them to deploy, disorder set in, and the 17th and 70th raced down-hill in headlong flight." Some of Foy's men had actually succeeded in crossing the communications road at the rear of the mountain and these were left stranded by Foy's flight. A few of these managed to surrender but most of them were killed.[22]

Reynier had only one regiment that had not been engaged, all the other twenty-two battalions had been badly beaten. The attack of the II Corps was clearly over. It had suffered over 2,000 casualties, including more than half its senior officers. General Graindorge had been killed and generals Merle and Foy were both wounded. The colonels of the 2nd, 4th and 31st Léger, and the 70th Line had also been wounded and of the twenty-three battalion commanders that had marched up the mountain four had been killed and seven wounded. Of the 421 officers in total that went into action, 118 had been hit. Amongst the 2,023 men lost by the II Corps – almost eighteen per cent of the troops committed to the attack – no less than 350 men and fifteen officers were in the hands of the allies.[23]

Over to the north of the battlefield, by the village of Moura, Ney was holding the VI Corps in readiness. He had been ordered to attack only when he was certain that Reynier was in possession of the heights and marching on the convent of Buçaco. Before daylight the artillery of the VI Corps had begun a heavy bombardment of the allied positions around the convent, and at approximately 06.30 Loison and Marchand assembled their divisions in columns of brigades ready for the assault upon the serra. As the early morning mist dispersed, Ney was able to see Merle's column massed on the edge of the plateau and he judged that the moment had come to launch his attack.

Loison moved off a few minutes before Marchand at around 07.00 hours. He put his two brigades side by side with the six battalions of Simon's Brigade on the right and Ferey's six battalions on the left. Both brigades started from the low ground in front of Sula, each with a strong line of tirailleurs and voltigeurs out in front. The allied artillery had already opened fire in response to the French bombardment and Craufurd had sent down three battalions of riflemen to meet the French advance. As soon as the VI Corps's leading files moved through the trees on the lower slopes, the tirailleurs encountered the allied light infantry. Craufurd had placed the 95th Foot and the 3rd Caçadores – more than 1,300 rifles – into the enclosures in front of Sula, and Pack had deployed the whole of the 4th Caçadores on the hillside in front of his line battalions. The allied skirmishers held their French counterparts in check and Loison was forced to detach whole battalions from his main column to assist his light troops. After a severe struggle the 95th and the Caçadores were driven back up to the village. Sula had been fortified and was now powerfully defended by the allied riflemen who again stopped the French tirailleurs. Instead of attempting to turn the flank of the village, Loison once again sent his battalions forward to support his skirmishers, this time through the narrow streets of the village. Gradually Craufurd's men were pushed out of the village and Loison's regiments reformed on the hillside above Sula.

Taking the windmill on the skyline as their objective, Simon's and Ferey's brigades moved confidently on up the mountain. As they left the village the leading battalions came under an intense cannonade from the heights above. Ross' guns were trained upon the exits from the village and they poured fire upon the heads of the columns whilst Cleeve's battery took Ferey's column in the flank. The 95th and the Caçadores had rallied some 1,200 yards above Sula and Craufurd sent down the 1st Caçadores to reinforce the skirmish line. Nevertheless, Simon's Brigade broke through the allied light infantry and the French general halted his men just 100 yards below the crest of the mountain before the final push for the summit. All that the French troops could see ahead of them was Spencer's 1st Division far to the left on the Cruz Alta and Ross' guns by the windmill. With the 26th Line leading the advance, Simon's Brigade reached the rocks protecting Ross' battery. Simon himself was the first Frenchman to leap over the rocks but he fell, shot in the face. Ross' battery was overrun, the guns being abandoned to the enemy.[24]

There now appeared to be nothing to stop the French from attaining the summit. They were completely unaware that the 43rd and 52nd Regiments were lying behind the crest. Craufurd, who had been standing watching the battle develop, now saw that the time had arrived for him to strike. His skirmishers had withdrawn from the side of the mountain and, with some passing through the gaps between the waiting battalions and others moving to the flanks, his front was now clear. He waited until the head of the enemy's column was within just a few yards of his position and he walked over to the 52nd and called out, "Now, 52nd, revenge the death of Sir John Moore!". From the sunken ground behind the crest the two regiments stepped forward up to the skyline. From a range of no more than ten yards the Light Division delivered a devastating volley that cut down the leading ranks of Simon's Brigade. Three companies of the 52nd wheeled round upon the right flank of the 26th Line and the 43rd did the same on the left to produce a deadly semi-circle of fire around the head of the French column. Simon's men halted but they refused to retreat, even though the French officers were unable to deploy their battalions into line with the British light infantry crowding in upon them. Volley after volley poured into the ranks of the French but still they held their ground until the 43rd and 52nd, supported by the reformed Caçadores and the 95th, lowered their muskets and charged.[25]

Under the pressure of this sudden onslaught, the foremost French files gave way and fell back upon those behind. The Light Division chased after Simon's leaderless brigade, which crashed into Ferey's Brigade taking it with them in their flight. "We kept firing and bayoneting till we reached the bottom," wrote Napier of the 43rd, "and the enemy passed the brook and fled back upon the main body, which moved down to support them and cover their retreat." The charge of the Light Division created a large gap in the allied line which Wellington filled by calling the battalions of the King's German Legion down from their position north of the convent.[26]

Only one French regiment remained on the hillside. The 32nd Léger, which had taken a small track to the south-west, had become separated from the rest. This solitary regiment, aiming for the eastern wall of the convent, wheeled into line opposite Coleman's Brigade and advanced towards the 19th Portuguese Regiment. But the Portuguese did not wait for the French to attack. As the 32nd Léger moved within musket range the Portuguese fired a volley and charged down the slope. The 32nd met the charge of the 19th and some of the Portuguese "got so wedged in amongst the French that they had not room to use their bayonets," wrote Major-General Macbean of the 19th. "They turned up the butt ends of their muskets and piled them with such vigour, that they promptly cleared the way." The 32nd Leger had met their match and they too were driven down the ridge to join the general rout.[27]

The failure of the 32nd marked the end of Loison's Division as a serious fighting force. Out of the 6,500 men used in the attack, Loison lost sixty-eight officers and 1,200 men, and his senior brigadier, General Simon, had been captured.[28]

The final engagement of the battle was the attack of Marchand's Division to the west of Moura. As the division marched through the village, Masséna urged them on: "My friends, this mountain is the key to Lisbon; it is necessary to seize it with the bayonet." Marchand took his brigades up the Coimbra road in a single column three files deep. Almost as soon as the column left Moura it came under fire from the shrapnel shells of the allied artillery which, according to one French officer, Guingret, "wiped out entire companies". In the face of this onslaught, Marchand's men marched on with Macune's Brigade in the lead. They pushed the 4th Caçadores before them until they reached the smooth slopes below the convent wall where Pack's Portuguese brigade was waiting. The French, although badly disorganised from the running battle with the Caçadores, made several attempts to storm the hillside but the Portuguese stood firm and Macune was unable to press home the attacks.[29]

Marcognet, in command of Marchand's second brigade, climbed the road behind Macune's Brigade but he halted when he came under the fire of Cleeve's and Passos' batteries and Ross' recaptured guns. Unable to get forward through the converging fire of eighteen guns, Marcognet's men could only watch whilst their comrades in the 1st Brigade were being slaughtered on the rise above them. Ney, who had gone forward with Marchand, could see that there was nothing to be gained from continuing the attack and the marshal ordered his divisions to withdraw.

Marchand's losses had been severe. Macune's Brigade had lost its brigadier, one colonel and thirty-three other officers, as well as 850 men. Even Marcognet's Brigade, though it had not managed to get within musket range of the allied positions, lost 300 men, killed or wounded.

Following the repulse of the VI Corps, a cease-fire was arranged between the two armies to permit the wounded to be recovered. Masséna still had the whole of Junot's 13,000 infantry and Mermet's Division of the VI Corps in hand. But he had lost over 4,400 men and he could see Wellington's army concentrated on the two points that had been attacked. Hill's strong division with Hamilton's Portuguese, totalling 10,000 men, had closed up to Leith's right wing and Cole had moved the 4th Division close to Craufurd's left.

Wellington had 33,000 men that had not yet been engaged and his army was victorious and confident. As he rode along the ridge his men cheered and waved their hats in salute. In the valley below, the troops of l'Armée de Portugal looked up in dismay at the towering heights and cursed the man who had ordered them to attack the Serra do Buçaco.[30]

Later in the day Loison sent a body of skirmishers up the hill to seize the village of Sula, where they came into contact with Craufurd's outposts. With this action Masséna was hoping to draw the allies into a fight on ground more favourable to the French. Wellington, seeing that the Light Division was exhausted from its earlier efforts, sent the light companies of the King's German Legion and the 6th Caçadores from the reserves to take over the fight. The French, however, managed to push some men into the village who were only evicted when Craufurd sent down a company of the 43rd. As it was clear that Wellington was only going to use his troops sparingly, Loison discontinued the engagement.

"We have been engaged with the enemy for the last three days, and I think we shall be attacked again tomorrow," Wellington reported a few hours after the battle, "as I understand they must carry our position, on which, however, they have as yet made no impression, or starve. Our position is an excellent one, and it is certainly no easy task to carry it, but I think they will make another trial." Masséna, though, was too experienced a commander to waste any more lives in such an unequal struggle and there was no further fighting that day. The evening passed without incident and the exhausted troops camped down around the positions that they had held the previous night.[31]

One of Masséna's aides – Baron Marbot – had alerted the Prince to reports of a road through the Caramula mountains north of Buçaco and early the following morning Masséna ordered his cavalry to find a way round the allied positions. Sainte-Croix's Brigade was sent along the route towards Mortágua, whilst General Soult led a reconnaissance along the Gondolem valley hoping to find a passage to the south. Soult found himself blocked by Lecor's Portuguese infantry and Fane's cavalry drawn up in front of the village of Quino. Soult tried to force the Portuguese position but without success and he returned to headquarters. Sainte-Croix, on the other hand, discovered the road through the Caramula mountains. A peasant captured in one of the deserted villages confirmed that the road ran for eleven miles from Mortágua via Boialvo to Sardão and on to the main Oporto to Lisbon highway, and that although the road was not a good one it was perfectly practicable for the passage of an army.

With this news Sainte-Croix returned to Masséna at about midday. It was the breakthrough that the French commander desperately needed and he immediately decided to make an attempt to turn Wellington's position along this road. There was some danger in such a manoeuvre. Wellington had an excellent view over the surrounding countryside and it was possible that the British commander might wait until a large part of the French army had withdrawn from his front and then descend from the heights and overwhelm the French rearguard. So while the Prince d'Essling made his arrangements for out-flanking the allied positions, his troops manoeuvred threateningly at the foot of the mountain in an attempt to disguise the Armée de Portugal's real intentions.[32]

At daybreak on the 28th, French skirmishers were sent up the lower slopes to engage the allied pickets and at noon the French artillery opened fire all along the line at the allied positions. Other troops began erecting abattis and digging trenches on the flanks of the Mortágua road and around San Antonio to help the rearguard cover the withdrawal of the army. In the late afternoon the VIII Corps moved off towards Boialvo with orders to hold the Caramula defile at all costs. By early evening Wellington was receiving reports of Junot's movements and at 18.00 hours the rearmost units of the VI Corps could clearly be seen moving off along the Mortágua road, despite their attempting a smoke screen by setting fire to the surrounding trees.

Wellington was perfectly aware of Masséna's intentions. "Having thought it probable that he would endeavour to turn our left by that road, I had directed Col. Trant, with his divisions of militia, to march to Sardão, with the intention that he should occupy the mountains," Wellington informed Lord Liverpool, "but unfortunately he was sent round by Oporto, by the General Officer commanding in the north, in consequence of a small detachment of the enemy being in possession of S. Pedro do Sul; and, notwithstanding the efforts which he made to arrive in time, he did not reach Sardão till the 28th, at night, after the enemy were in possession of the ground.

"As it was probable that, in the course of the night of the 28th, the enemy would throw the whole of his army upon the road, by which he could avoid the Serra do Buçaco and reach Coimbra by the high road of Oporto, and thus the army would have been exposed to be cut off from that town, or to a general action in less favourable ground, and as I had reinforcements in my rear, I was induced to withdraw from the Serra do Buçaco." Wellington, therefore, was determined to make no attempt to stop Masséna's turning movement even though, if he had acted promptly, the left wing of his army could have reached the exit from the Caramula defile well before the VIII Corps. Colonel Trant had in fact arrived at Wellington's headquarters at midday on the 28th with the news that his brigade would be at Sardão by 14.00 hours. Trant, of course, could not possibly stop the entire French army with just his 1,500 infantry and a squadron of dragoons but Wellington refused to give Trant any assistance: "It would have been impossible to detach a corps from the army to occupy the Serra do Caramula after the action of the 27th." He later wrote in defence of his decision not to block Masséna's flank march: "That corps might have been hard pressed and obliged to retreat, in which case it must have retreated upon Sardão and the north of Portugal. It could not have rejoined the army, and its services would have been wanting in the fortified positions in front of Lisbon. It was therefore determined to rely upon Colonel Trant alone to occupy the Serra do Caramula, as his line of operations and retreat was to the northward. Nothing could have been done, except by detaching a large corps, to prevent the French from throwing a large force across the Caramula. When, therefore, they took that road, there was nothing for it but to withdraw from Buçaco."[33]

In the fading light of evening Wellington watched the French columns marching into the distance and he knew that his position had been turned. At 18.50 hours Wellington issued the first of his orders for the evacuation of the mountain. By dawn the following morning the positions upon the Serra do Buçaco were deserted except for the Light Division and a brigade of cavalry which had been brought up to the rear of the mountain.

Throughout the early hours of 29 September the two armies marched away from each other. The Anglo-Portuguese army retired in two columns. Hill, with the 2nd Division and Hamilton's Portuguese, marched for Espinhal and Thomar. The other column marched for Mealhada and Coimbra. The small force that had been stationed behind the Alva – Lecor's Portuguese division and Slade's cavalry – joined up with Hill's column. The Light Division, along with Anson's cavalry, remained at Buçaco for another twelve hours before following the main column.

As the allies withdrew through the night, Sainte-Croix's dragoons led l'Armée de Portugal along the Caramula pass. Behind the dragoons was the rest of the VIII Corps, followed by Montbrun's cavalry reserve, then came the reserve artillery with the baggage train and the wounded. The VI Corps brought up the rear of the French column, with the II Corps remaining throughout the night opposite Buçaco. "This night march on narrow roads, crossing irregular terrain, was extremely difficult," wrote a French officer, Captain Guingret. "The slow march of this column transporting the wounded looked like a long funeral procession. The silence was only broken by whispers and the lugubrious rolling of the artillery … The bodies of those who died in the midst of this distressing march were placed on the edge of the road to point the way for the troops that followed."[34]

In the afternoon of the 30th, Sainte-Croix came up against Trant's militia in front of Sardão. Part of Trant's weak force bolted with the first shots fired, obliging Trant to retreat and leave the road open to the French.

Slade's and De Grey's cavalry brigades were given the task of holding back the French cavalry and at Mealhada they were joined by Anson's four squadrons. The three brigades retired, with the French dragoons pushing them hard all day. The VI Corps and VIII Corps, having marched through the Caramula defile, bivouacked on the night of the 30th at Mealhada.

The previous day the main allied column had marched through Coimbra. Despite the publication of the proclamation demanding the evacuation of the countryside, as many as four-fifths of the 40,000 inhabitants of Coimbra remained in their homes. Wellington was furious. "The fact is that the government ... conceived that the war could be maintained upon the frontier, contrary to the opinion of myself and of every military officer in the country, and instead of giving positive orders preparatory to the event which was most likely to occur, viz, that the allied army would retire, they spent much valuable time in discussing, with me, the expediency of a measure which was quite impracticable, and omitted to give the orders which were necessary for the evacuation of the country between the Tagus and the Mondego by the inhabitants."[35]

When, on the night of the 28th, Wellington sent a dispatch stating that he was abandoning Buçaco and that the French would be in the city within two or three days, the celebrations over the defeat of the French gave way to "indescribable panic" and a sudden, mass exodus of the place. The bridge out of the city over the Mondego was immediately choked by the crowds that were desperately trying to cross the river and for twenty miles south of Coimbra the roads were "littered with smashed cases and boxes, broken wagons and carts, dead horses and exhausted men", remembered an officer of the Commissariat. "Every division was accompanied by a body of refugees as great as itself, and rich and poor alike, either walking, or mounted on horses or donkeys, were to be seen all higgledy-piggledy, men and women, young and old, mothers leading children or carrying them on their backs ... The nearer the procession came to Lisbon, the greater was the number of animals belonging to the refugees that fell dead, either from fatigue or hunger; and very soon ladies were to be seen wading in torn silk shoes or barefoot through the mud. Despair was written on all faces. It was a heartrending sight ... The tail of the procession was made up by exhausted, weeping and wailing refugees."[36]

As the fugitives streamed out of Coimbra, "all in one dense mass of misery, wretchedness, and confusion", the French continued their march southwards. Masséna added most of Montbrun's dragoons and Soult's light cavalry brigade to Sainte-Croix's vanguard and the allied cavalry were pushed back to the northern outskirts of Coimbra where the Light Division was deployed. With the approach of the French, Craufurd retired through the town, driving the last of the stubborn inhabitants before him.

That night l'Armée de Portugal halted at Coimbra. For the first time since they had entered Portugal the French troops found a town full of food and as soon as they marched into Coimbra they broke ranks and went on the rampage. "Houses were broken into, shops upset, nothing was left untouched," recorded Pelet. "A great quantity of food was lost in the streets … and there were frequent fires endangering the city." In two days Masséna's men wasted food that would, with care, have lasted two or three weeks.[37]

Masséna remained at Coimbra until 3 October. Part of the reason for this delay was due to the fact that his army was out of control, running riot throughout the city, but he also needed time to consider his strategy. Masséna was surprised that Wellington had not made a stand at Coimbra. He never imagined that the allied commander would abandon such a large town to its fate and it now appeared that, despite the victory at Buçaco, the British army was in full retreat for the coast.

Reynier and Montbrun urged Masséna to pursue the retreating army immediately. Ney and Junot, on the other hand, wanted time to allow the troops to recover from the hard marching and fighting of the previous few days. They argued that a hasty pursuit might bring l'Armée de Portugal up against the Anglo-Portuguese drawn up in another strong defensive position and the French troops would have little enthusiasm for a second battle. But the same reasons that compelled Masséna to fight at Buçaco drove him on from Coimbra, and on 3 October Montbrun's cavalry led the advance across the Mondego.

Masséna decided to leave behind the sick and wounded at Coimbra rather than allow them to hinder the pursuit. Unless protected by a large garrison, these men would be in a position of extreme danger from the Ordenanza and Trant's militia, which had closed in on the French rear. But Masséna simply could not spare men from the battle line and he chose to garrison the town with a single company of 156 men and a few hundred convalescents. He reasoned that the "best security" he could afford them was "by pursuing the allies with the whole of his force and driving them from the country". Yet just three days after the French marched out of Coimbra, Trant, with a squadron of cavalry and six battalions of infantry, swept down from the north. The few able-bodied defenders resisted for over an hour before the officer that Masséna had left in charge of the city (with the extravagant title of Governor of Coimbra!) surrendered. Trant took over 4,000 prisoners and marched them off to Oporto.[38]

The two days that Masséna spent at Coimbra gave the allied infantry a start which they never lost. If Masséna had pressed hard upon the rear of the allies he might have presented Wellington with considerable problems, for the mass of fugitives choked up the road creating "disorder beyond words" in the ranks of the retreating army. "Fortunately the Enemy is extremely cautious in advance," wrote a British staff officer, "for if he had been otherwise there is no calculating how far the confusion might have spread." However, for the next seven days Wellington's main column continued its march on Torres Vedras uninterrupted by the l'Armée de Portugal but with "thousands, and tens of thousands" of Portuguese refugees "mixing with and impeding the retreating army". The Light Division and Anson's cavalry brought up the rear one day's march behind the main column. As the allies approached the Lines, the weather broke and "to complete the misery of all" the autumnal rains lashed the retreating columns, "pouring rain down in torrents, accompanied by severe thunder and lightning, filling the streams and watercourses, and rendering the roads deep and heavy".[39]

Wellington now ordered the occupation of the Lines by the militia infantry and the British and Portuguese artillery crews and told Jones to be prepared for the imminent arrival of the army. Wellington's main column moved to Alcobaça, the next day to Rio Maior and the following day to Alenquer. On 9 October the first units of the Anglo-Portuguese army took up their positions behind the great range of redoubts. Two days later the French cavalry arrived before the Lines, almost exactly a year after Wellington had ordered their construction.

CHAPTER VII
'Dug in to the Teeth'

On the morning of 11 October 1810 the advance units of l'Armée de Portugal continued to lead the march upon Lisbon. Pierre Soult's light cavalry division probed towards Vila Franca da Xira along the main road which runs alongside the Tagus whilst the rest of Montbrun's cavalry pushed up the road from Alenquer.

At Vila Franca, Soult found his way blocked by Hill's outposts. Soult drove the British pickets from the town only to see before him the long line of redoubts crowning the hillside behind Alhandra. Leaving a small force to hold Vila Franca, Soult withdrew to Castanheira and reported back to Montbrun. The main body of Montbrun's Division had arrived at the village of Sobral de Monte Agraço, which was occupied by the 71st Regiment from Spencer's 1st Division. Montbrun did not try to seize the village, as his scouts had informed him of the presence of a line of fortifications flanked by the rest of the 1st Division on the heights above Arruda and Zibreira. He sent his troopers as far westwards as Runa but they could not find any way past the line of fortifications. Montbrun made no attempt to advance any further, reporting back to Masséna that he had discovered a continuous line of fortifications stretching from the Tagus to beyond the Upper Sizandro.[1]

Throughout the previous few months work on the Lines had been "pushed on at high pressure" and by 6 October the Superintending Engineer, Captain John Jones, was able to report to Colonel Fletcher that "every preparation for an instant defence of the lines is now complete, and you need be under no apprehension for our credit, even if the enemy attack as the rear division enters the works". The fact was that the time lost by Masséna at Ciudad Rodrigo and Almeida and the long march to Buçaco had given the British engineers far more time than they had ever expected to have. The result was that the discontinuous range of independent strongpoints which formed the basis of Wellington's original plan for the first line had been turned into a chain of defences almost as strong as the second, or principal, line.[2]

As the spring turned into summer and l'Armée de Portugal was still encamped around Ciudad Rodrigo, Fletcher travelled up to Wellington's headquarters at Celorico. At their meeting it was considered that if the French laid siege to Almeida, rather than simply bypassing the fortress, they would be unable to advance upon Lisbon until the autumn. Almost all the 27-30 inches of annual rainfall of this region falls between October and March, turning gentle streams into fast-running rivers and open plains into swamps. This meant that along the whole twenty-five miles from Alhandra to the mouth of the Sizandro there would be only seven miles of ground not protected by natural obstacles, and Wellington decided to try and make the outer defensive front of the lines as secure as the main line. On 17 July, Fletcher issued orders to strengthen the right flank of the advance ground upon which the principal works at Torres Vedras and Monte Agraço had been established and to throw up additional works on the left flank.

As a result of these proposals as many workmen as possible were employed on the outer line. The conscription for labour was extended to a distance of fifty miles and no excuse for the withholding of service was accepted, even women and children took turns in digging trenches and building parapets. A third militia regiment was also added to the workforce. The rates of pay for the workers were increased to ten vintems a day for labourers and sixteen for skilled mechanics. Women were paid a half and children one quarter the rate of men. Fletcher remained at Wellington's headquarters and three other engineers (Captains Chapman, Squire and Goldfinch) joined the field army. Jones was left in "command and superintendence of all works and duties" connected with the Lines, along with eleven British, three Portuguese and two German engineers.[3]

The musketry trench (No. 1) across the marsh between the Tagus and the heights of Alhandra and the trench (No. 2) from the marsh up to the summit of the heights were converted into strong lines, including emplacements for fifteen guns. The left flank of trench No. 1 was developed to accommodate two 12-pounders and 800 men, and a redoubt for another two cannon and 200 men was begun on the hillside behind the trench. The heights above Alhandra were rendered virtually unassailable by cutting or blasting away the top fifteen to eighteen feet of the heights to form a perpendicular scarp along the whole of the north- and east-facing slopes (a distance of almost two miles). These scarps were covered by infantry trenches and redoubts Nos.114-120, which between them mounted twenty-seven guns and supported over 1,000 men.

131

The Alhandra position, though now considerably enlarged, was still isolated and easily turned on its open western flank. In order to prevent this, Jones ordered the heights above Calhandriz to be occupied by a chain of mutually supporting redoubts. On 6 September, 1,500 men under the supervision of Lieutenant Forster began work on four redoubts (Nos. 121-4) whilst miners dug and blasted the flanks of the ridge into a steep scarp. Eventually the Calhandriz heights, which was the only range of hills over which artillery could travel to turn the Alhandra defences, was formed into an immensely strong detached position. A flotilla of fourteen gunboats was stationed in the Tagus opposite Alhandra, and every structure along the northern bank of the river at this point, was levelled to the ground to offer the sailors an unimpeded field of fire.

In order to block up the valley between the heights of Alhandra and Calhandriz, and to connect the defences of the two positions, an abattis was placed across the valley slightly behind the westernmost redoubt of the Alhandra position (No. 6) and the easternmost redoubt on the Calhandriz ridge (No.21) so that the guns from these works could sweep the front of the abattis line. This line was formed mainly from complete olive trees pushed together so that their branches became inextricably tangled. It constituted an almost impassable barrier yet it afforded absolutely no cover for an assailant. Along the rear of the abattis a covered communications trench was dug and a number of stone buildings on both sides of the valley were converted into fortified musketry posts to provide flanking fire.

Time was even found for the construction of a redoubt (No. 125, for four 12-pounders and 250 men) behind Mata Cruz, which extended the line of defences from Alhandra through Calhandriz to the Serra de Serves. All the most accessible parts of this mountain were also scarped along their north-facing fronts as far as the pass of Bucelas.

Over on the western flank of the outer line, a chain of new redoubts was built along the left bank of the River Sizandro as far as the defences at Torres Vedras. During the summer months the Sizandro is reduced to a small stream but is turned into a significant river by the autumn rains. Obstacles were placed in the bed of the river which caused it to overflow its banks, turning the entire front into an impassable bog. With the guns of the new redoubts sweeping the length of the Sizandro this westernmost section of the line, from the Atlantic to Torres Vedras, became completely safe from attack. At the eastern extremity of the line the Alhandra and Alverca streams had been similarly obstructed, causing an inundation a mile wide across the low ground bordering the Tagus.[4]

132

With the two flanks of the outer line secured, all effort was concentrated on developing the centre of the line. In particular, attention was given to the construction of a road suitable for infantry and cavalry to connect Alhandra with Monte Agraço. As the hills along this sector are high and in parts very steep, no additional redoubts were considered necessary but all non-essential points of access were blocked and several bridges and paths leading to this front were destroyed.

When completed, the outer line included sixty-nine works with 319 pieces of artillery manned by 18,683 men. It comprised twenty-nine miles of fortifications, measuring twenty-five miles in a direct line from river to sea. It was approximately five miles longer than the inner line and the ground was generally far less formidable than the mountainous regions around Montachique, Bucelas and Mafra on the second line. Nevertheless, the outer line was now regarded as being strong enough to withstand a French assault and considerable manpower was switched to the works around the embarkation point at St Julian.

On the eastern side of the semi-circle of defences at St Julian, a very strong detached fort was built on a rise to the north-east of the town of Oeiras. Numbered 109, this fort mounted seven 9-pounders, one 5.5-inch howitzer and had a 500-strong garrison. All the approaches to this redoubt were also shaped and scarped. This work suffered from being overlooked by higher ground some 600 to 700 yards in its front, so in order to help protract the defence of this work after its parapets had been destroyed by plunging fire from enemy guns placed on the heights, a gallery, loopholed for reverse-flanking fire, was formed behind the counterscarp at the salient angle of the front faces. A communications trench was made along the bottom of the ditch from the interior of the fort to the gallery. This was the only redoubt throughout the entire three lines of fortifications that was built with a crenellated parapet. The rest of the defences were extended to completely encompass Oeiras. This was achieved through the addition of a line (No.110) from the Fort das Maias to the Tagus for 1,000 men and three cannon, and by connecting redoubts Nos.106-8 to the west with a covered road or musketry trench. This trench had a parapet but was without external revetting and was constructed without a ditch to permit the defending troops to advance from the trench in any direction.

The work at St Julian included the construction of four jetties to facilitate boarding and to enable a more rapid embarkation of stores as Wellington did "not now think anything safe in Lisbon". The jetties were built by Captain Holoway at a cost of £15,000. To the surprise of many local people, the jetties withstood the battering of the Atlantic gales for many years after the end of the war and made an embarkation possible even in extreme weather conditions.[5]

Wellington's conviction that the French would attempt a secondary invasion south of the Tagus was never far from his thoughts. As the invaders would not be able to bridge the river below Alhandra, the only aggressive action that they could take would be to establish batteries on the Almada heights which overlooked the Tagus estuary and the city of Lisbon. Initially, Wellington had rejected the idea of defending the southern bank of the Tagus but guns situated on these heights could prevent the passage of shipping into Lisbon harbour and even bombard parts of the capital, something which Forjaz was quick to point out would "succeed in exciting disturbances in Lisbon". Consequently, Wellington ordered Almada to be heavily fortified and Captain George Ross (followed later by Captain Goldfinch) was transferred from Mafra to take charge of the work.

The defences at Almada covered a distance of over 7,000 yards and consisted of seventeen detached redoubts with a number of advanced flèches. They were connected by adapting an existing sunken road which crossed the Almada heights behind the line of redoubts. The northern face of the road was dressed to form a short glacis and a section of the road was cut to create a banquette for infantry. The dilapidated fortifications of the Almada castle were also rebuilt and in total the defences were to hold 7,500 men and eighty-six guns. They were to be manned by some of the Lisbon militia and members of the Civic Volunteer Corps supported by British marines and sailors from Berkeley's squadron. A signal station was erected at Almada castle, which could communicate directly with Lisbon. If the French broke through the line of redoubts, the defenders could easily and safely be brought off by boat and transferred back across the Tagus.[6]

When the allies began their retreat from the frontier after the fall of Almeida Wellington issued Fletcher with a memorandum instructing him to divide the Lines into districts with an officer appointed to regulate the troops designated for the defence of the works in each district. These arrangements were as follows:

No.1 District. From Torres Vedras to the sea. Headquarters at Torres Vedras.
  2,470 Militia Infantry
  250 Ordenanza Artillery
  140 Portuguese Line Artillery
  70 British Artillery

No.2 District. From Sobral de Monte Agraço to the valley of the Calhandriz. Headquarters at Sobral.
    1,300 Militia Infantry
    300 Ordenanza Artillery
    140 Portuguese Line Artillery
    40 British Artillery

No.3 District. From Alhandra to the valley of the Calhandriz. Headquarters at Alhandra.
    400 Militia Infantry
    60 Ordenanza Artillery
    60 British Artillery

No.4 District. From the banks of the Tagus near Alverca to the pass of Bucelas. Headquarters at Bucelas.
    1,100 Militia Infantry
    500 Ordenanza Artillery
    80 Portuguese Line Artillery

No.5 District. From the pass of Freixal to the pass of Mafra. Headquarters at Montachique.
    2,400 Militia Infantry
    480 Ordenanza Artillery
    120 Portuguese Line Artillery
    50 British Artillery

No.6 District. From Mafra to the sea. Headquarters at Mafra.
    700 Militia Infantry
    350 Ordenanza Artillery
    230 Portuguese Line Artillery
    40 British Artillery

As soon as these troops were gathered at their respective assembly points the infantry were exercised in various defensive manoeuvres and the artillerymen familiarised themselves with their cannon and howitzers. The naval contingent of signallers practised sending messages up and down the line and Portuguese "arm" telegraphs, which had been fabricated in Lisbon, were erected at each signal post as a back-up system in case any of the main masts or yards were damaged. Wellington arranged for tents for 2,500 men to be sent to No. 1 District, for 2,000 men to No. 2 District, for 5,000 men to No. 3 and No. 4 Districts, and for 10,000 men at both No. 5 and No. 6 Districts. The whole of the

Portuguese irregular force occupying the Lines was placed under the nominal command of the British Colonel, later General, Peacocke.[7]

An engineer was selected for each district to escort the brigades of the field army to their allotted places in the line and to explain the nature and the purpose of the various defences. Each engineer was then to join the staff of the divisional commander of that district. The engineers were assisted by locals who were very familiar with the area and who acted as mounted guides. The guides (who received the same pay as British cavalry troopers) were stationed on the approach roads so that they could direct the retreating troops to their positions without confusion even if the French were in close pursuit. A commissary was also appointed to organise the supply and distribution of food and equipment in each individual district. It was arranged that the 2nd Division would be stationed at Alhandra, with Hamilton's Portuguese at Vila Franca. The Light Division would cover the ground from the west of Alhandra to Monte Agraço. The 5th Division was to be posted to the rear of the Monte Agraço, with Pack's Portuguese brigade placed in the great redoubt. The 1st and 4th Divisions were to occupy the districts between Monte Agraço and Torres Vedras (Zibreira, Ribaldeira, Runa etc.) and the 3rd Division was to occupy Torres Vedras and watch the line of the River Sizandro.[8]

On 10 October, the day that the troops took up their positions, Lecor's Portuguese brigade was stationed at Alverca. La Romana's Spanish corps was placed at Enxara dos Cavaleiros, the strongpoint situated midway between the first and second lines. Three squadrons of Fane's cavalry brigade formed the outpost line ahead of Hamilton at Vila Franca, with De Grey's cavalry brigade at Ramalhal to the north of Torres Vedras and the 14th Light Dragoons in front of Sobral towards Abrigada. The remainder of Fane's brigade was at Loures whilst the main body of the cavalry was cantoned behind the second line, where they could manoeuvre on the open plains bordering the Tagus. Cavalry headquarters was at Mafra, where Anson's brigade was also stationed. Headquarters of the army was located at Santa Quintina near Sobral.[9]

This was now the time for the engineers to complete all the defensive measures that could not have been carried out earlier because they would have impeded either military or normal commercial communications. Roads approaching the Lines were broken up and acres of trees were felled in front of the works to allow unrestricted fields of fire and their branches and stems were cut to form lines of abattis many yards deep. Bridges on all the rivers and streams were destroyed and only those bridges that were considered to be of importance to the allied army were left standing, each one being mined and placed under the supervision of the Portuguese Artillery. Houses were pulled down, hollow roads filled up, olive groves and orchards were cut to the roots and walls removed to the last stone so that the entire countryside was turned into one vast glacis. As Jones was to report: "We have spared neither house, garden, vineyard, olive-trees, woods, or private property of any description." Despite these efforts, when the troops marched into Torres Vedras only 126 of the scheduled 152 redoubts had been finished and only 427 of the 534 guns were ready for action.[10]

The retreat to the Lines had been conducted without serious incident but Wellington had found himself under constant attack from political opponents in his rear. As soon as the French marched from Almeida, Wellington had been engaged in an endless conflict with the Portuguese Government. Although the Regency had agreed to Wellington's scheme of permitting the French to advance as far as the Lisbon peninsula and for the depopulation and devastation of the countryside, when the first reports reached Lisbon of the evacuation of villages and the destruction of crops the members of the Council became appalled at the sacrifices that the nation was being expected to make. "Never," wrote one observer, "did any unfortunate country feel, with greater severity, the miseries of war than this country, through which the English and the Portuguese armies are slowly retreating and are pursued by the still more destructive armies of France." A proposal was put before the Regency that Wellington should be formally requested to force a pitched battle on the frontier before retiring upon the lines in front of Lisbon. The Principal Sousa also presented documents to the Council which were intended to show that the system of devastation was impossible, as the peasants would attempt to hide rather than destroy their food stocks, which the French would then inevitably find – a prediction that was to prove disappointingly accurate.[11]

After Wellington's failure to turn back the invaders at Buçaco, the Portuguese were convinced that the British were intent upon abandoning Portugal. *"Los Ingleses por mar"* – the English are for the sea – was the Portuguese cry. "Our movements have brought such distressing consequences upon the people of the country we have retired from," wrote one young British officer on 9 October, "that not all our declarations will convince the world for some time to come that our retreat is not a run-away." At Torres Vedras, John Jones reported that "everything is in confusion; the people are all running away; and a string of men, women, and children in carts, on animals, and on foot, are crowding every road to Lisbon. No-one will believe that the army will halt till it reaches St Julian and all authority and order is beginning to be lost." This disorder soon spread as far as Lisbon, where it manifested itself on 7 September in a riot when the militia planned to seize the castle and Fort St Julian because of a widely accepted rumour that the British garrisons were about to evacuate and put to sea. Sousa added to the confusion in the capital by insisting that the Portuguese troops should offer battle to the French instead of withdrawing into the Lines, even if the British refused to stand with them! This prompted an angry response from Wellington: "His Majesty and the Prince Regent having instructed me with the command of their armies, and exclusively with the conduct of the military operations. I will not suffer them [the Council] or anybody else, to interfere with them." But the capital was kept in a constant state of upheaval, with arbitrary arrests of supposed traitors and da Sousa even suggested that the Regency Council should evacuate to the Algarve.[12]

It was therefore with considerable unrest in his rear that Wellington awaited the first attacks by the French army upon his defensive lines behind Sobral. The exhausted French infantry did not arrive before the Lines until 12 October, which gave Wellington a further day to settle his troops into their respective positions. At Alhandra, Wellington ordered Hill to hold the redoubts of both the main position and those at Calhandriz with Hamilton's Portuguese Division and Lecor's brigade of militia, and to place one British brigade of the 2nd Division on the low ground from the high road to the Tagus. Hill was also instructed to hold the town of Alhandra, keeping a few guns in the church and barricading the streets, and to occupy the villages of Loureiro and A dos Melos to the west of Alhandra. One squadron of British cavalry and two of Portuguese were kept in advance of Alhandra to observe the movements of the enemy along the high road. In total Hill's area of responsibility extended for approximately four miles.

To Hill's left was stationed the Light Division and Wellington told Craufurd to pay particular attention to the pass of Arruda and to place either the 43rd Regiment or the 52nd Regiment on the high ground to the left of the pass. As arranged, Pack's Portuguese brigade was posted in the great redoubt on the Monte Agraço. A special independent force was assembled under General Sontag to occupy Torres Vedras and the redoubts from there to the sea to enable Wellington to concentrate his field army in the centre of the Lines. This independent force consisted of the 58th Regiment and two regiments of Portuguese militia, in addition to the British, Portuguese and Ordenanza artillery already assembled at Torres Vedras. Picton's 3rd Division was also stationed at Torres Vedras, with De Grey's Dragoon Brigade watching the high road.

A brigade of reinforcements from Britain had arrived at Torres Vedras a few days earlier. Another two battalions arrived from Cadiz shortly afterwards, followed by three more from Britain. With these additions to his strength Wellington was able to form a 6th Division, command of which was given to Alexander Campbell. The total force occupying the Lines had now risen to 57,000 British and Portuguese regulars, with a further 12,000 militia and Ordenanza. Wellington's personal headquarters were established at Pero Negro, where he remained during the allied army's occupation of the Lines.[13]

The first reports from the local peasants indicated that the French were advancing beyond Vila Franca and it appeared that Masséna intended to attack Alhandra. Wellington was convinced that the French "can make no impression upon the right, positively" and that they "must therefore endeavour to turn Hill's position upon the Serra of Alhandra by its left". Yet Wellington considered this "a tough job also, defended as the entrances of the valleys are by redoubts, and the villages by abattis, etc". If such an attack became certain, Wellington intended to move Spencer's 1st Division to Craufurd's right on the heights of St Romão, which overlooked the western edge of the Calhandriz valley.[14]

It soon became evident that the force marching from Vila Franca was not the main body of l'Armée de Portugal when, on 12 October, the advance guard of the VIII Corps attacked Spencer's outposts at Sobral. Clausel drove the light troops of Lowe's and Erskine's brigades out of the village but he did not pursue them beyond the lower slopes of the Monte Agraço. This was the only action of the day apart from a remarkable incident on the Tagus. General Sainte-Croix, with his Dragoon Division, was searching for abandoned boats along the banks of the river north of Vila Franca when he was struck and killed by a shot fired from one of the British gunboats that had been patrolling the Tagus.

Wellington wasted no time in concentrating his divisions around Sobral and that night he ordered Picton down from Torres Vedras to occupy approximately 800 yards of ground from Spencer's right wing at Sobral as far as the village of Patameira, with his light companies posted in Patameira itself. The 1st Division held a line 1,000 yards long, extending from the Sobral redoubts to an old mill to the left of Zibreira. Cole's position ran for 1,700 yards from a ravine in line with Patameira to the Portela on the Ribaldeira to Enxara dos Cavaleiros road, with his light troops out in front. The 6th Division was placed on the high ground to Cole's left, with the Lusitanian Legion at the extremity of the line. The 5th Division was kept in reserve on the right behind the 1st and 3rd Divisions. Campbell's and Coleman's Independent Portuguese brigades formed the reserve on the left near the Ribaldeira-Enxara road.[15]

The following day Junot again probed the allied line, this time sending his voltigeurs to the west of Sobral. Here they encountered the outposts of the 4th Division and a prolonged skirmish ensued. Cole eventually withdrew his picket line to the heights below the Portello redoubts but, as Wellington observed, the attack was "without much effect". Over at Alhandra, Reynier also probed the allied lines on the 13th but he found Hill's position "inattackable".[16]

On the 14th, Massena arrived at Sobral just as Junot was making another weak, and therefore unsuccessful, attempt to drive back the outposts of the 1st Division. Masséna had been told by the Portuguese officers on his staff that "the heights of Montachique are rounded plateaux, accessible to all armies, and adequate for marching or manoeuvring in any direction". When he saw "a gigantic wall of rocks extending on both flanks ... crowned by every kind of field fortification that can be constructed, along with formidable artillery" Masséna was furious. The Portuguese advisors tried to defend themselves by pointing out that Wellington had only recently built the Lines. "*Que diable,*" he shouted, "Wellington didn't make the mountains!"[17]

Junot did not renew his attack upon Sobral and as the fighting ceased Masséna and his staff rode as close to the Lines as they could to inspect the allied defences. "Opposite Sobral," wrote Masséna's senior aide, "I could see the Crest of Monte Agraço ... where a large work of 360 to 400 yards deployment with 14 to 15 feet of relief was covered with seventeen embrasures. We noticed some countersinks and palisades, and inside the fortification were barracks or traverses covered with sod ... To the left, on the slope, we saw a redoubt or some kind of lunette; another work was on the right and further back at the bottom of a rock-step; and finally there was a third one forward. They were like three satellites around a great retrenchment of two thousand men which seemed to be the centre of the first enemy line."[18]

Masséna rode eastwards along the Lines beyond Arruda. Opposite the Calhandriz valley he dismounted and laid his telescope on a low stone wall to examine the works. He studied the area for so long that a warning shot was fired from No. 120 Redoubt. The shot struck the wall and Masséna acknowledged the warning with a wave of his hat and moved on. Some of Masséna's staff continued eastwards until they met up with the II Corps opposite Alhandra. But the marshal had seen enough and he returned to his headquarters, which he had established at Alemquer.

Masséna now "clearly discerned" Wellington's campaign strategy. For months the French had "scorned" Wellington's refusal to help the garrisons of Ciudad Rodrigo and Almeida, his retreat from the frontier and his abandonment of the Buçaco heights. Now they knew why. On the 15th, Masséna explored the Lines to the west of Sobral and on the 16th he wrote the following note to Ney: "The enemy is dug in to the teeth. He has three lines of works that cover Lisbon. If we seized the front line of redoubts, he would throw himself into the second line … I have already visited the line three times to the right and left and I see great works bristling with cannon … I do not believe this is the moment to attack the enemy. A check would destroy all our hopes and would overthrow the state of things, so we will indulge in temporising."[19]

Whilst the French temporised, the men of the Anglo-Portuguese army waited for the attack that they believed was inevitable. Since their arrival at the Lines the troops had remained out in the open, exposed to the incessant rains, fully clothed and accoutred, in expectation of an immediate assault. "There is much appearance that the enemy will attack this position with his whole force," wrote Beresford's Quartermaster-General."Alhandra is too strong for him to attempt, and Torres Vedras, under his present circumstances and the state of the roads, too long a detour for him to make. He cannot well retire, and it is hoped that his distress for provisions will compel him to bring matters to a speedy decision." Wellington was confident that his arrangements had now made the allied position "tolerably secure" and if the French should attack the outcome would not be in doubt. "Each individual division has now more than sufficient troops to occupy the space allotted to it, and the overplus forms a first reserve for each respectively," D'Urban recorded in his diary. "If the force thus posted beats the attacking enemy, of which there can be no doubt, our telegraphic communications will bring Craufurd from Arruda and Hill from Alhandra on to their flank – and the affair will be complete."[20]

Masséna, however, had no intention of playing into Wellington's hands by throwing his weakened and somewhat demoralised army at the Lines. The memory of the humiliation at Buçaco was still fresh in his mind and it would appear that once he had fully assessed the magnitude of Wellington's defences he never seriously contemplated an attack. "The Marshal Prince d'Essling has come to the conclusion that he would compromise the army of His Majesty," he was to report to Napoleon, "if he were to attack in force lines so formidable defended by 30,000 English and 30,000 Portuguese, aided by 50,000 armed peasants." Not everyone in the French camp agreed with Masséna. Junot suggested an immediate attack upon the Sobral lines and the Baron de Marbot argued that "a position of this extent cannot present the same difficulties everywhere and must have its weak spots … it seemed to us that the ground was sufficiently irregular to conceal the movements of a portion of our army, and that by employing one corps to make a feint on the front while the other two pushed real attacks on the weakest points of this long line, they would find the English troops too widely scattered, or at any rate with their reserves at a considerable distance from the points attacked … We thought that at some point of their vast extent it would be easy to pierce the English lines". But Ney and Reynier were against any offensive action, as was Pelet: "the attack of the three enemy Lines would have cost us half of our actual army. Then what would we have done at Lisbon? … It was clear that we must wait for reinforcements."[21]

This was exactly what Masséna proposed to do. With the force at his disposal he could not penetrate the Lines but, if considerably reinforced with troops from Spain, the conquest of Portugal might still be effected. Masséna hoped that, if requested to do so, the IX Corps would move up from Old Castile and that Mortier with the V Corps would join him from Andalusia. Consequently, messengers were dispatched to the border to urge Mortier and Drouet to march without delay and General Foy, with a strong escort, was sent to Paris to explain the situation to Napoleon. Meanwhile, l'Armée de Portugal settled down in the deserted countryside to await their arrival.

Foy reached Ciudad Rodrigo on 8 November. He issued Gardanne with instructions to gather together every available man from the garrisons of Rodrigo and Almeida and take a convoy of ammunition to the front to replenish l'Armée de Portugal's depleted stocks. Continuing into Spain, Foy found the IX Corps at Valladolid. Foy urged Drouet to march immediately for Almeida and re-establish communications between Masséna and the frontier. Foy then rode on to Paris, arriving at Imperial headquarters on 22 November.

Masséna intended to adopt an aggressive stance in front of the Lines to maintain the impression that the invaders were still on the offensive. This, however, would place his troops within immediate striking distance of the allied army. Consequently, Junot, whose VIII Corps was to remain at Sobral, fortified the village with earthworks around the front and the sides of the hill upon which Sobral stands, and Reynier left only his outposts at Vila Franca and withdrew the rest of the II Corps to Carregado. Ney was placed between Junot and Reynier, with a single brigade of the VI Corps stationed opposite Arruda and the remainder of the VI Corps held in reserve far to the rear around Otta and Alemquer. The artillery and cavalry reserves went back to the town of Santarém some twenty miles to the north on the banks of the Tagus.

Masséna was wise to take such precautions, as Wellington most definitely considered attacking the French positions. Hundreds of deserters from l'Armée de Portugal had made their way into the allied camp throughout previous days and Wellington was well-informed about both the dispositions and the condition of the enemy. He estimated that Masséna still commanded around 55,000 men, including 6,000 or 7,000 cavalry, against which Wellington could bring approximately even numbers. In addition, there was the 6,000-strong garrison of Abrantes which could operate "with impunity" as far south as Punhete plus the 8,000 militia of Trant, Wilson and Millar based on Coimbra and Silveira's six regiments on the Coa. But Wellington refused to include the Portuguese irregulars in his calculations. "I should deceive myself," Wellington told Lord Liverpool, "if I could expect, or your Lordship if I should state, that any advantage would be derived from their assistance in an offensive operation against the enemy."[22]

Wellington could also call on the services of the 8,000 men from two divisions of the Marquis de La Romana's Estremaduran army, which had joined the allies behind the Lines to "share our fortune". La Romana's corps was the most effective body of Spanish troops still under arms and Wellington brought them into the Lines "in order to save them for the Spanish nation" and to increase "the disposable force which I should collect in these positions." Napoleon had ordered the V Corps to track La Romana's every move and prevent a junction with the Anglo-Portuguese army but Mortier could not have advanced into Portugal whilst the Spaniards still held Badajoz and his route through the Alentejo was blocked by the strongholds of Elvas and Abrantes. La Romana therefore reached the Lines without interference, having left the other two divisions of his army around Badajoz. The Spaniards were moved from Enxara into cantonments at Mafra on the second line. This meant that Wellington had a slight numerical advantage over his adversary, but the factors that had led to his decision not to fight the French in the open in the earlier days of the campaign were just as relevant now. He had drawn his enemies on ever deeper into the country and now they were stranded in the heart of a vast, empty desert. "Before them was a wall of brass," wrote a French Hussar, "behind them a region of famine." Wellington had planned and worked for this moment for over twelve months. He had Masséna exactly where he wanted him and nothing would induce him to gamble everything that he had accomplished in a battle beyond the Lines.[23]

There were also tactical factors related to an assault upon the French positions that served to further deter Wellington from taking offensive action. "Although the enemy's position is not so strong as that which we occupy," he told Lord Liverpool on 3 November, "there is no doubt that it has its advantages; one of which is, that in attacking it we could hardly use our artillery. I would also observe, that as in every operation of this description by the British army in Portugal, no attempt can be made to manoeuvre upon the enemy's flank or rear; first, because the enemy show they are indifferent about their flanks or rear, or their communications; and secondly, because the inevitable consequences of attempting such a manoeuvre would be to open some one or other road to Lisbon, and to our shipping, of which the enemy would take immediate advantage … We must carry their positions, therefore, by main force, and consequently with loss; and in the course of the operations I must draw the army out of their cantonments; I must expose the troops and horses to the inclemencies of the weather at this season of the year, and must look to all the consequences of that measure in increased sickness of the men, and in loss of efficiency and condition in horses."

Wellington could see no advantage in attacking Masséna whilst the marshal still commanded a large and powerful army: "I observe that … there is yet no other military body in the Peninsula which is capable of taking, much less of keeping, the field … We still stand alone in the Peninsula as an army; and if I should succeed in forcing Masséna's positions, it would become a question whether I should be able to maintain my own, in case the enemy should march another army into this country. But, when I observe how small the superiority of numbers is in my favour, and know that the position will be in favour of the enemy. I cannot but be of opinion that I act in conformity with the instructions and intentions of His Majesty's Government, in waiting for the result of what is going on, and in incurring no extraordinary risk." It was, he explained to Lord Liverpool, "the sure game" that he was going to play. Starvation and disease would, in the end, destroy l'Armée de Portugal just as effectively as a major defeat on the battlefield. "Every day's delay, at this season of the year, narrows our line of defence, and consequently strengthens it," Wellington continued, "and when the winter shall have set in, no number, however formidable, can venture to attack it; and the increase of the enemy's numbers at that period will only add to their distress, and increase the difficulties of their retreat."[24]

There can be little doubt that Wellington missed an ideal opportunity to inflict considerable damage upon Masséna's army. The VIII Corps at Sobral was very close to the allied lines and, despite the fieldworks in front and on both flanks of the village, it was in an exposed and isolated position. Only Ferey's Brigade of the VI Corps was within effective supporting distance. The rest of Ney's corps could not have marched to Junot's assistance in under four or five hours, and Reynier could not move from Vila Franca to help the VIII Corps without inviting Hill's two divisions to fall upon his flank or rear.

144

Masséna was aware of the danger that the VIII Corps would be in if the allies attacked in overwhelming numbers. Consequently, Ferey and Junot were told that in the event of an attack they should fall back to Alemquer, at which place Ney was ordered to concentrate all his reserves. Reynier was also instructed to abandon his position and retire to Alemquer if the VIII Corps was attacked.

That Masséna's plan would have worked is extremely doubtful. The troops in front of the VIII Corps – those of the 1st and 5th Divisions and Pack's Portuguese – were less than a mile from Junot's position, and the 4th Division and Campbell's Portuguese on the flanks were only two miles away. Both columns had an easy down-hill march to Sobral. Wellington could have brought 30,000 men against Junot's force of under 10,000 in about half an hour. Junot could not have escaped without suffering heavy losses. Yet Wellington would not be tempted down from the security of the Lines. "I could lick those fellows any day," he is reported to have said, "but it would cost me 10,000 men, and, as this is the last army England has got, we must take care of it." But with the passing of each day his army grew in strength and spirit whilst that of the enemy declined in numbers and in health.[25]

Masséna was well aware that he could not maintain his position in front of the Lines for more than a few weeks. At first the troops had fared well. Large magazines full of grain were found at Vila Franca and at other ports along the Tagus stores of imported rice, sugar and coffee were discovered; the dismantled windmills in the area were all repaired and each mill was allocated to one or more regiments, allowing the soldiers to receive a daily ration of bread. Biscuits were also baked at Santarém from the grain found along the Tagus. Yet by the first week of November l'Armée de Portugal was reduced to half-rations of boiled maize flour supplemented occasionally with a little meat. The incessant rain made the situation even more problematical for the French. "The roads had become torrents," remembered Marbot, "and the difficulty of seeking provisions, and especially forage, was much increased." There was no longer any food to be found in the immediate locality (the VIII Corps having already begun to slaughter and eat its mules) and the foraging parties had to travel ever further in search of cattle and grain. The bands of marauders had to search as far as fifty miles from their regiments and between a third and a half of the men were absent from the ranks on foraging missions. The foraging parties were composed of men taken from each company and they were expected to find food for the rest of the regiment. Organised in columns of 200 to 300 under the command of an officer, they were sent far to the rear to obtain food by any possible means. The problem was that these columns would be divided into smaller units led only by non-commissioned officers. These sub-divisions soon degenerated into undisciplined bands that remained away from their parent units for up to ten days, filling their own haversacks with food or plunder. Masséna did try to control this unlicensed marauding and he issued strict instructions that the roll-call be read each day in every regiment. But, as Clausel was to report, "The last detachment which came back to camp had been nine days away. Generals and soldiers agree in stating that for some time to come it has only been possible to collect a little corn with extreme difficulty."[26]

The fact that the invaders were able to find any food at all in the area angered Wellington. "At this moment the enemy are living upon grain found close to the lines," he wrote to Admiral Berkeley on 16 October, "and they grind it into flour with the mills in our sight which the [Portuguese] Government were repeatedly pressed to order the people to render useless, and which could have been rendered useless only by taking away the sails." Yet the French positions in front of the Lines were rapidly becoming untenable and Masséna was already planning to withdraw to an area that could sustain his army through the winter months until reinforcements arrived from Spain. The regions behind had suffered the passage of both armies. The land had been wasted and the towns ransacked. In front of him stood the impenetrable lines of the enemy and to the east was the sea. There was only one direction in which Massena could turn, and that was south to the land beyond the Tagus – the Alentejo.[27]

The town of Santarém rests on the northern bank of the Tagus approximately twenty-five miles upstream from Alhandra. To this town Masséna had sent all the craftsmen from every regiment of l'Armée de Portugal. He had placed them under the command of General Elbé of the Artillery and told them to build him a bridge across the river. "It will be necessary to surmount all obstacles," he told Elbé on 18 October; "we must demolish the houses to obtain planks and beams, and iron and nails. Collect all the rope in the country … You will employ all the extraordinary means at your disposal to succeed there." This walled town stands on a commanding height overlooking the Tagus. In medieval times it was regarded as one of the strongest fortresses in Portugal and it was ideally suited for defence. It was to be Masséna's centre of operations. From here he could still threaten the allied positions at Sobral along the roads from Leiria and Tomar, and when the bridge over the Tagus was laid the army would be able to dominate both banks of the river and open up the whole of the Alentejo to the famished troops.[28]

146

Wellington was informed of the bridge-building operation from the large number of French deserters that were being driven into the arms of the allies by starvation, and by reports from the Ordenanza patrolling the southern bank of the Tagus. He immediately ordered the removal of all valuable property, boats, cattle and grain and the dismantling of all the mills throughout the Alentejo. He instructed the population to evacuate to Elvas or Setúbal or even down to the Algarve. Wellington was also worried about the Almada heights. The Portuguese authorities had failed to press sufficient numbers of labourers into service and the defensive works on the Almada heights were not complete. He realised that he might be compelled to cross the Tagus to defend the Alentejo and he instructed the Regency Council to collect together all the registered boats in the Lisbon area. On 2 November Wellington decided to send a small corps of observation across the Tagus under the command of General Fane. All the Ordenanza of the upper Alentejo were called out to assist Fane and to watch the banks of the river. In addition to this, he asked Admiral Berkeley to strengthen his advanced flotilla of gunboats near Salvaterra so as to prevent the French from attempting to capture the small island of Lyceria, or Leziria.

Berkeley sent 400 sailors and several hundred fleet marines to assist Fane and eventually a battery was established on Leziria, which was also manned by seamen. With Fane was a detachment of artillery which was supplied with a number of Congreve rockets, a new weapon which Wellington had been asked to trial. On 13 November, Fane used the rockets in an attempt to set fire to the dockyard at Santarém. The rockets proved to be hopelessly inaccurate and they did little damage to the dockyard but it served notice to Masséna that any move to establish a bridge-head on the south bank of the river would be met with force. Nevertheless, the French continued their preparations for the crossing of the Tagus. "Forges and saw-mills were built; tools, planks, beams, anchors and ropes manufactured," a French officer observed, "numerous boats were constructed, and the work progressing as it were by magic."

Altogether the French engineers collected or built approximately 200 boats even though a battery was erected on the south side of the river and a gunboat was moored opposite the mouth of the Zezere to stop the French floating captured boats down the Tagus to the dockyard.[29]

Every day during the allied occupation of the Lines Wellington ordered all his troops, including the garrisons of all the forts, to assemble under arms and in full marching order two hours before daybreak. "This was by no means a pleasant task," remembered Lieutenant Grattan; "scrambling up a hill of mud and standing shivering for a couple of hours in the dark and wet." Wellington himself rode from his headquarters at Pero Negro each morning to the great redoubt on the Monte Agraço. "Runners" were then sent out to examine the French encampments at close quarters. Mounted on thoroughbreds brought over from England, these officers would gallop from the Lines and "race with the speed of stags through the vines and over the rocks", as Marbot recalled, "to inspect the positions occupied by our troops". After carefully checking the French positions, the runners would return to the Lines and submit their reports. The defenders remained on the alert until Wellington had received confirmation from every one of the signal stations along the line that there had been no alterations in the dispositions of the enemy during the night or any obvious preparations made for an attack. The troops were then stood down.[30]

Each division established advanced pickets of approximately battalion-strength centred upon small hamlets or windmills, in some cases within 200 yards of the French outposts. Those men not detailed for picket duty were "kept pretty busy" strengthening their respective fronts, improving the lateral communications, and entrenching and sheltering their outposts.

At Arruda, Lieutenant Harry Smith reported that "the whole [Light] Division was at work". Craufurd had secured Arruda by erecting a dry-stone wall sixteen feet thick and forty feet high across the ravine on the left of the village and a double line of abattis, formed from full-grown trees pulled up by their roots, which completely blocked the Arruda valley. With breastworks and walls to defend this tree line, the Light Division's post was quickly rendered "impregnable".

To the east, at Alhandra the defences were made so secure that "a mouse could not get through". One day in October Wellington, escorted by John Jones, rode over to Alhandra to visit General Hill but after risking his horse's legs in several attempts to penetrate Hill's defences the British commander turned back. Upon investigation it was found that the troops of the 2nd Division had, with "more zeal than knowledge", blocked not only the front which the French might attack but they had also destroyed the lateral road built for the use of the allies! Hill's men had, according to Jones, "completely succeeded in obliterating a system of communications of the utmost value, which had been planned with care, and constructed with much labour". Wellington, we are told, "expressed much displeasure"! By the beginning of November all the allied positions were "twice as strong" as they had been when the troops first marched into the Lines just three weeks earlier – and General Hill was certain that the French "will not meddle with us now".[31]

CHAPTER VIII

'The Land they had Beggared'

L'Armée de Portugal remained in front of the Lines for four weeks. By 10 November the preparations had been made for a withdrawal of the troops to the area between Santarém and the River Zezere. A pontoon bridge had been thrown across the Zezere to open up a line of retreat upon Spain via Punhete and Castelo Branco and a brigade from Loison's Division held the bridge-head. Part of Marchand's Division had also been removed from in front of the Lines to occupy Torres Novas and Tomar whilst Montbrun's cavalry was watching the roads from Leiria and Caldas da Rainha. With his rear thus secured, Masséna ordered the withdrawal to Santarém to commence at 20.00 hours on the night of 14 November.

The following morning the allied troops were at their posts before daylight as usual. A thick fog had risen during the night and visibility was reduced to less than 100 yards. It was 10.00 hours before the outlying pickets realised that the French sentries they could see were in fact straw dummies topped with old shakos. "Some of them were cavalry, some infantry," remembered Kincaid of the 95th Rifles, "and they seemed such respectable representatives of their spectral predecessors that, in the haze of the morning, we thought that they had been joined by some well-fed ones from the rear; and it was late in the day before we discovered the mistake and advanced in pursuit."[1]

In Wellington's opinion, Masséna had three choices. "The enemy intend either to retire across the Zezere, into Spain, or across the Tagus into Spain, or across the Zezere to attack Abrantes," he explained to General Fane, instructing him to make another attack upon Santarém dockyard with the Congreve rockets if the boats were still there. In case Masséna should attempt either to cross the Tagus or attack Abrantes, Wellington arranged for boats to be sent upstream so that he could reinforce Fane in the Alentejo. Leaving the 3rd, 4th, 5th and 6th

Divisions guarding the Lines, Wellington then set off to follow the French with just the 1st, 2nd and Light Divisions and Hamilton's Portuguese.[2]

"We could not advance a hundred yards without seeing dead soldiers of the enemy," wrote a soldier of the Light Division. As the allies marched towards Alenquer they found the road covered with dead horses, mules and asses and more dead men. "Alenquer had been entirely sacked," remembered another member of the Light Division, "the windows and doors torn down and burnt, as well as most of the furniture … It was a dreadful sight to see so many fine towns and villages sacked, and without a creature in them." Such was the "accumulation of filth of every description" left by the French, Wellington published a General Order instructing the troops to thoroughly clean the quarters vacated by the enemy before the allied troops reoccupied them. On the 17th the advanced troops of the Light Division made contact with the outposts of the II Corps at Cartaxo. The latter withdrew during the night to join the main body of Reynier's corps at Santarém.[3]

On the opposite bank of the Tagus, Fane had seen French columns moving eastwards beyond Santarém and he assumed that Masséna was marching upon Abrantes. Upon receipt of this information Wellington ordered Hill, with the 2nd Division, Hamilton's Portuguese and the 13th Light Dragoons, to be ferried across the river by boats of Berkeley's squadron under the direction of Rear-Admiral Sir Thomas Williams. This move deprived Wellington of almost half of his force when nearly twice that number of the enemy were within half a day's march. He quickly called the 4th and 5th Divisions out of the Lines to join him, leaving the 3rd Division at Torres Vedras in case Masséna made a sudden dash round the Montejunto. In the belief that the French were retreating either to Abrantes or to the frontier, Wellington planned to attack Santarém, which he considered was only held by a rearguard.

The town of Santarém could only be approached from the south along a walled causeway which carried the main road from Lisbon across the flood plain of the Rio Maior. "A strong abattis, lined with tirailleurs, formed the French advance post along this road," recalled General Leith in command of the 5th Division, "and the height, close to the end of the causeway on the Santarém side, was armed with artillery [16 field pieces], which swept the whole extent of it." The slopes of the heights upon which Santarém stands were also strengthened with breastworks and obstructed by felled trees. Nevertheless, Wellington intended to send one brigade of the 5th Division, plus Pack's Portuguese, to ford the Rio Major to the west of the town, and the Light

Division to the east. The 1st Division, along with the remaining brigades of Leith's Division, were to storm the causeway. But more heavy rain on the night of the 18th rendered the fords impassable, turning the plain into a "morass", and the attack was cancelled. On the 20th, Fane sent a dispatch stating that the French had not passed the Zezere and Wellington realised that only the rain had prevented him from attacking Masséna's entire force with barely 16,000 men. "Their army," he wrote to Lord Liverpool on the 21st, "being collected between Santarém and the Zezere, are in a situation to be able to maintain themselves in their strong position till the reinforcements, which I know are on the frontier, can join them."[4]

For a further three days Wellington held his position in front of Santarém in case Masséna continued his retreat. "I am not quite certain yet that they are not going," he told Liverpool. "I am convinced that there is no man in his senses, who has ever passed a winter in Portugal, who would not recommend them to go now, rather than to endeavour to maintain themselves upon the Zezere during the winter." Although the Portuguese had not carried out Wellington's scorched-earth policy as thoroughly as he wished, he still hoped that starvation would eventually compel Masséna to abandon his position at Santarém. But, as Wellington was forced to admit to the Earl of Liverpool, "it is certainly astonishing that the enemy have been able to remain in this country so long; and it is an extraordinary instance of what a French army can do. It is positively a fact that they brought no provisions with them, and they have not received even a letter since they entered Portugal. With all our money, and having in our favour the good inclinations of the country, I assure you that I could not maintain one division in the district in which they have maintained not less than 60,000 men and 20,000 animals for more than two months." Or as General Hill wryly observed, "it is a difficult matter to starve a Frenchman!"[5]

Though the allied troops were regularly supplied with rations and their situation was "in every respect, better than that of the enemy", they were just as exposed to the weather as the French. "Our huts," an officer from Picton's Division recalled, "from want of any good materials to construct them, were but a weak defence against the heavy rains which fell at this time." They were "a delightful shelter in fine weather" but they afforded little protection against the "torrents that soon after inundated us". On the 24th Wellington ordered his troops to draw back and go into winter quarters where the men could find some protection from the "violent gusts of wind" and the "pouring rain which swept through the bivouacs." Headquarters were established at

Cartaxo, with the whole army cantoned in the adjacent villages except for the 5th Division which remained at Torres Vedras. Only Craufurd and Pack with Anson's cavalry were left in touch with the French, Hill and Hamilton remaining south of the Tagus. "The enemy have a position stronger than Buçaco or Sobral," Wellington observed, "and the rain, which is destroying them, enables them to maintain it." Despite the weather, work continued on the Almada defences. Fletcher made repeated trips across the Tagus and every available engineer was transferred to this area.[6]

Whilst the Anglo-Portuguese army settled into its quarters l'Armée de Portugal pushed out the boundaries of the area of land upon which it hoped to feed itself. Montbrun's cavalry, supported by small detachments of infantry from the VI Corps, pressed northwards as far as Espinhal and Coimbra, where the presence of Wilson's and Trant's militia deterred the French from any further excursions. As winter closed in, the blockade of the invaders remained unbroken but, on 20 November, General Gardanne set off from Ciudad Rodrigo with 5,000 men in an attempt to cut his way through the cordon of partisans with a large convoy of munitions. Gardanne encountered dreadful weather which hampered the progress of the heavy wagon train and he was harassed continually by the Ordenanza. Nevertheless, by 27 November, he had reached Cardigos, only fifteen miles from Loison's Division at Punhete. It was as far as he was to go. He had no real idea where Masséna was and he had been told by a number of Portuguese deserters that Hill's corps was marching to intercept him. This was enough for Gardanne, who turned round and retreated back to Ciudad Rodrigo as fast as he could travel.

Throughout December both armies remained on the defensive. Masséna could attempt no offensive operations until reinforced and Wellington considered that it "would still be impossible to make any movement of importance upon the right flank of the enemy's position at Santarém without exposing some divisions of troops to be insulated and cut off". Wellington was not going to place "the fate of the campaign on the result of a general action on ground chosen by them," and he still expected the French to be starved out of Portugal even though the Portuguese had "left behind them everything that could be useful to the enemy". Though Wellington was certainly exaggerating when he made this complaint to the Regency Council, the French foraging parties initially found a great deal of food in Golegão plain. "Workshops were started in every battalion," wrote the Baron de Marbot, "and each regiment, organising a system of raids on a large scale, sent out detachments, armed and well led, who returned driving thousands of

152

donkeys laden with provisions of all kinds, and immense herds of sheep, pigs and goats, the booty being proportionately divided on its arrival.[7]

The peasants, quite understandably, could not bring themselves to waste good food and instead of burning it as ordered they hid it in the hope of recovering it when the French had gone. In fact as early as December 1809, many months before the first of Wellington's proclamations, the Portuguese had begun to bury and hide their food and belongings in anticipation of an invasion. The French troops soon learnt that large quantities of grain had been hidden in caves in the Cartaxo and Azambujeira hills and at one time a continuous line of soldiers carrying grain could be seen stretching from the hills to the French positions. Many peasants had buried the food in their gardens or underneath their houses but these caches were soon discovered. The troops, knowing this, would flood the ground and watch for any points where the water drained away unusually quickly or they would observe, as one Frenchman explained, "the vapours rising from the ground early in the morning". Excavations at these points often turned up large chests full of grain. Because of requisitioning by their own government, and the "exorbitant demands" of the priests, the Portuguese had become accustomed to building secret storage places within their homes to hide grain, wine and oil. To find these stores the French measured the outside of a house and then measured the inside. If the two measurements did not correspond the marauders knew that they had found a hiding place and they immediately smashed the walls down. Individual houses and even whole villages were pulled down by the ravenous troops in their desperate search for food and any of the Portuguese that had disobeyed the Government and had remained near their homes were captured and tortured into revealing where the food stocks had been hidden.[8]

A number of those peasants who had refused to make the long trek to Lisbon escaped to Peniche. At night some of the menfolk would slip out of the fortress back to their villages to collect their hidden food stocks but many were unable to do this and they died in alarming numbers. An average of 25 to 30 people died each day in Peniche alone (reaching a peak of 65 in a single day) and a British cavalry officer who visited in February saw entire families lying on the ground, too weak to move. "The scenes of misery are beyond anything I ever saw," wrote Lieutenant Tomkinson of the 16th Light Dragoons, "and if the enemy continue long in their present position, half the poor of the country will be in their graves."[9]

Those civilians who had evacuated to the area behind the Lines were also experiencing considerable hardship. "It becomes very necessary that this state of things should have an end," urged one of Beresford's officers on 18 December, "for the complete destruction of the Peasantry by Famine will be the consequence of its continuance as well as the ruin of the better orders." Weeks after the occupation of the Lines many peasants were still making their way towards Lisbon. Donaldson of the 42nd Regiment watched them passing through Torres Vedras: "It was a melancholy sight to see the poor natives, carrying their children, and any little thing which they were able to bring with them, moving along the road, after having left their homes and property – travelling they knew not whither, desolate and friendless. In a few days they might be reduced to beg, or perhaps die of hunger." It has been estimated that approximately 300,000 evacuees crowded into the capital during the winter of 1810-11 (including 87,000 in one day) and some refugees crossed the Tagus and moved into the Alentejo.[10]

Feeding the refugees was the biggest problem and, as Alexander Dickson noted, "everything which prudence and humanity could suggest was done by the inhabitants of Lisbon to alleviate the public misfortune. Charitable institutions were set on foot and food was daily distributed to such of the fugitives as were necessitous and helpless". Corn, regardless of the price, was sought for in Ireland, the United States, Morocco, Greece and Egypt and 1,000 tons of Government shipping were lent to merchants to fetch grain from Algiers. Distribution of the food was left to the Portuguese authorities but they were quite incapable of dealing with the crisis. Mules and carriages – the means of distribution – were "injudiciously" seized by the Government and then, as an exasperated Wellington was to complain, the animals and their owners were kept "starving and shivering" and were never put to use. As a result the "misery and wretchedness of the refugees is beyond description, numbers are perishing from disease and want", wrote one eyewitness. "It is quite melancholy to see the state of the poor people; women are to be seen in all directions gathering herbs which they cook and nearly live on." Around 40,000 people are reported to have died in the Lisbon area during that terrible winter and there was a real fear that when the warmer weather arrived disease would increase to epidemic proportions right across central Portugal.[11]

L'Armée de Portugal had been out of touch with every other French force in the Peninsula since it marched from Ciudad Rodrigo in July when the Duchess d'Abrantes watched "an army of 60,000 men cross a stream, [the Agueda] reach the further bank, only to disappear the following day into a profound silence". Almeida was blocked by Silveira's militia, Trant held Coimbra and the line of the Mondego, with Wilson at Leiria pressing close upon Masséna's rear. To the north-east was the garrison of Abrantes which, with the strong garrisons of Elvas and Badajoz, supported by a division of La Romana's Estremaduran army, completed the encirclement of the French. De Grey's cavalry brigade (replaced from the end of October by Anson's brigade) also patrolled beyond the Lines north of Torres Vedras as far as Obidos. This beautiful old walled town had been rendered defenceless and its guns spiked by the allies as they retreated to the Lines. A small detachment (250 men) from Peniche under Major Fenwick had reoccupied the place and "with no small degree of labour" had lifted its cannon back onto the battlements, made new platforms and unspiked the guns. From Obidos, Fenwick, in conjunction with one troop from each of Anson's regiments, two companies of Caçadores and one of the militia regiments from Torres Vedras, attacked the foraging parties of the VIII Corps that ventured towards the coast. With captured French weapons Fenwick was able to arm many of the local peasants and Junot's hungry troops were unable to scavenge anywhere between Caldas da Rainha and Torres Vedras. Wellington was justifiably able to claim that the enemy "really possess no part of the country excepting that on which their army stands." Scores of men were deserting to the allies each day, reporting that "almost everyone is sick", and the army of 65,050 that had left Almeida on 15 September had declined to 46,171 by the end of December.[12]

For three months the army was totally isolated, until 26 December when Drouet, with a division of the IX Corps and Gardanne's detachment, broke through the cordons of partisans and arrived at Espinhal where he made contact with the VI Corps. Napoleon had ordered Drouet to open a communication between Masséna and Almeida. Consequently Drouet had left Claparéde's division of the XI Corps at Celorico and cleared Trant's militia from Coimbra, moving on to Espinhal with the remaining 8,000 men. Drouet had done all that Napoleon had required of him but Masséna still dreamt of capturing Lisbon and he demanded that the IX Corps joined l'Armée de Portugal. Drouet was moved down to Leiria and almost immediately Wilson's militia brigade re-occupied Espinhal, severing Drouet's link with Claparéde. Masséna's communications with Spain had been open for just four days, and these reinforcements barely replaced the losses suffered over the previous three months, adding nothing to l'Armée de Portugal other than 8,000 more empty stomachs.

Another six weeks was to pass before l'Armée de Portugal's isolation was broken again when, on 5 February, Foy returned from Paris at the head of 1,800 men, with dispatches from the Emperor. "It is necessary that the Prince organise his food, that he entrench himself, that he construct bridges, that his communications with Spain be established with strong posts at a distance of two or three marches apart," Napoleon had told Foy. "I will send the IX Corps to Coimbra and the V Corps to Alentejo." So now Masséna knew that the assistance of the V Corps was the only extra help that he was to receive. Before Mortier could advance into the Alentejo he would be compelled to either blockade or lay siege to the fortresses of Badajoz and Elvas which guarded the main road from Madrid to the southern bank of the Tagus. It was obvious that it would be weeks before Mortier and Soult could provide any effective assistance and an abortive attempt to occupy the island of Boavista opposite Santarém had made it clear that the bridging operation could only succeed if supported by a corps on the southern bank of the river.

Though Masséna hung on for another two weeks, sending reconnaissance patrols along the upper reaches of the Tagus in the hope of making contact with the V Corps, when he read Napoleon's dispatch he must have realised that the campaign was over. On 18 February, Masséna called his senior officers together to discuss the situation. The Prince opened the meeting by outlining the current military situation. He then asked his corps commanders if the army could remain in its present positions any longer. Loison believed not, urging an immediate retreat before the few remaining horses became too weak to pull the guns. Masséna, therefore, proposed a withdrawal to the Mondego but Ney saw such a retreat as "terrible and dishonourable" and instead he suggested marching through the Alentejo to Castelo Branco, from where the army could make contact with the V Corps. All the other generals agreed that the army could not maintain itself on the northern bank of the Tagus yet they were unable to decide upon a satisfactory method of forcing the passage of the river with the allied army holding both banks in strength. The meeting broke up without conclusion but Masséna had already decided to retreat. He planned to fall back to Coimbra or, if he was unable to maintain a secure position on the Mondego, to Guarda and the banks of the Coa. There he hoped to find "the means of supporting his army without entirely abandoning Portugal", a French staff officer was later to record, "and to invade again as soon as reinforcements arrived".[13]

Marshal Soult, with 20,000 men, including Mortier's V Corps, had in fact already set off from Andalusia on 2 January. His objective, however, was not to enter the Alentejo but merely to capture Badajoz in order to create a "diversion in favour of the imperial army in Portugal". The assembly of such a force could not pass unnoticed and Wellington had received warning of Soult's expedition before the V Corps had even begun to march. He feared that this marked the start of the much-dreaded and long-anticipated secondary French attack south of the Tagus, and all the Spanish troops that had followed La Romana into the Lines set off on 14 January to re-join the Spanish forces in Estremadura. Before La Romana reached the frontier he died of a heart attack. He was the only Spanish general that Wellington trusted and he regarded the loss of La Romana as "the greatest which the cause could sustain".[14]

Command in Estremadura was left with General Mendizábal. Wellington advised Mendizábal to entrench a strong position on the San Cristóbal heights adjacent to Badajoz. This position, with the River Guadiana on one flank and the River Gebora to its front, could have been made virtually unassailable and the presence of a large Spanish force so close to the fortress would have severely hampered the French siege operations. But Mendizábal ignored Wellington's suggestion. His army was destroyed by Soult at the Battle of Gebora and, Wellington lamented, Spain lost "the last body of troops which their country possesses". Badajoz now lay unprotected and the Alentejo exposed.[15]

Whilst Soult's guns bombarded Badajoz, l'Armée de Portugal was preparing for the retreat. The heavy baggage was ordered to the rear, followed by the guns of the divisional artillery, and in a remote spot hidden from the allied outposts the boats and bridging equipment was destroyed. Finally the rations which Masséna had carefully accumulated in the central magazines were distributed to the regiments with strict instructions that the food should not be consumed until the retreat began.[16]

On 4 March, Marchand's Division of the VI Corps took the first steps northwards on the long march that was to end a month later when l'Armée de Portugal crossed the Agueda into Spain. One by one the divisions broke camp and moved to the concentration point around Leiria, which was still held by Drouet's small force. They left behind them almost half their numbers, Kincaid observed, "to fatten the land which they had beggared". Only three divisions were left occupying their existing posts by the morning of the 5th.

Masséna had made his move at exactly the right moment. The first of eight battalions of reinforcements were disembarking at Lisbon and Wellington had decided to attack the French positions as soon as the reinforcements arrived at the front. He planned a wide encircling movement, with the main body of the army falling upon the VIII Corps at Rio Maior whilst Beresford (who had taken over command of Hill's corps south of the Tagus after Hill had been struck down with a severe fever) crossed the Tagus via the boat-bridge at Abrantes and struck at Loison's Division of the VI Corps at Punhete. Alerted by reports of a significant French re-deployment, Wellington undertook a reconnaissance of the

Santarém defences on the 5th but, as he told Beresford, he could "perceive no difference" in the French positions: "It is probable that the baggage, stores, and the heavier part of the artillery, have been sent off, but that the effective part of the army still remains." Twenty-four hours were to pass before Wellington realised his mistake.[17]

Shortly after dusk Heudelet's and Clausel's divisions slipped away to the north, leaving Loison's Division of the VI Corps holding the line of the Zezere. Wellington sent the Light and 1st Divisions off in pursuit and he occupied Santarém with the 5th and 6th Divisions. They found "the houses torn and dilapidated, the streets strewn with house-hold furniture half-burnt and destroyed, many streets quite impassable with filth and rubbish, with an occasional man, horse or donkey rotting, and corrupting the air with pestilential vapours; a few miserable inhabitants like living skeletons". On the night of the 6th, Loison set fire to the bridge on the Zezere and marched off towards Tomar in the same general direction as the rest of l'Armée de Portugal and Wellington was at last convinced that Masséna was in full retreat for the frontier. The French no longer made any attempt to disguise their intentions and whenever the pursuers gained high ground, as Sergeant Cooper of the Royal Fusiliers observed, "the track of their march might be discovered by smoking towns and villages."[18]

The retreat continued on the 7th, with the allied cavalry following on the heels of the II and VIII Corps. "Every village on their route was pillaged; while the people were murdered, and the women assaulted," recalled one of the pursuers. "Nothing can exceed the devastation and cruelties committed by the enemy during his retreat," wrote another witness, "he has set fire to all the villages and murdered all the peasantry for leagues on each flank." The town of Leiria was put to the torch and the ancient monasteries of Alcobaça and Batalha were ransacked. At the burnt-out convent of Porta de Mós, Donaldson of the 42nd "found the half-consumed skeletons of human beings on every side ... and the agonised expression of their scorched and blackened features was awful beyond description". In the countryside the peasants had been dragged from their hiding places and killed. At the entrance to a cave Grattan saw "an old man, a woman, and two young men, all dead. The cave, no doubt, had served them as an asylum in the preceding winter, and appearances warranted the supposition that these poor creatures, in a vain effort to save their little store of provisions, fell victims to the ferocity of their murderers".

It is an appalling fact that the destruction of the towns and historic buildings was an organised act sanctioned by Masséna's headquarters staff and there is evidence that an orderly book found near the Convent of Batalha indicated how many soldiers had been detailed each day for such tasks. The convent of Alcobaça was systematically pulled apart, even to the extent of scaffolding being erected so that troops could destroy the top of the building and Wellington, on 14 March, told Lord Liverpool that the convent "was burnt by order from French headquarters".[19]

The suddenness of the French withdrawal had taken Wellington by surprise. The divisions had taken up the pursuit with only the rations that they carried with them and nothing could be gleaned from the ravished countryside through which they advanced. The speed of the allied pursuit was therefore restricted to the speed at which food could be brought up from the rear. Nevertheless, the leading allied units made contact with the rearguard of Ney's corps at Pombal on the 9th, where the II, IX and IV Corps were standing their ground with every appearance of being prepared to fight. Only the cavalry and the Light Division (under the temporary leadership of General Erskine), with Pack's Portuguese, were in contact with the French and Wellington could not attack Pombal with such a force. It took two days for the 3rd and 4th Divisions to reach the front and Wellington threw them into battle as soon as they arrived. By this time Ney had evacuated Pombal, leaving Mermet's division posted on the heights behind the town with Marchand's division in close support. Wellington sent the Light Division into the town whilst Picton swept round to the west to threaten Ney's flank. This placed the VI Corps's baggage train in danger and Ney decided to send down Macune's brigade to contest possession of the town. Macune barricaded the main street and then, as Pombal and the surrounding hills formed a long and narrow defile through which the allies had to pass, they set fire to the houses. Macune abandoned the burning town and Ney concentrated his force upon the heights. The fire delayed the allied attack and the day ended with the VI Corps still in possession of the heights, which Ney vacated during the night.

The remainder of Wellington's divisions had come up to Pombal throughout the course of the day and before dawn the next morning the allies were on the road in pursuit of the French. The VI Corps was also on the move by first light, following the II Corps in the direction of Celorico.

As before, Erskine and Pack took the lead, now accompanied by Picton. These advance columns came upon the VI Corps, which still formed the French rearguard, at Redinha. The II and VIII Corps were in support of Ney just two hours' march to the north and east. Wellington halted to allow the rest of the pursuing divisions to catch up, then he sent the 3rd and Light Divisions to the left and right of Ney's position in an encircling movement designed to cut off Ney's rearmost division. After some heavy skirmishing, Ney fell back to a second position some two miles beyond Redinha and when Wellington again tried to turn Ney's flanks the French marshal broke contact and retired upon Condeixa. Ney had very intelligently delayed Wellington for a whole day without becoming embroiled in a full-scale battle and, in fact, the allied army had advanced only ten miles in the previous twenty-four hours.

There was little comfort in this, though, for Masséna. He had planned to occupy Coimbra and "to take a position there and to maintain the troops as long as possible on the banks of the Mondego". His first difficulty was in crossing the Mondego. The only bridge in the area, actually at Coimbra itself, had been destroyed and a reconnaissance party under Montbrun had reported that Coimbra was held by Trant's and Silveira's militia, with a battery of guns in position covering the river. Montbrun's attempts at fording the river failed due to the strength of the current. Masséna's engineers also reported that even if Coimbra was seized they would require two days to put the bridge into a sufficient state of repair to permit the passage of artillery. Despite Ney's success at Redinha, Wellington was still close behind and it was unrealistic to expect that Ney would be able to delay the full weight of the allied army long enough for Masséna to capture Coimbra and repair the bridge. So, on the morning of 13 March, Masséna issued instructions for l'Armée de Portugal to march for Celorico and the frontier.[20]

Wellington, for his part, was content to pressurise the French into continuing their retreat without becoming involved in a serious engagement. "The whole country affords advantageous positions to a retreating army," he wrote to Liverpool on the 14th, "of which the enemy have shown that he knows how to avail himself. They are leaving the country, as they entered it, in one solid mass, covering their rear on every march by one (or sometimes two) corps de armée." With the allies snapping at his heels and the forbidding range of the Serra da Estrela ahead of him, Masséna decided to abandon his entire baggage train and on the 14th he ordered the destruction of all wheeled vehicles other than the artillery and ammunition wagons. All the draught animals that were no longer fit for service were hamstrung and left "floundering in the mud", wrote a witness to this heart-rending scene, "some with throats half cut, the rest barbarously houged".[21]

The destruction of so much equipment by the French finally convinced Wellington that Masséna would not stop until he had reached Almeida and on 20 March he allowed all the units of the militia and Ordenanza occupying the Lines to return to their homes. Wellington also permitted Beresford's corps, which had moved slowly along the south bank of the Tagus as far as Abrantes, to march upon Elvas. Wellington even reduced the force under his command by detaching the 4th Division and De Grey's cavalry brigade to reinforce Beresford. With some 20,000 British and Portuguese troops and four brigades of artillery, Beresford was now strong enough to advance into Estremadura and confront Soult, allowing Wellington to follow Masséna all the way to the frontier with his flank and rear secure.

Six days after l'Armée de Portugal had broken camp at Santarém Soult accepted the surrender of Badajoz. Six months earlier the capture of Badajoz might have influenced events in Portugal. Now its loss would have no bearing on the outcome of the campaign. Soult took possession of the fortress on 11 March but he had received news of a break-out from Cadiz by the Anglo-Spanish garrison and immediately after the capitulation Soult marched back to Andalusia, leaving Mortier in Estremadura with little over 11,000 men.

After abandoning its heavy baggage l'Armée de Portugal could travel much faster and by the 22nd the three principal corps had reached the region around Celorico and Guarda. Contact had been made with Claperéde's Division of the IX Corps and Masséna was once again in communication with Almeida.

Wellington had been left far behind. The allies had outmarched their supply convoys and Wellington had been "induced" to halt almost half his force at Ponte da Murcela, "or see them perish for want", leaving just three infantry divisions and two cavalry brigades to track l'Armée de Portugal. The French troops now expected Masséna to retire behind Almeida "in order to let them recover a little from their fatigues and long privations", as Masséna had originally intended, "and to allow me to replace so much equipment which is now entirely lacking". But having brought his men safely back to the Beira, this remarkable old campaigner chose instead to turn his army round and "menace once more Central Portugal and the Lines of Torres Vedras". Masséna's plan, according to his aide-de-camp Marbot, was to "regain the Tagus" via Guarda and Alfaiates. He would re-build the broken bridge at Alcantara, cross the Tagus, and join forces with Soult at Badajoz. From there the combined armies of Soult and Masséna would march upon Lisbon through the Alentejo. This decision led to open defiance from his corps commanders and a downright refusal by Ney to obey Masséna's instructions. Masséna promptly relieved Ney of his command and sent him back to France. This brought his mutinous subordinates back into line and on the 23rd l'Armée de Portugal turned south-eastwards towards the Serra da Estrela.[22]

For five days the French trudged through the bleak mountains before both Junot and Reynier proclaimed that their men could travel no further. So Masséna bowed to the inevitable and he ordered the exhausted and demoralised divisions of l'Armée de Portugal to return to Almeida where they took up the line of the Coa.

There was to be no respite, however, for the much-abused French soldiers. Whilst Masséna marched and counter-marched around the frontier, the British and Portuguese troops that had been delayed on the Alva awaiting supplies had re-joined the main body. By the end of March, Wellington had 38,000 men under his immediate command. This number included the 6,000 reinforcements that had marched up from Lisbon, 4,000 of which were formed into a 7th Division. With this force Wellington was determined to push Masséna not merely over the Coa but over the frontier.

To accomplish this, Wellington intended to force the passage of the Coa at Sabugal some twenty or more miles upstream of Almeida. Here was posted the II Corps in an isolated position ten miles to the south of the nearest other French unit, Junot's VIII Corps, which was stationed at Alfaiates. Wellington planned to send a small force – the Light Division and two brigades of cavalry – over the Coa to block the Alfaiates road whilst the main body of the army crossed the river by the bridge and fords at Sabugal and attacked the II Corps. In the face of considerably superior numbers Reynier would be compelled to withdraw northwards towards the VIII Corps, only to find his line of retreat severed by Erskine and the cavalry. If all went according to plan, the II Corps would be surrounded and destroyed long before Junot could march to Reynier's assistance.

On the morning of 3 April the Light Division began its turning movement above Sabugal. But a dense fog, "as difficult to see as in the fogs on Buçaco", Wellington was later to tell Marshal Beresford, reduced visibility to such a degree that the leading brigade found the wrong ford. Instead of reaching the Alfaiates road undetected, the Light Division stumbled into the very midst of the II Corps. Because of the prevailing conditions (it had also started to rain heavily), the main allied body had not attempted to cross the Coa and the Light Division was completely unsupported. Undeterred, the two brigades continued to advance, becoming embroiled in a fierce contest with Merle's Division. The fog and rain made it impossible for Reynier to see the size of the attacking force and he deployed his troops with caution. Though Wellington later claimed "the action fought by the Light Division with the whole of the

2nd Corps, to be one of the most glorious that British troops were ever engaged in", there is no doubt that the Light Division, alone and with the river at its back, would have been in the gravest of danger if Reynier had known from the outset that he was being challenged by little more than 3,500 men. The fog suddenly lifted and Reynier saw not only the Light Division but also the rest of the allied army poised to cross the river. He disengaged rapidly and the rain, which had strengthened into a torrential storm, covered his retreat.[23]

Two days later l'Armée de Portugal trudged back into Spain. "They marched in disorderly crowds," wrote one Frenchman. "Hardly did there remain horses enough to manoeuvre the guns in the presence of the enemy, and the cavalry were in such a state of exhaustion that the riders could not venture to give their steeds the rein for a charge. The soldiers, blackened by the sun, attenuated, ragged, shoeless … vented their ill-humour on all the world for so many sufferings undergone for no purpose."[24]

A French presence was still maintained in Portugal by the garrison of Almeida. In itself the occupation of Almeida was not important, as l'Armée de Portugal in its current condition and without considerable reinforcement could not re-invade Portugal. But the country's war of independence could not be considered won, nor accepted as lost by Masséna, whilst the French held one of the country's principal fortresses. Yet Almeida was surrounded by the allies and the 1,300-strong garrison was desperately short of food. Its fall was inevitable unless the blockade could be lifted and the fortress re-supplied. Masséna was acutely aware of the garrison's predicament and within days of his return to Spain he began to assemble a convoy of provisions for the relief of Almeida.

At the head of 42,000 infantry and 4,500 cavalry Masséna re-crossed the Agueda on 2 May and advanced upon Almeida. Wellington knew that Masséna was coming and he tried to find the best defensive position possible on the rolling plateau upon which, just a year earlier, he had refused to fight. Along a line of low hills near the village of Fuentes d'Oñoro, five miles from the fortress, Wellington posted his entire disposable force – just 36,000 men – with the River Coa at its back. The rest of the Anglo-Portuguese army, the 2nd and 4th Divisions and Hamilton's Portuguese, had moved up from Abrantes and was now blockading Badajoz over 100 miles to the south.

This was exactly the kind of situation Wellington had tried to avoid. He was faced with the prospect of encountering a numerically superior enemy in open country with his army divided. Worse still, was that

Marshal Soult was marching back from Cadiz to the relief of Badajoz and both halves of Wellington's army would be under simultaneous attack. A defeat now could undo everything that the British commander had achieved. "There was not during the war", wrote Colonel Napier, "a more dangerous hour for England."[25]

At last Masséna had found the allied army in a relatively exposed position and on 3 May he launched the first attacks of the battle that he had desired since the campaign began. The front of Wellington's position was defined by the narrow gorge of the River Dos Casas. With this difficult ground in front, and a clear field of fire before it, the centre of the allied army's line was comparatively secure. The weak point in Wellington's defence was on his right, where the main road from Ciudad Rodrigo crossed the Dos Casas at Fuentes d'Oñoro. In and around the village Wellington had placed four of his six divisions and, predictably, it was here that Masséna struck with almost his entire force.

At one o'clock in the afternoon eight divisions of l'Armée de Portugal advanced directly upon Fuentes in three huge columns. The combined British, German and Portuguese light infantry posted in the village were driven through the streets and up the slopes of the main allied position. Wellington immediately counter-attacked and the allied troops re-occupied Fuentes. The struggle for possession of the village continued until nightfall put an end to the fighting.

As at Buçaco, a frontal assault upon Wellington's line had failed. It was time for more subtle methods. The ground north of Fuentes was too difficult to be assaulted but to the south the terrain was much easier and the Dos Casas far less of an obstacle. On the morning of the 4th, Montbrun probed Wellington's southern flank. He found that Wellington's right wing rested on the hamlet of Pozo Bello and was composed of no more than a light cavalry screen supported by a single battalion of infantry. Montbrun's reconnaissance patrols, however, had not gone unobserved and Wellington transferred the recently formed 7th Division to strengthen his right where it occupied Pozo Bello and the wooded ground around it. The afternoon of the 4th passed without further incident but as soon as darkness fell the French troops began to move.

At daybreak on the 5th, four brigades of cavalry followed by three divisions of the VI and VIII Corps – 21,000 men – burst through the woods and fell upon Wellington's exposed right flank at Pozo Bello. The isolated and utterly outnumbered 7th Division could do nothing but retreat and Wellington sent the Light Division to cover its withdrawal. Craufurd, re-established in his old command, formed his men into battalion squares and shepherded the 7th Division back towards the heights behind Fuentes whilst the French cavalry, "trampling, bounding, shouting for the word to charge", swarmed all around them. Across more than a mile of open plain the Light Division withdrew, with Montbrun's horsemen poised to exploit the slightest disorder in its ranks. In what was regarded by onlookers as "a masterpiece of military evolutions", the Light Division saved Wellington's right flank for the loss of just sixty-seven men."[26]

By abandoning Pozo Bello Wellington had uncovered his communications with Torres Vedras but he had also narrowed his front into a compact L-shape, with the village of Fuentes forming the angle. Masséna made every effort to break the allied line at this angle, throwing almost the whole of the IX Corps against Fuentes. But by early afternoon Drouet's attack had been driven off and the village was in the firm grip of the 3rd Division.

Masséna had lost over 2,000 men and Wellington's position was, if anything, even more secure than before the first French attack two days earlier. L'Armée de Portugal remained in front of Fuentes d'Oñoro until 8 May when, its rations consumed, it returned to Ciudad Rodrigo, leaving the garrison of Almeida to meet its destiny alone.

Masséna had fought his last battle. With no prospect of relief, General Brennier's garrison destroyed the fortifications of Almeida, broke through the allied blockade and escaped over the border back into Spain. Just a few days later, Beresford repulsed Soult at Albuera in the bloodiest battle of the war. Beresford re-established his blockade of Badajoz and Soult retreated back to Andalusia. The invasion of Portugal was over.

CHAPTER IX

'Europe will not be lost'

PROCLAMATION

10 April,1811

The Portuguese nation are informed that the cruel enemy who have invaded Portugal, and had devastated their country, have been obliged to evacuate it, after suffering great losses, and have retired across the Agueda. The inhabitants of the country are therefore at liberty to return to their occupations.

Wellington[1]

The tide of French conquest, which had flowed unstemmed across Europe for nearly two decades, had finally begun to ebb. The high-water mark of French conquest in Europe, Sir Charles Oman observed almost a century later, was reached on a wet and windy day in October 1810 when l'Armée de Portugal stopped at Sobral and looked up in awe and dismay at the Lines of Torres Vedras. It marked the turning point of the entire war and was, Sir Charles wrote, the beginning of the end for Napoleon. By January 1811 Wellington had recaptured Almeida and Ciudad Rodrigo; three years later the last of Napoleon's soldiers were driven out of Spain, never to return.[2]

In the 1810-11 campaign l'Armée de Portugal suffered the heaviest defeat experienced by any of Napoleon's armies until the disastrous Russian campaign of 1812. After his failure at Fuentes de Oñoro Masséna was relieved of his command in favour of a far younger man – the thirty-six year-old Marshal Marmont – and ordered back to Paris. It is reported that Napoleon would not speak to Masséna for many months after his return and when they did eventually meet Napoleon greeted him with the words, "Well, Prince d'Essling, so you're no longer

Masséna!" He was never to lead an army in the field again.[3]

Masséna was held to be entirely responsible for the failure of the invasion and he was roundly condemned by his subordinates, both officers and men, in his handling of the campaign. His march by way of Buçaco, however, cannot be criticised. He was aware of the defences at Ponte da Murcela, which he had been told were of "surprising strength", and by taking the road through Viseu he intended to turn those defences. Though the Alcoba range and the Buçaco Alta are shown as prominent features on the Lopez map, Alorna and the other renegade Portuguese officers were either unaware or unappreciative of the strength of the Serra do Buçaco as a defensive position and Masséna was misled by their advice. It is possible that Masséna may have received reports of a road through Boialvo and he directed Ney and Junot to reconnoitre all the roads from Viseu that crossed the Caramulo. Either through neglect or incompetence, Masséna was informed that none existed. It must be noted, as an aside, that there was a considerable quantity of good military surveys available to the French, particularly those made by Junot's engineers in 1807-8. Why these documents were not issued to Masséna has never been satisfactorily explained.[4]

Masséna halted at Viseu for three days and this pause allowed Wellington time to concentrate all the divisions of his army at Buçaco and gave his engineers the opportunity to break up the approach roads and prepare the lateral road along the rear of the ridge. This delay was quite justified. The reserve artillery pare, which had experienced great difficulty travelling to Viseu due to the poor state of the roads, had fallen far behind the main body and had almost been captured by a brigade of Portuguese militia. Masséna could not afford to lose his artillery so he waited at Viseu for it to catch up. "We were stopped at Viseu not only by the delays of the grand parc which could not be left behind, but also because we still had to wait for the food wagons in order to give the troops a fresh supply of biscuit," wrote Pelet. "Finally we were obliged to make repairs on all the artillery wagons of the army corps since they were badly damaged by the poor roads." However, Baron de Marbot claimed that "the fatigues experienced" by Madame Leberton "contributed greatly towards delaying Masséna and holding him up there, for with the country in a state of insurrection it was impossible to leave her behind without exposing her to the risk of capture". Even if this were true it was not until his army arrived before Buçaco that Masséna began making the mistakes that made defeat inevitable.[5]

Whilst his army advanced without being stopped by the allies it was not necessary for Masséna to march with the vanguard; but as soon as his corps commanders were forced to halt because the enemy were blocking the road in a strong position, he should have ridden up to the front immediately to see the situation for himself. Contemporary reports suggest that it was because his mistress was feeling unwell that he stayed at Mortágoa to "secure lodging" for her. Consequently, Masséna and his staff did not leave for the outposts until 14.00 hours. Whatever the reason may have been, vital hours were lost. On the morning of the 26th Masséna's corps commanders were confident of a successful assault upon the allied army, which was still taking up its final positions on the heights, but by nightfall some, particularly Ney, Masséna's second-in-command, were predicting defeat and suggesting a withdrawal. Masséna arrived at the front late in the day. He had only one eye, due to a hunting incident in which he was shot in the face by Napoleon, and the light was fading rapidly. He then chose to attack a position that he had not thoroughly reconnoitred, not knowing the strength of the enemy nor where they were posted. His orders for the attack were consequently flawed. He assumed Picton's division to be the end of the allied line and that Reynier's columns, on striking the enemy at that point, would turn Wellington's right. Instead of finding Wellington's flank, Reynier struck almost the centre of Wellington's position, with disastrous results. The attacks of the II and VI Corps, as mentioned before, were separated by a distance of two miles and were therefore delivered in isolation against each other as two separate engagements.[6]

Masséna accepted the risk of battle only because he totally disregarded the effectiveness of the Portuguese contingent of Wellington's army. In 1807 Junot had seized Portugal without a shot being fired in its defence and both Masséna and Napoleon left the Portuguese out of their calculations. Masséna also believed that Hill's division could not join Wellington at Buçaco. Pelet wrote: "One must never forget our ignorance of the topography of this country, especially what we had been told about the impassability of the Zezere and the Serra da Estrella; we believed that direct communications between Wellington and Hill were impossible except through Thomar." Masséna reckoned that he was, in effect, going to fight a British army of some 20,000 when, in fact, he was about to engage an allied force almost as strong as his own. He made the unpardonable error of underestimating his enemy.[7]

By attacking a steep mountain Masséna was unable to make effective use of his artillery whilst his enemy made full use of all his seventy guns. Worse still his cavalry could not make any contribution whatsoever, being compelled to remain inactive in the rear. How different it might have been had they been scouting around Wellington's flanks on the 25th and 26th and reported back to Masséna about the Boialvo road before the battle. "If that position had been turned," remarked one French officer, "the enemy would have been taken in flank and would have retired upon Lisbon, and our army, in full strength and ardour, would have attacked the Lines on its arrival, and certainly have carried them ... But our heavy losses at Buçaco had chilled the ardour of Masséna's lieutenants, and bred ill-will between them and him; so that now all were trying to paralyse his operations and representing every little hillock to be a new height of Buçaco." The campaign may have lasted for a further six months but, effectively, it ended at Buçaco.

Napoleon, inevitably, was also critical of Masséna's attack at Buçaco. "Why the devil did Masséna thrust himself into that muddle at Buçaco?" He asked General Foy when he arrived at Paris to plead for reinforcements for l'Armée de Portugal. "Even in a plain country columns do not break through lines, unless they are supported by a superior artillery fire."[8]

Masséna's tenacious stand at Santarém throughout the winter of 1810-11 has been applauded almost unreservedly by soldiers and historians alike. Through the resilience of the troops and the determination of their commander was certainly remarkable, the five months of deprivation that l'Armée de Portugal endured outside the Lines accomplished nothing. "It is difficult to account for the length of time which he passed in front of the lines after he had reconnoitred and ascertained the impracticability of carrying them," wrote one of Wellington's generals, because this delay "daily added strength to his opponent, and made his own situation more critical." Masséna firmly expected significant support from the other French forces in Spain and he was encouraged by Napoleon into believing that mounting pressure in England for the army to be withdrawn would induce the Government to order the evacuation of Portugal, and that the longer he remained before the Lines the louder would be the cries of the Opposition. In fact the Tory administration (admittedly by "a small and unwilling majority") fully supported the war and even reinforced Wellington's army during this period "for the purpose of maintaining the contest in the Peninsular for an indefinite time" and whilst Wellington remained undefeated there was no likelihood of Portugal being abandoned. As Johnny Kincaid of the 95th Rifles was to observe, "the Prince of Essling ought to have tried his luck against them [the Lines], as he could only have been beaten by fighting as he afterwards was without it".[9]

As at Buçaco, Masséna could only have succeeded in an assault upon the Lines if he had attacked before the defenders had become established in their positions. Morale in the French camp was still good at this stage. Though they had been repulsed at Buçaco, the invaders had compelled the allies to withdraw from very strong defensive ground simply by threatening Wellington's flank. Victory was still possible. All Masséna had to do was find the weakest point in the defences, attack with all his force, and the allies would be on the run again. This Masséna attempted to do. His reconnaissance at Buçaco could only be described as cursory. Masséna did not repeat this error. He spent two days examining the Lines as far as the Calhandriz valley to the west of Alhandra. The ground in this area is a tangle of irregular hills and narrow passages and Fletcher's redoubts, with their low profiles, had been sculptured into the landscape. It was simply impossible for Masséna to gauge the depth of the defences or their probable vulnerability. The Serra de Buçaco is a relatively simple and clearly defined line of heights yet Wellington concealed his troops so effectively that Masséna misjudged the extent of the allied positions. How then was Masséna to tell where the main body of the Anglo-Portuguese army might lie behind the complex ranges of the Montejunto and the Montachique? He decided, therefore, that he could not risk the defeat that an attack might bring. With that decision went all hope of conquering Portugal.

The fact is that Masséna was not provided with the means to subjugate Portugal. "You will lack nothing in resources." Napoleon promised Masséna. "You will be absolute master and you will make your own preparations to open the campaign." But this was simply not true. There were over 300,000 French troops in Spain yet Masséna marched from Almeida with less than 70,000 men under his command and the IX Corps was never formally placed under his direct authority. Napoleon had also said that "the destruction of the English army is the only important concern", but instead of concentrating all his efforts against the British he allowed the majority of his troops to remain in occupation of the territory already conquered. Certainly Napoleon could not have anticipated the extent of Wellington's defensive arrangements and he genuinely believed that Masséna had been given sufficient resources to brush aside the British army and seize Lisbon. However, when Foy returned to Paris and explained the situation to Napoleon, the Emperor's response was wholly inadequate. Napoleon should have laid down his Spanish possessions and sent every available soldier to storm the Lines of Torres Vedras. The lost Spanish provinces would easily have been re-captured after the British had been defeated. Wellington had stated that he could defend Portugal against a force of up to 100,000 men. Napoleon could have invaded Portugal with double that number.[10]

Napoleon refused to appoint a general-in-chief in the Peninsula until the war was beyond any possibility of a successful conclusion. Like a distrustful Senate suspicious of Caesar's designs, so the self-crowned Emperor of the French was fearful of placing such power in the hands of one of his marshals. The detrimental effects of this were most severely felt when Masséna stood before the Monte Agraço and saw that he could only assault the Lines with a considerable reinforcement. There is no doubt that if the other French generals in Spain had been subordinated to Masséna he could have called Soult, Mortier, Drouet and even Victor to join him at Sobral. What price those earthen ramparts then?

L'Armée de Portugal lost approximately 25,000 men – almost forty per cent of the original force. Of these, only about 2,000 had been killed in action and a further 8,000 had been taken prisoner. All the rest perished from hunger or disease. It had lost almost half of the 14,000 horses with which it marched into Portugal, and it left behind all but thirty-six of its wheeled vehicles. Never again would the French make a serious attempt to invade Portugal.

How different it had been in 1807 when Junot had invaded Portugal with a mere 25,000 men and had occupied Lisbon unopposed. In 1811 it was a land upon which the French dare not tread. This had long been Wellington's objective. "If we are able to maintain ourselves in Portugal, the war will not end in the Peninsula," he had declared in 1809, and he had taken every possible measure to ensure that the French could not evict him from Portugal. It did not trouble Wellington that those measures resulted in the displacement of over a quarter of a million people, the deaths of tens of thousands of Portuguese peasants and the utter devastation of vast tracts of land, "bringing more evils", wrote one battle-hardened campaigner, "than twenty years of continual war". The fact also remains that Wellington did not need to permit such extensive damage to be inflicted upon the Portuguese nation. He had stopped Masséna's advance at Buçaco and he should never have allowed the French to march any further into Portugal. Even the French were shocked with Wellington's withdrawal "that instantly spread the evils and violence of war to a whole kingdom".[11]

Wellington's decision to fight at Buçaco has been a much debated subject. It must be remembered that his whole campaign strategy was based upon stopping the French at Torres Vedras and, if he was as certain of ending the French advance at the Lines as his dispatches indicate, he had no strategical reason to stand at Buçaco. It has been suggested that Wellington needed time to destroy or remove his magazines to save them from falling into the hands of the enemy. Many historical commentators have said that Wellington only fought at Buçaco to appease both the British and Portuguese Governments, who were unhappy with his apparent unwillingness to fight. "If you are unable to defend us, why do you arouse our resistance and cover our country with blood and ruins?" A Portuguese officer is reported to have said to Wellington. "If you are in force, deliver battle; if you are too weak and cannot obtain reinforcements, retire and leave us to compromise with the conquerors." It has also been suggested that Wellington decided to fight the French to give his troops confidence for the time when they would have to stand at Torres Vedras and that the strength of the Buçaco position gave him a perfect opportunity to do this. Wellington's words to his brother appear to support this view: "The battle has had the best effects in inspiring confidence in the Portuguese troops both among our croaking officers and the people of the country."[12]

Whatever Wellington's motives may have been, his decision to fight at Buçaco was justified by the fact that he achieved a notable victory for the loss of little more than 1,000 men. His decision to retreat from Buçaco, when his position was unassailable and his enemy was beaten, is far more difficult to support. He had been urged by the Portuguese Regency Council to fight the war upon the frontier to save the country from the ravages of a third invasion. It is clear that such a policy was impracticable and he had to fight his "battle to save the country" on the banks of the Alva or the slopes of Buçaco. But having fought and won his battle, why did he then retreat to Torres Vedras and expose another seventy miles of Portugal's richest countryside and fine, historic towns to despoliation and ruin? The Beira frontier was, and is, an infertile and sparsely populated region. No widespread evacuation of this area was required. As the French advanced so the peasants took to the hills, to return to their lands once the invaders had passed by. For the people of Coimbra and the province of Estremadura, though, the only escape route open to them was southwards to Lisbon, where the refugees perished in their thousands in the litter-strewn, vermin-infested streets of the capital.[13]

Wellington has, of course, given us his reasons for the withdrawal from Buçaco: "I would have stopped him [Masséna] entirely if it had not been for the blunders of the Portuguese General commanding in the North, who was prevented by a small French patrol from sending Trant up the road by which he was ordered to march. If he had come by that road, the French could not have turned our position, and must have attacked us again; they could not have carried it and must have retired." According to the Baron de Marbot such an excuse "is not permissible" for an experienced commander. It is not sufficient for a general simply to issue orders; he must also check that his instructions have been carried out. "Boialvo is only a few leagues from Buçaco," wrote the Baron, "and yet Wellington never ascertained that this pass, so important to the safety of his army, had been guarded according to his orders."[14]

Even if Trant had arrived at Boialvo much earlier, did Wellington seriously believe that 1,500 ill-equipped militia could have stopped an army of 60,000 men? It is inconceivable that a commander who had spent months building elaborate fortifications at Ponte da Murcela and Torres Vedras would have permitted the course of such a carefully planned campaign to hinge upon the actions of a few battalions of part-time troops whose absence or presence, according to Colonel Napier, "could have produced no effect whatever". Wellington had taken pains to widen the lateral road that ran behind the Buçaco summit, he had established infantry positions and batteries in the convent and his engineers had broken up the approach roads. Yet the only road by which his position could be turned was left untouched, despite the fact that his engineers had been working at Buçaco since 21 September – almost a full week before the day of the battle.[15]

If we are prepared to accept that Wellington really did hope to block Masséna's advance with Trant's militia, we then have to question the reason why Wellington did not send a proportion of his army to defend the Caramulo pass as soon as he was certain of Massena's movements. If he believed that Trant could stop the French, he could not have doubted that a brigade of British regulars would have successfully defended the pass. His army was only four hours' march from the end of the pass and a part of his force could have been in position long before the arrival of the French vanguard. Wellington, however, wrote in his Memorandum of Operations that "nothing could have been done, except by detaching a large corps to prevent the French from throwing a large force across the Caramulo". This completely contradicts his earlier statement that if Trant's tiny force had arrived in time Massena could not have turned his position! And why could Wellington not have detached this "large force"? The 1st, 2nd and 4th Divisions, the KGL, and Hamilton's, Campbell's and Coleman's Portuguese formations had not even been engaged at Buçaco. The Buçaco position had proved to be so strong that Wellington was able to defend it with less than half his army. He therefore could have spared at least two full divisions to block the Caramulo pass without seriously endangering his position at Buçaco.[16]

Wellington has told us that if the French had not found their way through the Serra do Caramulo, they would have been obliged to retreat. If he had blocked the pass, the campaign would have been won. Yet Wellington would not detach even a small part of his force to secure a complete victory. It would be a reckless critic indeed who would accuse Britain's most successful general of incompetence or excessive caution, so are we to conclude that Wellington intentionally permitted Masséna to outflank him?

Wellington, we must remember, had disagreed with the members of the Regency Council over his conduct of the campaign. They had demanded that he should make a stand against the French and he had argued strongly that they were wrong; "I know best where to station my troops, and where to make a stand against the enemy, and I shall not alter a system, framed upon mature consideration, upon any suggestion of theirs." At Buçaco, however, he had made a stand and, just as the Regency Council had suggested, the French had been beaten. Could Wellington, after such remarks as "there is not an arrangement of any description which depended upon them, or their officers, which has not failed", have conceded that the likes of da Sousa and the Patriarch might have been correct after all?[17]

Wellington's entire defensive strategy had been founded on permanent and semi-permanent fortifications. At Abrantes, Punhete, Ponte da Murcela, Almada, Torres Vedras and St Julian he had consumed the resources of a bankrupt nation in the construction of elaborate defensive works. Yet Masséna had not marched by way of Abrantes or Punhete, no secondary French army had penetrated the Alentejo, and when he stood and fought the invaders the French were beaten from a position created by the forces of nature, not by the hands of man. If Wellington could defeat the enemy so convincingly at Buçaco, could he not have stopped the French advance even earlier? We have read of the almost impassable terrain over which Masséna marched to reach Viseu and even the main Celorico-Coimbra highway was "intersected by many good military positions, on which a defending army can offer battle to an invader with advantage". Were Wellington's celebrated defences, which he claimed had "saved the country", in fact a waste of private land and public money?[18]

From a purely political standpoint, Wellington did not need to fight at Buçaco. However vociferous his detractors in Lisbon may have been, they did not have the power to seriously obstruct his actions, as he controlled the army and the militia through Marshal Beresford, and through Charles Stuart he controlled the huge British subsidy. He had originally planned, nevertheless, to give battle to the French at Ponte da Murcela before retiring upon the Lines, and when Masséna unexpectedly marched by way of Viseu rather than Celorico the

174

strength of the Buçaco heights offered Wellington "a favourable opportunity" to bring the "Portuguese levies into action with the enemy for the first time in an advantageous position". There were other reasons, of course, why Wellington fought at Buçaco. It enabled him to show Masséna "the description of troops of which this army is composed"; it likewise "removed an inference which began to be very general, that we intended to fight no more, but to retire to our ships: and it has given the Portuguese troops a taste for an amusement to which they were not before accustomed, and which they would not have acquired if I had not put them in a very strong position". Though Wellington claimed that the failure of Trant's brigade to reach the Caramulo pass in time was the reason why he was unable to stop the French at Buçaco, he only fought at Buçaco to reassure the civilian authorities of Britain's commitment to the defence of Portugal and to give the raw Portuguese troops some battle experience before they had to take up their positions along the Lines of Torres Vedras. He did not intend, nor expect, to stop the French at Buçaco. This is borne out by the words of his Adjutant-General, one of the two most important men on Wellington's staff, who stated that "as we never calculated upon retaining Buçaco after it should be executed, we made ready to abandon the high grounds, and continue our retreat". Even if Wellington took no one else into his confidence, the Quartermaster-General and the Adjutant-General would have been informed of his immediate plans, since it was their task to organize and control the movements of the army.[19]

On the evening of 28 September, Wellington stood on top of the Serra de Buçaco watching the French marching towards Mortágoa. He had given his Portuguese troops their first taste of battle and the confidence of l'Armée de Portugal had been severely shaken. All had gone according to plan, the next stage of which was an unimpeded withdrawal to the Lines of Torres Vedras. Yet Wellington had seen that Masséna's army was no stronger than his and that if he blocked the Caramulo pass there would be no tactical or strategical reasons for him to withdraw. He knew that if he allowed the French to turn the Buçaco heights there was no other strong defensive positions that he could take up north of Torres Vedras. He would therefore expose the whole of the province of Ribatejo and most of Estremadura to the ravages of war. Wellington did not see this as a great misfortune. The French would attempt to storm the Lines and would be repulsed. They would then retreat back to Spain. Lisbon was always well provisioned and could sustain the emigrant population for a short period of time. Wellington never imagined that Masséna would keep the refugees trapped inside

175

the Lines for nearly five months, despite Da Sousa's warnings that the Portuguese would attempt to hide their food rather than destroy it. Nor did Wellington anticipate the extent of the damage that the French committed both during their stays at Sobral and Santarém and throughout the retreat. He miscalculated, and 40-50,000 Portuguese – approximately 2% of the entire population of Portugal – lost their lives.[20]

We know that Wellington planned to fight a major rearguard action to stiffen his troops and bolster the civilian authorities before retiring into his prepared defensive position. We also know that he could have stopped the French at Buçaco but, as this was not his intention, he withdrew to the Lines, believing that once Masséna found that he could not force them he would return to Spain. But these are not the only reasons why Wellington allowed l'Armée de Portugal to march through the Caramulo pass.

Since his return to the Peninsula in 1809, Wellington had regularly asked the British Government for more and more money, but he never once revealed that large sums were being spent on the building of the Lines of Torres Vedras. In fact the Government were left in the dark about Wellington's plans for the defence of Portugal and he intentionally kept the Lines a secret from them. It was obviously essential that the Lines remained unknown to the enemy until the moment that they stood before them. If the French had been made aware of Wellington's plans they would never have spent months besieging Astorga, Ciudad Rodrigo and Almeida. Masséna would have masked these fortresses with a small blockading force and rushed down the Mondego valley in the spring of 1810 before Wellington's engineers had made the Lines secure. Knowing that Wellington's last stand was to be at Montachique, Masséna would never have attacked at Buçaco and his troops would have arrived at the Lines with their ranks undiminished and their morale high. Then would have been fought one of the greatest battles of the Napoleonic Wars. Amongst the incomplete redoubts and the partially scarped hills, 130,000 men would have fought for the possession of Iberia.

With naïve frankness (and alarming accuracy) the English newspapers had reported the British army's every move, The English press, hopefully unwittingly, provided Napoleon with a rich source of military intelligence and Wellington dare not disclose the details of his plans for the defence of Lisbon to anyone in London. Though it is usually stated to the contrary, both the Portuguese authorities and the officers of the British army were aware that fortifications were being prepared in front of Lisbon. Eventually the Government must have learnt of this massive construction project, which had been undertaken without its knowledge or consent, and if the French had been turned back at Buçaco Wellington would have had some difficult explaining to do. "I do not know, that, in these days of economy," he was forced to admit to Beresford, "I shall not be brought over the coals for having paid for all the works superintended by British engineers." Or, as Captain John Jones, the supervising engineer of the Lines, wrote the day before the army reached Sobral: "When I heard of the Buçaco business, I began to be alarmed for the consequences of having done so much; for if the lines had not come into play the expense would most likely have been cavilled at as unnecessary; but now, of course, only the benefit from the strength of the works will be considered." Was this the real reason why Wellington did not stop Masséna at Buçaco?[21]

Wellington also failed to take advantage of the weakened and increasingly dispirited state of Masséna's army at Sobral. Again Wellington gave his reasons: "I have frequently turned over in my mind the expediency of attacking the French army now in my front … and upon the whole, I am inclined to be of opinion that I ought not to do so," he told Lord Liverpool on 3 November. "I think the sure game, [is] that in which I am likely to lose the fewest men, the most consistent with my instructions and the intentions of the King's Government; and I therefore prefer to await the attack. Besides, although I have the advantage of numbers, the enemy are in a very good position, which I could not turn with any large force, without laying open my rear, and the road to the sea. This is the worst of all these strong countries, that they afford equally good positions to both sides". Wellington never lost sight of his goal. He would only commit his troops to battle if such a course of action was unavoidable. There was no indication that Masséna was likely to receive any reinforcements in the short term, nor was there any movement of French forces towards Spanish Estremadura. Therefore, there was no military imperative to induce Wellington to attack such a strong position. His reasoning was sound but there is little doubt that Wellington missed an exceptional opportunity to finish the campaign with a single blow, and minimise the distress of the displaced Portuguese.[22]

"Wellington has behaved like a clever man," Napoleon is reported to have said when first told of the Lines of Torres Vedras, "his total desolation of the kingdom of Portugal is the result of systematic measures splendidly concerted. I could not do that myself, for all my power." Napoleon and his generals now knew that Portugal might never be taken but if Wellington could be confined to that country the subjugation of Spain might still be accomplished. Even though Almeida had been evacuated, both Ciudad Rodrigo in the north and Badajoz to the south were still held by the French. Regarded as the "Gateways of Spain", whoever controlled these two strongholds controlled the Portuguese-Spanish border. Whilst they remained in French hands Portugal would never be spared the threat of invasion and Wellington would be compelled to remain impotently upon the defensive. It was even possible that, without some direct intervention by the Anglo-Portuguese forces on behalf of the Spaniards, the insurgents might become discouraged and seek an accommodation with the invaders. If Wellington was to perpetuate the war, he had to be able to attack the French forces in Spain.[23]

The weight of those French forces was still too great for Wellington to overcome. Any attempt upon Ciudad Rodrigo or Badajoz would lead to a concentration of two or more French armies and Wellington, once again, would have to withdraw. As if to test the speed of the French response, Wellington attacked Badajoz at the end of May, just two weeks after the last French troops had been expelled from Portugal.

Leaving half his army in the north around Almeida to watch l'Armée de Portugal and guard the road to Torres Vedras Wellington galloped down to join Beresford's corps at Badajoz to oversee the siege. The reaction of the French commanders in eastern Spain, however, was far swifter than Wellington had expected. After two unsuccessful assaults upon the Cristóbal heights that dominated the fortress, Wellington dismantled the breaching batteries and retired across the Guadiana having learnt that the armies of marshals Soult and Marmont – 60,000 men – were marching upon Badajoz.

Wellington immediately called down the rest of his army from Almeida and occupied a strong position near Elvas. Wellington had brought together every man he could muster yet his entire force numbered almost 10,000 less than combined strength of his opponents. The two armies faced each other for a full week with Wellington hoping, as always, to "get over the crisis of this moment without a battle". Eventually Soult and Marmont, with insurrection in their rear and starvation ahead of them, disengaged and returned to their respective operational areas.[24]

"The devil is in the French for numbers!" complained a frustrated Wellington. The French were simply too strong. Unless some dramatic event should reduce the number of French troops in western Spain, Wellington would never be able to break out of Portugal. For six months he waited and the event, when it came, was the most dramatic of the Napoleonic Wars – Napoleon had decided to invade Russia. As a result, Marmont's area of responsibility was greatly enlarged and his forces reduced, as Napoleon transferred large bodies of troops from Spain to join his Russian expedition. Wellington waited no longer. "The next operation that presents itself," he told Lord Liverpool, "is the siege of Ciudad Rodrigo."[25]

In direct contrast to Masséna's protracted siege operation against Ciudad Rodrigo the previous year Wellington, threw his men at the walls of the city only twelve days after the fortress had been invested. "We proceeded at Ciudad Rodrigo on quite a new principle in sieges." Wrote a gleeful Wellington. "The French ... who are supposed to know everything, could not take the place in less than forty days after it was completely invested." By the time Marmont could respond, the allied army was fully installed behind the re-built ramparts of the fortress.[26]

The loss of Ciudad Rodrigo was not, in itself, a serious misfortune to the French. They were not likely to use the fortress again as a base for an invasion of Portugal and Wellington could not move beyond the Portuguese frontier whilst Badajoz remained in French hands. Wellington still feared that a French force would cross the Tagus and cut the allied army off from Lisbon and the Lines. Unless the route through Badajoz was sealed, Wellington's flank would always be exposed and the security of Portugal always threatened. The French marshals with responsibility for western Spain were perfectly aware that Badajoz would be Wellington's next target and when the allied army concentrated on the banks of the Guadiana in the spring of 1812, Marmont invaded northern Portugal.

Brushing aside a collection of militia at Guarda Marmont marched into Lower Beira and occupied Castello Branco. Yet this move failed to draw Wellington away from Badajoz and the great fortress fell to the allies on 6 April, after a short but bloody siege. Nevertheless, the threat that l'Armée de Portugal posed to Wellington's communications could not be ignored and just two days after the capture of Badajoz the bulk of the allied army marched back to the north. Marmont, with his army on the verge of starvation, abandoned Castelo Branco and retired upon Salamanca.

With the loss of Badajoz the subjugation of Portugal was now utterly beyond the means of the French commanders in Spain. Work on the Lines had continued throughout the previous year and by 1812 the Lines (including St Julian) consisted of 165 fortified redoubts mounting no less than 628 guns, and were now considered strong enough to resist any assault. With the departure of the troops for the projected Russian invasion, the total number of French soldiers in the Peninsula in the summer of 1812 had fallen to little more than 200,000. Napoleon had failed to crush the Iberian revolt and so he was turning his back on it.

The war in the Peninsula was relegated to a holding action and command in Spain was delegated to his brother Joseph. Napoleon had never understood, much less solved, the logistical problems of campaigning in the Peninsula. He still could not accept that Wellington, with a field army of 50,000 men, might possibly succeed against almost a quarter of a million French troops. Yet Napoleon's famous victories had been won by achieving battlefield superiority against a numerically stronger enemy. His policies in the Peninsula allowed Wellington to fight his battles if not with greater numbers, then at least on equal terms, and although the French armies were now under a single authority, they would never be able to muster the resources to operate as one body.[27]

Wellington had never told his government that he would win the war. All he ever promised was that he would maintain the war in the Peninsula so that Napoleon's "Spanish ulcer" would continue to bleed away the military resources of the French empire. As Wellington was repeatedly to stress, his objective in the Peninsula was merely to assist and support the Iberian people in their fight for self-determination. "Our business is not to fight the French army," Wellington had explained to Lord Liverpool at the end of December 1810, "… but to give occupation to as large a portion of it as we can manage, and to leave the war in Spain to the guerrillas." With the capture of Badajoz, Wellington had largely accomplished his aim. Ciudad Rodrigo and Badajoz were important Spanish towns and their re-capture sent a signal to the guerrillas all over Spain that, if they continued to fight, their own towns would also be freed from the hated invaders.[28]

The consequences of the prolongation of the war in Spain were felt far beyond Iberia. "I truly believe that if we are to continue the war in the Portuguese and Spanish Peninsula," Wellington told Forjaz, "Europe will not be lost." With between a quarter and a third of Napoleon's entire disposable force locked into the struggle for the Peninsula, the French military presence in central Europe was considerably diminished and there is no doubt that this was one of the factors taken into account by the Tsar Alexander when he decided to resist Napoleon in 1812.[29]

In support of the Spaniards, Wellington could now strike at will into western Spain confident in the knowledge that, if he should suffer a reverse or find himself met by superior numbers, his line of retreat was secure. "We can advance with safety nearer to the centre of the scene of operations, and retire with greater ease," he explained to Lord Liverpool, "and make Lisbon the point of its communication with England." Any expeditions into Spain, nevertheless, would take Wellington into the midst of an enemy army four or five times stronger than his own. Consequently, his offensive actions were to be constrained by two self-imposed rules. These were, he explained to Lord Bathurst in the summer of 1812, as follows:

1. "above all, not to give up our communications with Ciudad Rodrigo"
2. "not to fight an action, unless under very advantageous circumstances, or it should become absolutely necessary".[30]

The only way that the French could stop incursions into Spain by the powerful allied army was by concentrating large bodies of troops to oppose it. But the ravaged countryside could no longer support such numbers. Until 1811, the French had been on the offensive and were able to move their forces into territories untouched by the war. All that had now changed. "We have already, in some degree, altered the nature of the war and of the French military system," claimed Wellington in August 1811. "They are now in a great measure on the defensive and are carrying on a war of magazines. They will soon, if they have not already, come upon the resources of France; and as soon as that is the case you may depend upon it the war will not last long." Furthermore, in order to be able to form large field armies, the French would have to strip their garrisons and remove troops from counter-insurgency operations, and as soon as the hastily assembled French forces marched against Wellington the guerrilla bands would converge upon the weakened French outposts. This was the great paradox of the war: to defeat Wellington in their front, the French must suffer defeat in their rear.

Reinforcements from England, plus a considerably reduced sick-list, meant that Wellington was now able to put 60,000 men into the field. None of the French armies taken individually could stand before such a force but Soult and Marmont had joined forces before and might do so again. Between Soult on the Guadalquivier and Marmont at Salamanca ran the mighty Tagus. The only bridge across the river that the French could use was at Almaraz. Before Wellington carried the war into Spain he intended to seize the bridge and snap the chain of communication. This mission was entrusted to General Hill who, on 12 May 1812, crossed the Guadiana and marched deep into French-held territory. It took almost a week for Hill's 6,000 men to reach Almaraz. The bridge was guarded by three redoubts and a fortified bridge-head, armed with eighteen cannon and held by a garrison of 1,000 men. Unable to bring forward his artillery because of the state of the roads, Hill had to storm the defences with the bayonet. For the loss of just 179 men, Hill took the whole position and destroyed the forts and the bridge before escaping back to the safety of the Portuguese border. The link was broken. Wellington could now resume the offensive.

His first target was Salamanca. After the fall of Ciudad Rodrigo Salamanca had become an important operational base for l'Armée de Portugal and it had been heavily fortified. The main position consisted of a triangular group of three forts standing on high ground to the south-west of the city. It took the Anglo-Portuguese army ten days to capture the forts, which allowed Marmont time to march to the assistance of the beleaguered garrison. Marmont, however, found Wellington's covering force posted on the heights of San Cristóbal some three or four miles north of Salamanca. The marshal declined to attack and he retired beyond the Douro, where he took up a strong defensive position behind the river. Wellington moved his army up to the Douro but, as he explained to General Graham, "Marmont will not risk an action unless he should have an advantage; and I shall certainly not risk one unless I should have an advantage". Consequently, the opposing armies marched and countermarched for three weeks within sight of each other without engaging in a general action. The breakthrough came on 22 July. Marmont overextended his line whilst attempting to race around the allied army's flank. This was the "advantage" that Wellington had been waiting for. He attacked immediately, cutting l'Armée de Portugal in two. Marmont was wounded and his army routed.[31]

General Clausel, in temporary command of l'Armée de Portugal, withdrew northwards with his shattered army towards Burgos. Wellington was tempted to pursue Clausel but this would have exposed his line of communications with Ciudad Rodrigo to an attack from the south. He chose instead to march on Madrid.

As the allies advanced upon the capital Joseph evacuated Madrid and the Anglo-Portuguese army liberated the city on 11 August 1812. Joseph moved to Valencia and then ordered Soult to abandon Andalusia and join him at Toledo. But Soult was unwilling to leave the sunny shores of southern Spain and submit himself to Joseph's authority, and it took him over two months to obey the King's summons. Meanwhile, Wellington, taking advantage of Soult's stubbornness, moved part of his army northwards towards Valladolid, which had recently been occupied by Clausel who, seeing that he was no longer being pursued, had started to move threateningly forwards again. Wellington pushed Clausel back as far as Burgos but, lacking siege equipment, he failed to subdue the castle's defensive armament and all three assaults upon the place were repulsed. By the middle of October, Soult had finally joined up with Joseph near Valencia. Together they mustered 60,000 men to the east and, with the Armée de Portugal now reinforced and totalling some 50,000 men pressing upon Wellington from the north, the British commander had little choice but to withdraw his troops once again over the frontier to the safety of Portugal.

For six months Wellington rested his troops and planned his next move secure in the knowledge that the French dare not follow him into Portugal. Reinforcements received throughout the winter had brought Wellington's fighting force up to a total of 52,000 British and 29,000 Portuguese, to which he was able to add 21,000 Spaniards that had been placed under his direct command. With such numbers, and supported by the growing guerrilla movement, Wellington could adopt a far more ambitious strategy than had previously been possible. Until this time his offensive campaigns had been little more than extended raids into Spain, in which he never ventured far from his Portuguese base. With southern Spain abandoned by the French, and Madrid liberated, the rest of the war would be fought in the north and every step that the allies trod would take them ever further from Lisbon. But now Wellington possessed the strength to match the combined armies of the enemy and to operate anywhere in the Peninsula. His new base was to be Santander in the extreme north of Spain and in the rear of Joseph's positions on the Douro. Under the pretext of reinforcing the Spanish army of Galicia, Wellington assembled transport ships, guns and ammunition at Corunna ready for the short journey along the Biscayan coast to Santander. The Lines of Torres Vedras, the cornerstone upon which Wellington had built his strategy for the last three crucial years, were now redundant.

Joseph's headquarters, and therefore the headquarters of the French in Spain, were at Valladolid, with his forces distributed between the Tagus and the Douro. Wellington knew that even though Joseph had only 60,000 men immediately at hand, he could call upon l'Armée de Portugal and the two divisions of l'Armée du Nord if the allies attacked. He intended, therefore, to hold Joseph's attention with a show of force in front of the French positions on the Douro whilst the main body of the Anglo-allied army would, in true Napoleonic fashion, cross the river further downstream and sweep around the enemy's flank.

On 22 May the advance began with six brigades of cavalry forming a dense screen to mask Wellington's movements. Behind this screen came only the Light Division, the 2nd Division, the Portuguese Division and two weak Spanish divisions. Such was Wellington's confidence, when he crossed the frontier he raised his hat and called: "Farewell Portugal! I shall never see you again!"[32]

The first contact with the enemy was on the outskirts of Salamanca. Immediately Joseph ordered the concentration of all his forces behind the Douro but a few days later the intrusive King realised that something had gone wrong with his plans. Six miles to the east of his concentration-point, the British 1st, 3rd 4th 5th and 7th Divisions – a mass of 42,999 men – had crossed the Douro and were bearing down upon his flank. Joseph had to abandon his position and retreat. He decided to fall back as far as Burgos but the British divisions did not pursue. Again Wellington marched around the French flank and again the French were compelled to withdraw. This time Joseph halted at Vitoria and he was determined to retreat no further. His men had been pushed back continuously for the previous month and morale was far from good. For his part Wellington, whose force now outnumbered his opponent's, was happy to accept battle. On 21 June the two armies clashed in the plain outside Vitoria. The result was a resounding victory for the allies. There was no orderly withdrawal by the French this time. Utterly routed, they fled back into France.

The allied army followed the French as far as the Pyrenees and occupied the mountain passes. Santander, which is less than 100 miles from the French frontier, was established as the new operational base from which Wellington planned to invade France. The French forces, now commanded by Soult, did force their way through the Pyrenean passes in an attempt to relieve the beleaguered French garrison in the fortified town of Pamplona, but without success. For the rest of the war the French were on the defensive, gradually being pushed deeper into France. Finally, on 12 April 1814, shortly after driving the French out of Toulouse, Wellington was brought the news of Napoleon's abdication. The Peninsular War was over.

Since those early days of the Peninsular War, Portugal has been spared the threat of invasion and the Lines of Torres Vedras, the greatest chain of fieldworks that Europe had seen until the trench networks of World War I, were allowed to slide into ruin. The Lines were maintained in good order by the Engineers until the end of the war and though they remained under military superintendence many of the redoubts were built on private land and the ground was soon returned to productive use. Though the São Vicente redoubt at Torres Vedras has recently been renovated, only the forts of St Julian and Cascais that guard the mouth of the Tagus remain as military establishments.

Despite their obvious success, the Lines of Torres Vedras had little immediate influence on the nature of warfare. Fieldworks and entrenchments had been a feature of battlefields for centuries and though the Lines were certainly unique there was nothing innovative in the strengthening of a defensive position with earthworks and redoubts.

Or so it was seen by the military men of Europe. The twenty-two years of conflict that had ended at Waterloo became known as the Napoleonic Wars and it was Napoleon's great battles in central Europe that attracted the attention of the leading military figures of the nineteenth and early twentieth centuries. The Peninsular War was regarded as a mere "sideshow". It was Napoleon's art of war, with its emphasis upon the destruction of the enemy's main army in a swift, offensive campaign, that was considered to be the manner in which "modern" wars would be fought. In 1903 Marshal Foch, who became Supreme Allied Commander in 1918, stated the following: "Defensive battle never brings about the destruction of enemy forces," he wrote, completely disregarding the destruction of Masséna's army in Portugal. "The offensive form must therefore *always* be adopted." The italics are Foch's.[33]

World War I – the first great war of the industrial era – changed everything. The new rapid-firing machine guns, breach-loading rifles and high-calibre field guns were so accurate and efficient that infantry and cavalry could no longer operate in the open. Fieldworks, some of a size and sophistication to equal even the Lines of Torres Vedras, marked every battlefield. A hundred years after the end of the Peninsular War vast ranges of earthworks and redoubts once again helped to determine the outcome of a major European war.

APPENDIX I

The allied army within the Lines of Torres Vedras, 1 November 1810

Total all ranks

CAVALRY DIVISION (Cotton)

De Grey's Brigade: 3rd Dragoon Guards & 4th Dragoons	804
Slade's Brigade: 1st Dragoons & 14th Light Dragoons	893
Anson's Brigade: 16th Light Dragoons & 1st Hussars KGL	808
Unbrigaded: 13th Light Dragoons	323
Fane's Portuguese Division: 1st, 4th & 10th Regiments	1,193
Total cavalry	4,021

1st DIVISION (Spencer)

Stopford's Brigade: 1st & 3rd Foot Guards; 1 company 5/60th Foot	1,685
Cameron's Brigade: 2/24th, 2/42nd, 1/79th Foot; 1 coy. 5/60th	1,539
Erskine's Brigade: 1/50th, 1/71st, 1/92nd Foot; 1 coy. 5/60th	2,043
Lowe's Brigade: 1st, 2nd, & 5th Battalions KGL, Detachment of Light Battalions KGL	1,681
Divisional total	6,948

2nd DIVISION (Hill)

Colbourn's Brigade: 1/3rd, 2/31st, 2/48th, 2/66th Foot; 1 coy. 5/60th	2,105
Houghton's Brigade: 29th, 1/48th, 1/57th; 1 coy. 5/60th	1,657
Lumley's Brigade: 2/28th, 2/34th. 2/39th; 1 coy 5/60th	1,489
Divisional total	5,251

3rd DIVISION (Picton)

Mackinnon's Brigade: 1/45th, 1/74th, 1/88th Foot	1,681
Colville's Brigade: 2/5th, 2/83rd, 94th Foot; 3 coys. 5/60th	1,655
Sutton's Portuguese Brigade: 9th & 21st Line	1,961
Divisional total	5,297

4th DIVISION (Cole)

Kemmis' Brigade: 2/27th, 1/40th, 97th Foot; 1 coy. 5/60th	2,572
Pakenham's Brigade: 1/7th, 1/61st Foot; Brunswick Oels Jagers	2,220
Collins' Portuguese Brigade: 11th & 23rd Line	2,535
Divisional total	7,327

5th DIVISION (Leith)

Hay's Brigade: 3/1st, 1/9th, 2/38th Foot	2,047
Dunlop's Brigade: 2/30th, 2/44th Foot	1,182
Spry's Portuguese Brigade: 3rd & 15th Line	2,163
Divisional total	5,392

6th DIVISION (Campbell)

British Brigade: 2/7th, 1/11th, 2/53rd Foot; 1 coy 5/60th	1,948
Eben's Portuguese Brigade: 8th Line; 1st & 2nd Lusitanian Legion	2,083
Divisional total	4,031

LIGHT DIVISION (Craufurd)

Beckwith's Brigade: 1/43rd, 4 coys.	
1st & 2nd 95th Foot; 3rd Caçadores	1,965
2nd Brigade: 1/52nd, 4 coys. 1/95th; 1st Caçadores	1,764
Divisional total	3,729

PORTUGUESE DIVISION (Hamilton)

Archibald Campbell's Brigade: 4th & 10th Line	2,407
Fonseca's Brigade: 2nd & 14th Line	2,414
Divisional total	4,821

UNATTACHED INFANTRY

2/58th (with Gen. Sontag). At Lisbon: 2/88th Foot, 1 coy. KGL	938
Pack's Portuguese Brigade: 1st & 16th Line; 4th Caçadores	2,267
Alexander Campbell's Portuguese Brigade:	
6th & 18th Line; 6th Caçadores	2,442
Coleman's Portuguese Brigade: 7th & 19th Line; 2nd Caçadores	2,196

ARTILLERY

Royal Horse Artillery (2 Troops)	322
Royal Foot Artillery (7 Companies, two incomplete)	845
KGL Artillery (2 Companies)	347
Portuguese Artillery (9 brigades)	701

ENGINEERS	43
TRAIN	422
STAFF CORPS	40
Total regulars	**57,380**

MILITIA & EMBODIED ORDENANZA

1.	Lecor's Division (Alhandra Forts):	
	Militia Regiments of Santarém, Idanha, Castello Branco,	
	Covilhã & Feira; 12th Portuguese Line	3,829
	Artillery	440
2.	At Bucellas Forts:	
	Militia Regiments of Lisbon, Thomar & Torres Vedras	1,907
	Artillery	1,065
3.	In the Sobral Forts:	
	Atiradores Nacionais (embodied Ordenanza)	761
	Artillery	450
4.	In the Torres Vedras Forts:	
	Militia Regiments of Lisbon (East & West), Setúbal,	
	Alcacer do Sal	2,231
	Artillery	398
5.	At the Mafra Forts:	
	Militia Regiment of Viseu	691
	Artillery	538
Total irregulars		**12,310**

THE SPANISH ARMY OF ESTREMADURA (La Romana)

Vanguard Division (La Carrera)	
Regiments of Principe, Vittoria, and 1st & 2nd Catalonia	2,500
2nd Division (O'Donnell)	
Regiments of Zamora, Rey, Toledo, Hibernia, Princesa & 2nd Seville	5,500
Total Spaniards	**8,000**
Total of all troops in the Lines	**77,690**

Note: The above details are assembled from Oman, *History of the Peninsular War*, vol. III, Appendix XIV and XV, with the kind permission of Lionel Leventhal, Greenhill Books.

APPENDIX II

Works comprising the Lines of Torres Vedras

1st Line
District No.1
From the Tagus at Alhandra to the Arruda road

Work No.	Garrison	Artillery Mounted In Each Works				Location	Altitude (metres)
		12-pounders	9-pounders	6-pounders	5.5" howitzer.		
1.	1,000	4	3	6	-	Line across low ground at Alhandra, resting on the Tagus	1
2.	800	2	-	-	-	Rising ground, left of No.1	40
3.	260	2	-	-	-	Redoubt, left flank of No.2	94
4.		2	-	-	-	Right flank of scarped face of the Alhandra position	94
114.	100-	-	2	1	-	Flanking redoubt to the scarped front of the Alhandra position	142
115.	100	2	-	-	-	Ditto	264
116.	100	5	-	-	-	Ditto	292
117.	150	-	-	-	-	Flèche, ditto	297
Unnumbered 195		-	-	-	-	Battery position, nova de Susserra	
118.*	400	8	-	-	-	Redoubt, top of Alhandra position	316
119.	350	6	-	-	-	Redoubt, closing the left of the position	299
6.		2	-	-	-	Gun platform, on the extreme of the left	-
120.	130	2	-	-	-	Redoubt, left of the Alhandra heights	309
5.	120	-	3	-	-	Ditto	309
121.	250	-	3	1	-	Heights of Calhandrix, advanced work	313
122.	300	3	-	-	-	Ditto, right	332
123.	300	3	-	-	-	Ditto, centre	345
124.	350	3	1	-	-	Ditto, left	342

125.	250	4	-	-	Rear redoubt, to connect the Calhandrix position with the rear line	227
7.	200	3	-	-	Redoubt on the heights in the rear of Alhandra, looking up the valley	286
Unnumbered		11	1	-	- Entrenchment across the Calhandrix valley.	
8.	200	3	-	-	Erected whilst the army occupied the lines	286
					Heights of rear of Trancoso, left flank of Alhandra, to prevent Alhandra being turned with artillery	355
9.	280	3	-	-	St Sebastian, right of pass of Matos	252
10.	400	2	1	-	Carvalhao, left of pass of Matos	394
11.	300	4	1	-	Windmill above Arruda road	323
	6,280	51	36	9	(Totals)	

S = Signal station.

District No.2
From the Arruda road to the left of the Monte Agraço

Work No.	Garrison	Artillery Mounted In Each Works				Location	Altitude (metres)
		12-pounders	9-pounders	6-pounders	5.5" howitzer.		
12.	120	-	3	-	-	Rocky bluff above Arruda road	283
13.	120	2	-	-	-	Fort de Canara, paved road to Bucellas	297
14.*	1,590	14	6	4	1	Main work, Mont Agraço	440
15.	460	3	3	1	-	Advanced work, Monte Agraço	417
16.	250	1	2	-	1	Ditto	431
17.	300	-	-	7	1	Ditto	424
152.	250	4	2	-	-	Advanced work, right of road to Sobral	384
	3,090	**24**	**16**	**12**	**3**	(Totals)	

*Signal station.

District No.3
From Zibreira to the Caduceira height

| Work No. | Garrison | Artillery Mounted In Each Works | | | | Location | Altitude (metres) |
		12-pounders	9-pounders	6-pounders	5.5" howitzer.		
151.	300	-	-	-	-	Redoubt for field guns near Ribaldeira	250
150?		-	-	-	-	Scarped plateau between Quinta de Anoteira and Ribaldeira prepared for field guns	255
128.*	500	6	-	-	-	Main work, Serra de Caduceira	350
129.	350	6	-	-	-	Ditto, centre	265
130.	200	-	5	-	-	Ditto, left	224
28.	270	3	4	-	-	Enxara dos Cavalleiros, north redoubt	236
	1,900	15	9	-	-	(Totals)	

*Signal station.

195

District No.4
From the left of the pass of Runa to the sea

Work No.	Garrison	Artillery Mounted In Each Works				Location	Altitude (metres)
		12-pounders	9-pounders	6-pounders	5.5" howitzer.		
149.	259	4	2	-	-	Heights above Matacaes, to command the Runa road	134
26.	300	-	3	-	-	Advanced work near Matacaes to block the Runa road	134
20.*	470	5	-	2	1	Torres Vedras main work, SE bastion	118
21.	270	-	2	6	1	Ditto, SW bastion	118
22.	380	5	-	3	1	Ditto, NW bastion	118
	600	-	-	-	-	Ditto, curtain walls (south curtain 150 men, west curtain 90 men, NE curtain 360 men)	118
23.	180	-	4	3	-	West redoubt, Torres Vedras	105
24.	300	-	7	-	-	East redoubt, Torres Vedras	68
25.	200	-	2	-	-	Convent of São Joa, Torres Vedras	40
27.	500	5	-	-	-	Castle of Torres Vedras, in the town	60
131.	90	4	-	-	-	Enclosed battery, left of Variatoja	125
132.	150	6	-	-	-	Ditto	101
133.	120	-	4	-	-	Enclosed battery, Pedrulhos	77
134.	110	4	-	-	-	Enclosed battery overlooking the village and heights of Benfica	76
135.	160	-	4	-	-	Ditto	86
136.	150	4	-	-	-	Ditto	107
137.	100	4	-	-	-	Ditto	97
147.	-	-	-	-	-	Open battery above Ponte do Rol	65

148.	–	–	–	–	–	*Ditto*	73
138.	100	–	–	2	–	Enclosed battery, rear of No.30	44
30.*	340	3	1	–	–	Redoubt above Ponte do Rol	65
139.	160	4	–	–	–	Enclosed battery between Nos. 30 and 31	40
140.	120	4	–	–	–	*Ditto*	38
31.	373	–	3	–	–	Redoubt at Algaterra	58
141.	180	4	–	–	–	Enclosed battery between No.31 and St Pedro	58
142.	150	4	–	–	–	*Ditto*	62
143.	150	–	4	–	–	*Ditto*	52
144.	130	4	–	–	–	*Ditto*	50
32.	260	3	1	–	–	Redoubt at St Pedro de Cadeira	34
145.	250	–	4	–	–	Quinta de Belmonte	53
111.	250	5	–	–	–	Between St Pedro and the sea	33
146.	250	–	6	–	–	Qunita de Bessuaria	34
112.	220	4	–	–	–	Between Quinta Bessuaria and the sea	40
113.	50	2	–	–	–	Enclosed battery at the sea	35
	7,413	78	47	16	3	(Totals)	

* Signal Station

197

2nd Line
District No.5
From the Tagus to the pass of Bucellas

Work No.	Garrison	Artillery Mounted In Each Works				Location	Altitude (metres)
		12-pounders	9-pounders	6-pounders	5.5" howitzer.		
33.	300	4	-	-	-	Banks of the Tagus, right of Via Longa	2
34.	200	-	3	-	-	Advanced redoubt to enfilade Calcada	21
5.	120	-	4	-	-	Ditto	75
36.	370	9	-	-	-	Ditto	80
37.	50	-	3	-	-	Redoubt at Calcada	9
38.	340	-	5	-	-	Ditto	53
39.	340	5	3	-	-	Ditto	85
126.	180	2	-	-	-	To close the right of the Cabo valley	90
127.	154	-	-	-	-	Ditto, the left	108
40.	150	-	-	-	-	To close the left of the Via Longa at Caza de Portella	280
41.	240	5	-	-	-	Ditto, right-hand redoubt	274
42.	350	6	-	-	-	Ditto, left-hand redoubt	287
43.	-	4	-	-	-	Open battery right of Bucellas pass	140
44.	-	-	2	-	-	Ditto, front emplacement	140
45.	-	3	-	-	-	Ditto, rear emplacement	130
46.	-	-	2	-	-	Open battery left of Bucellas pass, front emplacement	170
47.	-	3	-	-	-	Ditto, rear emplacement	185

APPENDIX II

No.						
48.	-	2	-	-	Rear of No.46 to enfilade Calcada	7
18.	300	4	-	-	Serra de Santa Ajuda, right redoubt	311
19.	200	-	3	-	*Ditto*, left redoubt	305
	3,602	47	25	-	(Totals)	

District No.6
From the pass of Freixal to the park of Mafra

Work No.	Garrison	Artillery Mounted In Each Works				Location	Altitude (metres)
		12-pounders	9-pounders	6-pounders	5.5" howitzer.		
49.	-	2	-	-	-	Pass of Freixal	300
50.	160	-	2	-	-	Ditto, right redoubt	255
51.	300	4	-	-	-	Ditto, left redoubt	305
52.	190	-	3	-	-	Right of entrance to pass of Montachique	215
53.	230	-	2	-	-	Pass of Montachique, right	234
54.	210	-	-	-	-	Ditto, on Enxara road	276
55.	150	3	-	-	-	Ditto, rocky bluff	273
56.	150	2	-	-	-	Ditto, pine wood	275
57.	270	3	-	-	-	Ditto, rocky height covering the right	332
58.	310	-	3	-	-	Montachique pass, left of entrance	232
59.	260	4	-	-	-	Ditto, mill on the Mafra road	261
60.	150	-	2	-	-	Ditto, fléche on left flank	289
61.	190	-	2	-	-	Ditto, covering left flank	286
62.	390	3	-	-	-	In front of, and covering, the road from Mafra to Montachique	249
63.	280	-	3	-	-	Serra de Cazal, covering the Mafra road	250
64.	210	-	3	-	-	Ditto, corner of the park wall	288
65.	270	3	-	-	-	Mafra road, Oiteira de Santa Maria	367
66.	350	4	-	-	-	Ditto, Malveira	266
67.	120	-	2	-	-	Ditto, right of No.66	295

68.	260	4	-	-	*Ditto*, Monte de Zinho	357
69.	240	4	-	-	*Ditto*, Pinhal de Fidalgo	270
70.	240	4	2	-	Quinta de Estrangeiro	287
71.	240	-	4	-	*Ditto*,	289
72.	130	-	2	-	Mafra road, Astradaieros	265
73.	340	3	-	-	*Ditto*, Cazal de Conto	261
	5,640	43	30	-	(Totals)	

District No.7

From the park at Mafra to the sea

Work No.	Garrison	Artillery Mounted In Each Works				Location	Altitude (metres)
		12-pounders	9-pounders	6-pounders	5.5" howitzer.		
74.	190	-	2	-	-	Park of Mafra, right of the park, within the entrance	326
75.	70	-	2	-	-	Within the park walls	302
76.*	390	4	-	-	-	Cabeca de Sincout	356
77.	380	4	-	-	-	Juncal	317
78.	110	2	1	-	-	Serra de Chypre, advanced work	238
79.	290	3	-	-	-	Ditto, redoubt, advanced mill	265
80.*	310	3	-	-	-	Ditto, second mill	266
81.	280	-	3	-	-	Ditto, lower redoubt	249
82.	210	2	2	-	-	Left of village of Morugueira, right flank	225
83.	240	-	3	-	-	Ditto, centre	215
84.	290	3	-	-	-	Ditto, right	215
85.	290	3	-	-	-	Alto de Arriero on Ereceira to Mafra road	201
86.	280	3	-	-	-	Alto de Paz, Ericeira to Mafra road	211
87.	340	3	-	-	-	Mill, south of Ericeira road at Pinheiro	207
88.	200	3	-	-	-	To command road from Sobral des Alvares to Mafra	197
89.	200	3	-	-	-	Defence of Picanceira road	153
90.	230	3	-	-	-	Peneyaixo, to command the roads leading to Picanceira and Encarnacoa	158
91.	200	3	-	-	-	Ditto, commanding three roads from Encarnacoa at Lagoa	131

92.	180	3	–	–	–	Defence of the road to Morvao	112
93.	330	3	–	–	–	Ribamar, right	115
94.	320	2	–	–	–	*Ditto*, left	85
95.	250	2	–	–	–	Rear line, right at Monte Gordo	102
96.	280	3	–	–	–	*Ditto*, centre at Carvoiera	98
97.*	350	2	–	–	–	*Ditto*, left, at St Julian	74
	6,300	57	13	–	–	(Totals)	

* Signal Station

District No.8
From embarkation point at Oeiras (St Julian)

Work No.	Garrison	Artillery Mounted In Each Works				Location	Altitude (metres)
		12-pounders	9-pounders	6-pounders	5.5" howitzer.		
98.	1,340	20*	-	6	-	Main work, St Julian	42
99.	70	6	-	-	-	Right battery to flank the valley and beach at Oeiras	14
100.	50	6	-	-	-	Left battery to flank Oeiras valley	15
101.	250	10	-	-	-	Advance to main work, right	29
102.	260	8	-	-	-	Ditto, left	28
103.	130	-	3	-	-	Advanced work in front of Oeiras	47
104.	100	-	2	-	-	Ditto, south	47
105.	170	-	4	-	-	Ditto, north	47
106.	320	6	-	-	-	Vineyard, left of No.98	27
107.	800	6	-	-	-	Qunita Nova, building and redoubt	18
108.	360	6	-	-	-	Left flank of the position	5
109.	500	-	7	-	1	Advanced work on a hill NE of Oeiras	72
110.	1,000	-	3	-	-	A line extending on the right from No.114 to Fort das Mais	23
	5,350	68*	19	6	1	(Totals)	

*This number includes twenty 24-pounders.

Note: This list of the works is compiled from Jones, *Journal of Sieges*, vol.III, pp.95-100, Norris & Bremner, pp.67-76 and *Supplementary Despatches*, vol.VI, pp.538-46.

APPENDIX III

A visitor's guide to the Lines of Torres Vedras

Many of the redoubts and forts of the Lines have disappeared or are scarcely recognizable as defensive works. However, some parts of the fortifications are still in reasonable order and a few have been restored to their original condition. To visit all of the remains would take many days but a visitor to Lisbon or the coastal resorts of Estoril and Cascais can see the more interesting remains of the Lines in just one or two days. Traffic can be very heavy around the Lisbon area and an early start is essential.

From Lisbon centre take the coast road to Cascais. This road is easily found and adequately signposted. The first stop should be made at Oeiras. The Fort of São Julião is very clearly identifiable on a low, rocky headland projecting into the sea. The small, sandy beach to the east of the fort was the intended embarkation point for Wellington's army. Four jetties were built here to facilitate the loading of stores. There is a left turn off the Lisbon-Cascais road and free car parking overlooking the beach. The fort is still a military establishment.

Returning to the main road, pass through Estoril and take the right-hand turn to Sintra. Again this is well signposted. It was from Sintra that Sir Hew Dalrymple sent his dispatch to London announcing the terms of the infamous Convention of Cintra (the Convention was actually negotiated in Lisbon and signed at Torres Vedras). From Sintra follow the N9 to Mafra. The massive Convent of Mafra became Junot's headquarters when he led the first French invasion in 1807. Continue on the road past the convent to Murgeira and Gradil. Look out for the blue signposts to the Tapada. Soon will be seen the old wall of the Tapada (or Royal Park) on the right running alongside the road. This is the pass of Mafra, one of the most important positions on the second, or main, line. The wall was fitted with a banquette to allow infantry to fire over the top and four redoubts were built inside the enclosure. The road itself was blocked with abattis. This road drops steeply through heavily scarped hillside before ascending towards Gradil and the Chypre ridge on which were built Forts Nos.78-80.

Travelling through Gradil and Enxara de Cavalleiros (where redoubts 28 and 29 were situated) the road runs into the village of Pero Negro. Pass through

205

the village and at the last bend before reaching a railway level-crossing, is a driveway on the left. This leads to a large house on a low rise. This was Wellington's headquarters during his army's occupation of the Lines and it is marked by a plaque situated on the front of the house. Passing over the level-crossing, the road eventually leads to a junction where there is a signpost for Sobral de Monte Agraço.

The Great Redoubt was built on the summit of the Monte Agraço, which is found just off the Sobral to Bucellas road. The redoubt is indicated by a brown sign on the left of the road. It reads "Forte de Alqueidão", pointing across the road to a rough track that leads to the redoubt. The whole of the lower part of the summit is now covered in trees but it is still possible, with persistence, to find the remains of the defensive works higher up. At 440 metres it is the highest point in the Lines, and it was up to here that Wellington galloped from Pero Negro every morning before sunrise. Signal station No.4 was located here.

By returning towards Pero Negro, signs will be seen for Torres Vedras. This famous old town is dominated by the ruins of its Moorish castle built on a conical hill in the centre of the town. The castle was incorporated into Wellington's defensive system as Fort No.27. It is worth a visit and is very easy to find. Just outside the town, along the N9 to Lisbon, is Fort São Vicente, the largest fort of the Lines. The turning to the fort is clearly signposted on the right-hand side of the road. The approach to the fort and the fort itself have been restored and the revetted gun embrasures, walls, traverses and powder rooms are all to be seen. The position actually consists of three forts surrounded by a perimeter wall about 1,500 metres long. In the southernmost fort are the remains of the ancient chapel of São Vicente, where signal station No.2 was erected.

The other principle position to visit is at Alhandra on the Tagus. This is best approached from Lisbon. Again locate the coast road but this time take the eastern carriageway past the docks along the Avenida Infante Henrique. The road runs parallel with the Tagus though the river is not always in sight. Follow signs for Vila Franca de Xira. The turning to the "Linhas de Torres" is on the left just before the town of Alhandra. The road climbs up the hillside and branches near the summit. Take the left fork which leads to the top of the hill and Fort No.114. Of particular interest here is the original dressed stone on the front of one of the gun embrasures. After the winter of 1809-10 the earthen ramparts of many of the works were faced with this stone to avoid erosion of the soil in wet weather.

Return to the fork and turn left to the "Monumento". Built on the site of No. 2 redoubt is a statue of Hercules set on a large marble column looking out over the Tagus. There are excellent views down to the river from where the Royal Navy operated its flotilla of gunboats. Inscribed on the plinth of the column are tributes to both Colonel Fletcher and Neves Costa, and in large letters are the defiant words proclaiming Portugal's determined stand against invasion – "NON ULTRA" – No Further! Anyone who wishes to investigate the Lines in more detail is advised to contact the British Historical Society of Portugal, 13 Rua da Arriaga, 1200 Lisbon.

References and Notes

Chapter 1.

1. F. Wilkie, *Peninsular Sketches by Actors on the Scene*, vol.i, p.4. G. Gleig, *The Hussar*, vol. i, p.248. W. Warre, *Letters from the Peninsula*, p.21.
2. Grant and Temperley, *Europe in the 19th and 20th Centuries*, p.114.
3. For a translation of Vincent's report of 28 June 1808 see *Correspondence, Despatches and other papers of Viscount Castlereagh*, vol. VI, pp.376-81.
4. *Proceedings upon the Inquiry Reletive to the ARMISTACE and CONVENTION etc. made and concluded in Portugal, in August 1808,* p.197. See also Burrard's address in the Public Records Office, PRO WO1 415, pp.191-214.
5. M. Dumas, *Souvenirs,* pp.321-2, quoted in D. Chandler, *The Campaigns of Napoleon,* p.620.
6. Napoleon to Joseph, 11 January 1809, *Correspondance de Napoléon ler,* 14,684, quoted in Charles Oman, *A History of the Peninsular War,* vol.11, p.17. Carola Oman, *Sir John Moore,* p.559.
7. "The Burial of Sir John Moore after Corunna", poem by Rev. Charles Wolfe. See A. Bryant, *Years of Victory,* p.255.
8. *Correspondance de Napoléon,* ibid. Moore to Castlereagh, Salamanca, 25 November 1808, quoted in Oman, *History,* vol. II, p.286. Craddock to Villiers, 20 December 1808, quoted in J. Fortescue, *A History of the British Army,* vol.7, p.125. J. Gurwood, *The Dispatches of Field Marshal the Duke of Wellington,* vol.4, pp.261-3. A. Wellington, *Supplementary Despatches, Correspondance and Memoranda of Field Marshal the Duke of Wellington,* vol. VI, p.210.
9. Wellington's *Dispatches,* vol.5, pp.50-1, 90 & 94.
10. Ibid, pp.556-9.
11. J. Pelet, *The French Campaign in Portugal, 1810-11,* p.157. *Dispatches,* vol.5, p.89 & vol.6, p.6. J. Marshall-Cornwall, *Marshal Massena,* p.177.
12. *Dispatches,* vol.5, pp.274-9.
13. *Dispatches,* vol.4, p.261. Oman, *History,* vol. II, p.293. *Dispatches,* vol.6, p.6.
14. *Dispatches,* vol. 5, pp.94-6. Wellesley to Frere, 24 April 1809, quoted in Oman, *History,* vol.III, p.293.
15. *Dispatches,* vol.4, pp.261-3.
16. Ibid, vol.5, pp.544-5.
17. R. Southey, *History of the Peninsular War,* vol.4, pp.326-54.
18. J. Aitchison, *An Ensign in the Peninsular War,* p.74. Aitchison's father had actually stopped writing to his son in Portugal in the belief that the army had already embarked! (p.78). E. Sidney, *The Life of Lord Hill,* p.116. *Supplementary Despatches,* vol.VI, pp.493-4. *Dispatches,* vol.5, pp.538-42.
19. *Supplementary Despatches,* vol. VI, pp.493-4. *Dispatches,* vol.6, pp.6-10.

20. Southey, vol.4, p.328. *Supplementary Despatches,* vol. VI, pp.438-41.
21. Southey, ibid, pp.462-3. *Dispatches,* vol.6, pp.328-9 & 434-7.

Chapter 2.
1. R. Ford, *Gatherings from Spain,* pp.133-4. See also Ford's *A Handbook for Travellers in Spain,* vol. I, pp. 138-47.
2. M. de Rocca, *Memoirs of the War of the French in Spain,* p.191.
3. Ford, *Gatherings,* ibid.
4. *Dispatches,* vol.5, pp.244-5.
5. Ibid, p.234-9.
6. R. Jones, *An Engineer Officer under Wellington in Peninsula,* p.70. *Dispatches, vol.7,* pp.83-5.
7. Oman, vol. II, p.286. W. Eliot, *A Treatise on the Defence of Portugal,* pp.5 & 7. Portugal had been invaded four times from the north through Valenca-do-Minho, three times through Ciudad Rodrigo and Almeida, see S. Ward, *Wellington,* p.67.
8. *Dispatches,* vol. 5, p.555. There were no fixed bridges in Portugal across the Tagus at that time and the boat-bridge at Abrantes was really only semi-permanent. See R. Bremner, "The Building and Manning of the Lines of Torres Vedras", *New Lights on the Peninsular War,* p.111. Wellington was later to realise that artillery on the Almada heights could bombard Lisbon and prevent the passage of shipping through the Tagus estuary. The Almada heights were therefore heavily fortified. See *Dispatches,* vol.5, pp.590-2.
9. *Dispatches,* vol.5, p.234-9.
10. *Dispatches,* vol.5, pp.418-9. Napoleon did, in fact, envisage a two-pronged attack upon Portugal. In *Correspondence* No. 16504, dated 27 May 1810, he proposed that Reynier, with the II Corps, should advance towards Lisbon along "the right bank of the Tagus". See D. Horward, *Napoleon and Iberia,* pp.114-5.
11. *Dispatches, vol.7,* p.304. Eliot, pp.102-3.
12. Instructions given to Colonel Wilson, 18 February 1810, for the destruction of the Estrada Nova are found in *Dispatches,* vol.5, pp.503-4. The Estrada Nova was so completely destroyed that it has never been repaired; see J. Weller, "Wellington's Peninsula Engineers" in the *RE Journal* for 1963, p.299.
13. *Dispatches,* vol.6, p.7.
14. *Dispatches,* vol.6, pp.494-5 & vol.5, pp.244-6.
15. Sidney, p.132.
16. B. D'Urban, *The Peninsular Journal,* p.74. *Dispatches,* vol.6, pp.10-11. The regiments at Peniche were Infantry Regiments Nos. 1, 4, 7, 13, 16, 19 & 22, and the 1st Regiment of Artillery. See G. Nafziger, *The Armies of Spain and Portugal,* p.78.
17. Eliot, pp.8-9 & 83. There were other batteries along the banks of the Tagus, notably at the castle of Bélém. See Eliot, pp.68-9.
18. A. Dickson, *The Dickson Manuscripts,* vol. 2, pp.201 & 161-3. *Dispatches,* vol.5, pp.436-7, 474-6 & 503.
19. P. Guedalla, *The Duke, p.189. Dispatches,* vol.5, pp.534-6.
20. *Dispatches,* vol.5, pp.457-8 & 505-6. Ward, *Wellington,* p.76.
21. *Dispatches,* vol.6, pp.318-22, 329-30 & vol.7, pp.456-7.
22. *Dispatches,* vol.6, p.104 & vol.5, pp.374-5.
23. *Supplementary Despatches,* vol. VI, p.450.
24. *Supplementary Despatches,* vol. VI, pp.467-8 &489-90.
25. *Dispatches,* vol.6, pp.329-30.
26. Wellington to Bacellar, 1 March 1810, *Dispatches,* vol.5, pp.534-6. Oman, vol. Ill, p.187. *Dispatches,* vol.5, pp.528-9.
27. *Dispatches,* vol.5, pp.274-79 & 479-82.
28. A. Halliday, *Observations on the Present State of the Portuguese Army,* pp.53-4. *Dispatches,* vol.6, p.556. M. Foy, *History of the War in the Peninsula,* vol. I, p.229, states that the population of Portugal exceeded 2,800,000 persons.

29. Halliday, ibid. Foy, ibid, p.266. *Supplementary Despatches*, vol. VI, p.518.
30. *Dispatches*, vol.5, pp.529-30 & 534-6. D'Urban, p.76.
31. Aitchison, p.68.
32. Oman, vol. Ill, pp.178-80.
33. *Croker Papers*, vol. i, p.337. *Dispatches*, vol.5, p.376-7. Oman, vol. II, pp.213-7. The 2nd Cavalry Regiment (Moura) and 3rd (Estremoz) never took the field. The 9th (Chaves) was dismounted and sent to the fortress of Almeida and the 12th (Miranda) was dismounted at Lisbon in March 1810. See Halliday, pp.34-40.
34. C. Oman, *Wellington's Army*, pp.232-3 and Oman, *A History of the Peninsular War*, vol.III, pp.172-5. Only the initial batch of twenty-four British officers that transferred to the Portuguese service were granted the double step in rank, all the subsequent transferees received only a single step in the Portuguese army with no advancement in their British rank. This led to much acrimony. See *Dispatches*, vol.4, pp.369-71, 393-6, vol.5, pp.151-3 & 283-5. D'Urban, p.60. See the circular from Beresford dated 17 May 1810 in Dickson, vol.2, pp.221-2, confirming the right of transferred officers to receive the pay from both commissions.
35. Warre, p.78. Warre was an aide-de-camp to Beresford. See also Halliday, pp.14-5 and D. Chandler, "The Lines of Torres Vedras 1810-11", in *History Today*, April 1976, pp.262-8. Translations of the Portuguese infantry drill book and the *Instrucções para a Cavallaria* courtesy of Antonio Manuel Ram-inhos Cordeira Grilo, Lisbon 1996. The story of John Schwalbach comes from the *Illustrated London News*, 2 January 1847.
36. *Dispatches*, vol.5, pp.411 & 427. The first complete returns available for the reformed Portuguese Army was that of 15 September 1809. See Oman, *History*, vol.11, Appendix V, pp.629-31. Permission to take the Portuguese troops with him if Wellington was forced to evacuate was refused due to the cost. Instead they were to march through the Alentejo to the Algarve, from where it was hoped they would join up with the Spaniards at Cadiz. See *Supplementary Despatches*, vol. VI, pp.466-7.
37. Wellington disapproved of the Portuguese supply system and he suggested that a commissariat should be attached to each Portuguese brigade. See *Dispatches*, vol.5, p.444. *Supplementary Despatches*, vol. VI, pp.476-80. Dick-son, ibid, p.275: "since I entered this service not a man has received a pair of shoes, shirts or anything". Dickson was a major in the Portuguese artillery. *Dispatches*, vol.5, pp.452-7, 481 & 426.
38. J. M. das Neves Costa, *Memória Militar respectiva ao Terreno ao Norte de Lisboa, Maio 1809, acrescentada com observacões e notas do mesmo autor em 1814*, (Lisbon 1888). *Dispatches*, vol.4, pp.179. D. Francis, *Portugal 1715-1808*, p.224. Southey, vol.2, p.500. *Dispatches*, vol.4, p.193. Castlereagh, vol.VI, pp.376-81.
39. *Dispatches*, vol.4, pp.263, 289, 439, 384, 312 & vol.9, p.81. There is also a map in the Public Records Office (WO 78 1004) which shows the ground occupied by Wellesley's division on 31 August 1808. This ground was the country around Sobral de Monte Agrago – the exact position which became the centre of the Lines of Torres Vedras during the time that they were occupied by the allied army.
40. *Dispatches*, vol.5, pp.234-9. The fords were at Le Redimoinhos, Barquinha (2), Pinheiro, Chamusca (2), Santarém (2), Benfica do Ribaiejo, Escarrofin and Salvaterra de Magos (2). See Beresford's *Further Strictures on those parts of Col. Napier's History of the Peninsular War*, p.34.
41. J. Pelet, *The French Campaign in Portugal, 1810-11, p.224. Dispatches*, vol.5, pp.235 & 244-7.
42. *Dispatches*, vol.5, p.89.
43. D'Urban, p.74.
44. *Dispatches*, vol.5, pp.244-6. J. Jones, *Memoranda Relative to the Lines thrown up to cover Lisbon in 1810*, p.5-7.
45. J. Jones, ibid. *Dispatches*, vol.6, pp.77-8. Lieutenant Rice Jones was already preparing sketches for defensive works at St Julian as early as 14 October – almost a week before Wellington's memorandum to Colonel Fletcher. See *An Engineer Officer under Wellington*, p.45.
46. *Dispatches*, vol.6, pp.418 & 10-11. It is usually thought that the army had very little

knowledge of the Lines but John Aitchison – a mere Ensign – was not only fully aware of the "fortified positions of Vila Franca and Torres Vedras", but he was also aware of Wellington's original survey of the area in October 1809 and of his inspection of the works in January 1810. See *An Ensign in the Peninsular War*, pp.109, 67 & 82. There were, of course, official plans of the embarkation points and these are now held in the Public Records Office. The fortified area around Setúbal and Palmela is found under WO 78 2533, and Almada, St Julian and Oeiras are listed under MR 939, WO 78 1004 and WO 78 1766. See also A. Norris and R. Bremner, *The Lines of Torres Vedras, pp.57 & 61-2*.

47. *Dispatches*, vol.4, pp.261-3.
48. Oman, *History*, Preface to vol. III. If Wellington was forced to evacuate the army 6,000 men were to be shipped to Gibraltar and the rest of the British force was to lie off Cadiz, disembarking only if the Spaniards agreed to submit to Wellington's authority. See *Supplementary Despatches*, vol.VI, pp.465-6 & 66-7.

Chapter 3.
1. *Dispatches*, vol.5, pp.234-9. Plans and sketch maps of the Lines can be found in the Public Records Office Map Room. The main collection is under WO 78 1660. The other important collection of maps is listed under WO 78 1004, which includes a sketch of the fortress of Abrantes and the bridge of boats; a map of the Lines in 1809 by Lt Joaquim de Olivera of the Portuguese Army; and a plan of Fort São Julião dated 1810. A plan "Shewing the fortified ground in front of Lisbon" is in WO 78 1221 and a later Portuguese map of *"des famosas linhas de Lisbon"* is in WO 78 460. A survey of the ground fortified on the south side of the Tagus is in WO 78 1768.
2. *Dispatches*, vol.5, p.502. J. Jones, *Memoranda*, p.21-2. T. Connolly, *History of the Royal Sappers and Miners*, vol.1, p.175.
3. MS *Autobiography of Major-General Sir John Jones RE*, pp.38-9.
4. *Dispatches*, vol.5, pp.264 & 399. J. Jones, ibid, p.20. R. Jones, pp.47-9.
5. J. Jones, ibid, pp.77-8. Fletcher MS Letter Book for 1810, p.40.
6. J. Jones, ibid, pp.78-9. Connolly, ibid.
7. *Supplementary Despatches*, vol.VI, pp.459-62 & 473.
8. R. Jones, p.51. Norris & Bremner, pp.65-76. *Supplementary Despatches*, vol.6, pp.538-46.
9. *Supplementary Despatches*, vol.VI, p.451. R. Jones, pp.51-2. George Ross, MS letters for 25 April and 25 May 1810.
10. *Supplementary Despatches*, vol.VI, pp.452-5. J. Jones, ibid, p.9-11.
11. J. Jones, ibid, pp.11-2. *Supplementary Despatches*, vol.VI, p.487.
12. J. Jones, ibid, pp.13-5. J. Burgoyne, *Life and Correspondence*, pp.64-5.
13. J. Jones, ibid, pp.139-41.
14. J. Jones, ibid, pp.170-6. *Dispatches*, vol.6, pp.196-7. *Supplementary Despatches*, vol. VI, p.537.
15. J. Jones, ibid, pp.16-7
16. Ibid, pp.82-94.
17. Ibid, pp.101, 97,104 & 94.
18. Initially eleven telescopes were purchased by Lieutenant Rice Jones (R. Jones, p.54). J. Jones, ibid, pp.104-5 & 162. See *Supplementary Despatches*, vol.VI, pp.546-7 for some of the different types of signalling equipment. The Admiralty in fact refused to supply the additional rations and pay for the sailors to serve ashore, and Wellington was only able to retain the services of Berkeley's men after the Government had intervened to provide the necessary funding. See *Dispatches*, vol.6, pp.196-7, 224, 421 & 525-6.
19. S. Ward, *Wellington's Headquarters*, p.126. J. Jones, ibid, pp.105-6 & 108. R. Jones, p.53.
20. P. Kealy, MS *follow the Sapper*, p.287. G. Ross MS letters for 25 May & 20 June 1810. *Dispatches*, vol.6, pp.493-4. Ross was not the only engineer to express such doubts. Captain Goldfinch (MS letter dated 4 April 1810) considered the idea of defending Lisbon as "impracticable" and he doubted whether or not the redoubts would hold the enemy in check for more than a few hours.

Chapter 4.

1. Correspondence *de Napoléon,* XIX, 15871, quoted in Oman, vol.III, p.197. "I wish to enter Lisbon myself as soon as possible. When I show myself beyond the Pyrenees the terrified leopard [the British] will seek safety in the ocean, from shame, defeat and destruction" – speech to the Corps Legislatif, 3 December 1809, *Correspondance,* XX, 16301, quoted in D. Horward, *Napoleon and Iberia,* p.14. J. Fortescue, *A History of the British Army,* vol.7, pp.374-6.
2. Napoleon to Berthier, 31 January 1810, *Correspondance* XX, 16192. "In Poland I am in the centre of Europe; in Lisbon I would be at the edge of the world" – M. Foy, *Vie Militaire du Général Foy,* p.110.
3. Oman, *History,* vol.III, pp.202-6. Napier, *History,* vol.III, Appendix I.
4. M. de Rocca, pp.342-3.
5. J. Haswell, *The First Respectable Spy,* p.113. Foy, ibid, p.100-1. J. Hulot, *Souveniers Militaires du Baron Hulot,* p.303. Pelet, p.21. Napier, ibid, vol. Ill, p.347. *Memoirs of the Baron du Marbot,* pp.416-7. *Journal of the International Napoleonic Society,* vol.1, no.l, pp.5-21.
6. Southey, vol.4, p.107.
7. Oman, ibid, vol.III, p.145-7. *Dispatches,* vol.5, p.90. The Portuguese troops at Cadiz came from the 20th Regiment of Infantry. See also *Supplementary Despatches,* vol.VI, p.436.
8. *Dispatches,* vol.5, p.482.
9. Ney's instructions are found in Napoleon to Berthier, 12 February 1810, *Correspondance,* 16245. See Oman, ibid, vol.III, p.213. *Correspondance,* XX, 16192, Napoleon to Berthier, 31 January 1810, which can be found in *Supplementary Despatches,* vol. XIII, p.386, "The English are the only danger in Spain; the rest are a rabble who can never stand and fight."
10. J. Belmas, *Journaux des sièges fails ou soutenus par les français dans la peninsule, de 1807 a 1814* vol. III, p.270. Herrasti to Ney, 12 February 1810, quoted in Horward, p.11. For Wellington's assessment of the situation at this time see *Dispatches,* vol.5, pp.511-3.
11. Oman, ibid, vol.III, pp.231-2. Fortescue, vol.7, pp.456-9. Napier, ibid, vol.III, pp.262-3. *Dispatches,* vol.5, pp.429-30, 430-1 & 431-2.
12. *Dispatches,* vol.6, pp.51-3. Wellington to Charles Stuart: "I do not consider the possession of Astorga, by the enemy, to be an object of very great importance in the existing situation of affairs." Dickson, pp.187-8.
13. *Dispatches,* vol.5, pp.610-11. Wellington's instructions to his divisional commanders are found in *Dispatches,* vol.5, p.466 to Cole, p.473 to Craufurd and pp.474-6 to Sherbrooke. See also pp.555-6.
14. Lord Burghersh, *Memoir of the Early Campaigns of the Duke of Wellington,* pp.137-8. *Dispatches,* vol.6, pp.74 & 94-5.
15. A. Herrasti, *Relacion histórica y circumstanciada de los sucesos del sitio de la plaza de Ciudad Rodrigo en al anon de 1810,* pp.78-81, quoted in Horward, p.55. *Dispatches,* vol.6, p.120.
16. Pelet, p.34.
17. Horward, pp.81-3.
18. G. Wrottesley, *Life and Correspondence of Field Marshal Sir John Burgoyne,* vol.1, pp.154-5. The Teson is actually 105 feet above the valley floor and 600 yards from the fortress. It rose forty-two and a half feet above the main enciente, Horward, pp.86-91. J. Grehan, *The Forlorn Hope,* pp.47-8. Pelet, pp.44-6. J. Koch, *Memoirs de Masséna,* vol.VII, pp.50-2.
19. Horward, pp.91-5.
20. Oman, ibid, vol. III, pp.239-42.
21. *Dispatches,* vol.6, pp.171-2. See also pp.80-1.
22. *Correspondance,* XX, 16519 to Berthier, 29 May 1810, quoted in J. Marshall-Cornwall, *Marshal Masséna,* p.190.
23. *Dispatches,* vol.6, pp.212-4. See also Wellington to Craufurd, pp.221-3. Horward, pp.105 & 107-8.
24. Pelet, p.62. E. Sprunglin, *Souveniers d'Emmanuel-Frédéric Sprunglin,* pp.429-30. Horward, pp.107-8. *Dispatches,* vol.6, pp.195-6 & 197-8. Koch, vol.VII, p.57.

25. Pelet, p.63. Horward, pp.120-1.
26. Masséna to Berthier, 5 June 1810, quoted in Pelet, p.60.
27. Horward, pp.128-9.
28. *Dispatches*, vol.6, pp.186-8. Pelet, p.64. Horward, p.136.
29. Pelet, p.65.
30. Belmas, *Journaux des siéges*, vol. III, pp.286-7. Herrasti to Ney and Ney to Herrasti, 28 June 1810, quoted in Pelet, p.66.
31. *Dispatches*, vol.6, pp.202-3. Burgoyne, vol.1, p.83. D'Urban, p.113. *Dispatches*, vol.6, pp.221-3 & 227-9. Napier, ibid, vol.III, p.282.
32. The Little Teson is fifty-six feet above the valley floor and less than 200 yards from the breach. Pelet, p.77.
33. Pelet, p.78. Napier, vol.III, p.281. T. Picton, *Memoirs of Lieutenant General Sir Thomas Picton*, vol.1, p.271.
34. Pelet, p.79. Horward, p.177.
35. Pelet, p.80.
36. Herrasti, *Relacion histórica*, pp.86-91, quoted in Horward, p.181. *Dispatches, vol.6*, pp.295-6. Herrasti, ibid, pp.112-3, quoted in Horward, pp.184-5.

Chapter 5.
1. Pelet, pp.83-4. The Cortez, acting as the government of Spain, opened its first session on 24 September 1810 in the besieged fortress-port of Cadiz. The members were elected from each of the Spanish provinces but, as many areas of Spain were under French control, representation was very uneven. See Oman, *History*, vol.III, pp.511-3. *Dispatches*, vol.6, pp.257-8.
2. *Correspondance de Napoléon*, XX, 16732, Napoleon to Masséna, 29 July 1810 and 16519, Napoleon to Berthier, 29 May 1810.
3. Horward, p.225. Pelet, pp.85 & 98. Belmas, vol.III, pp.373-5. Elbe, who commanded the artillery of l'Armée de Portugal, stated that as many as fifteen horses a day died during this period.
4. *Dispatches*, vol.6, p.220.
5. Ibid, pp.285-6.
6. E. Costello, *The Peninsular and Waterloo Campaigns*, p.32. G. Simmons, *A British Rifleman*, p.76.
7. Simmons, p.77.
8. Simmons, ibid. W. Napier, *The Life and Opinions of General Sir Charles James Napier*, vol.1, pp.137-8.
9. J. Leach, *Rough Sketches of the Life of an Old Soldier*, pp.149-50. Simmons, p.93.
10. H. Smith, *The Autobiography of Lieutenant General Sir Harry Smith*, vol.1, p.31.
11. *Supplementary Despatches*, vol.VI, pp.561-4. *Dispatches*, vol.6, pp.292-4. Masséna to Berthier, 29 July 1810, in Belmas, vol. III, p.375-80, quoted in Oman, *History*, vol.III, p.264. See also Horward, pp.217-8.
12. Rev. A Craufurd, *General Craufurd and his Light Division*, p.115. Wellington's instructions are to be found in *Dispatches*, vol.6, pp.149-50, 238-40 & 258-9. Picton confirmed these instructions in a letter to Craufurd dated 4 July (*Craufurd and his Light Division*, p.121) in which he suggested that a dragoon should be placed at Valverde to enable direct communications between the two divisions so that Picton could "co-operate" with Craufurd's movements. Napier, *History of the War in the Peninsula*, vol.III, pp.294-5, observed that Craufurd and Picton did not often meet without a quarrel!
13. Napier, *History*, vol. III, p.269. *Dispatches*, vol.6, p.306.
14. *Dispatches*, vol.6, pp.300-2.
15. Southey, vol.4, pp.434-9.
16. Pelet, p.96. Cox to Beresford, 1 July 1810, in *Ministerio dos Negocious Extrangeiros*, Maço, 168 (2), quoted in Horward, p.273. Horward (p.273) puts the figure of the garrison at

3,000 effective infantry, 222 artillery and 61 Dragoons. Oman, *History*, vol.III, p.267, gives 4,000 infantry and 400 gunners plus the cavalry.

17. Cox to Beresford, 12 May 1809, quoted in Horward, p.268.
18. Pelet, p.85. Pelet (p.108) also tells us that the soldiers developed an organised system of marauding to gather food: "Each one brought back any thing he found. Then a value was determined for every item – a measure of grain, a cow, a pig, a goat etc. Each soldier or company could get what they wanted by exchanging these items."
19. Pelet, p.120. Horward, pp.300-1.
20. Oman, ibid, p.272. This was only one version of the cause of the disaster. A Portuguese officer claimed that a French shell ignited a barrel of powder in the courtyard and the fire from this reached the main magazine, whilst Governor Cox surmised that a shell crashed through the door of the magazine. But the fact is that no eye-witnesses survived the explosion and we will never know for certain the exact events of the evening of 26 August 1810. See J. Noel, *Souvenirs militaires d'un premier empire* (1895), p.107, E. Sprunglin, *Souvenirs, Revenue Hispanique* (1904), p.445 and J. Hulot, *Souvenirs militaires du baron Hulot* (1868), p.316.
21. Napier, *History*, vol.III, p.306.
22. Pelet, p.122. Horward, pp.300-2.
23. Oman, ibid, pp.273-4. Belmas, vol.III, p.382-3, Masséna to Cox, 27 August 1810, quoted in Pelet, p.122.
24. Cox's new terms were "that the garrison would be free to go home on their word of honour, that the British would be allowed to return to England on the same terms, and that the gates would not be opened until the next day at noon", Pelet, p.124. This time of the capitulation is given by Oman (ibid, p.275) but Masséna did not accept the capitulation until about 03.00 hours on the 28th and the French guns ceased firing shortly after dawn, Horward, p.308.
25. Pelet, p.126.
26. *Dispatches*, vol.6, pp.394-5 & 389-92. Horward, p.311.
27. *Dispatches*, vol.6, pp.385-6 to Hill & 389-92 to Liverpool on 29 August. Aitchison, p.110.
28. *Dispatches*, vol.6, pp.408-9 & 422-4.
29. Oman, ibid, p.276. Horward, p.316. *Dispatches*, vol.6, pp. 396-7.
30. Oman, ibid, pp.277-9. *Dispatches*, vol.6, pp.397-9 & 402-4. Sidney, pp.138-9. Napier, *History*, vol.III, p.310.
31. *Dispatches*, vol.6, p.363. *General Orders of the Duke of Wellington*, vol.2, p.62.
32. *Dispatches*, vol.6, pp.405, 378-80, 402-3 & 403-4. Sidney, ibid.
33. Pelet, pp.145-6.
34. Masséna to Berthier, 8 September 1810, quoted in Oman, ibid, p.342. Wellington to Masséna 9 September 1810, "It disturbs me greatly to learn that you have issued orders to the French army not to take prisoners among the Portuguese ordenanza, and that the French army, obeying this order, shoot all of this corps that fall into their hands ...If the French army continue to shoot the prisoners of the ordenanza ... these orders ... will be the cause of misfortune for the soldiers of the French army who fall into the hands of the Portuguese troops." *Dispatches*, vol.6, pp.419-20.
35. Oman, ibid, pp.342-3.
36. Pelet, pp.133-41. Oman, ibid, pp.343-4. Napier, *History*, vol.III, pp.315-6.
37. Napier, *History*, vol.III, p.309.
38. H. Mackinnon, *A Journal of the Campaign in Portugal and Spain*, p.71. *Dispatches*, vol.6, pp.441 & 450.
39. Pelet, p.138.
40. Pelet, pp.55 & 135. J. Marbot, *The Memoirs of the Baron de Marbot*, pp.417-8. The actual Lopez map used by Masséna was captured by the British during the rout of the French after the Battle of Vitoria. Masséna's line of march is marked in red ink in parts iii, iv and v of the map. It is currently held in the Special Collections section of the Library of The Queen's University of Belfast. The two Portuguese generals were the Marquis d'Alorna

and the Count de Pamplona. See also W. Walker, "Masséna's Lines of March in Portugal", *English Historical Review,* July 1901.
41. Noel, pp.112-5, quoted in D. Horward, *The Battle of Bussaco,* p.53.
42. *Dispatches,* vol.6, p.374. Marbot, pp.415-6.
43. *Dispatches,* vol.6, pp.451 & 453-4. 41. *Dispatches,* ibid, pp.459-60.

Chapter 6.
1. Masséna to Berthier, 22 September 1810, in Koch, vol. VII, pp.183-4. D. Horward, *The Battle of Buçaco,* p.60. Marbot, p.415.
2. Oman, *History,* vol. III, pp.354-8.
3. Reynier to Ney, 08.00 hours, 26 September 1810. Ney to Reynier, 10.30 hours, quoted in Napier, *History,* vol. III, Appendix VII, Section 3.
4. Koch, vol. VII, pp.191-2. Horward, ibid, p.72. According to Major Dickson of the Portuguese artillery (Dickson, vol.2, p.296), Hill's infantry was not fully established upon the serra until 15.00 hours and the artillery until midnight of the 26th.
5. E. Longford, *Wellington, Years of the Sword,* p.224. Tomkinson, p.42. *Dispatches,* vol.6, pp.466-7.
6. G. Chambers, *Wellington's Battlefields Illustrated, Buçaco, 1810,* pp.12-20 & 183.
7. Chambers, pp.130-4. D'Urban, pp.147-8. Major Duncan in the second volume of his *History of the Royal Regiment of Artillery* (p.276) was critical of the distribution of the allied artillery at Buçaco. Wellington, he stated, "displayed an ignorance of Artillery tactics … At Buçaco, instead of massing his Artillery in reserve until the attack should develop itself the guns were placed …where it was supposed the French *would* attack." The allied artillery was particularly effective at Buçaco but this, according to Duncan, was not due to Wellington's correct assessment of where the attacks would be delivered but on the "intelligence and gallantry" of the gunners! Duncan clearly had never visited Buçaco, though, or he would have seen how difficult the ground is for the rapid movement of artillery. If the guns had been left in reserve many of them may not have been deployed in time to meet the French attacks.
8. S. Ward, *Wellington's Headquarters,* p.112. Bathurst to Beresford, 19 September 1810, 19.00 hours, *Dispatches,* vol.6, p.455. Burghersh, pp.172-3.
9. M. Sherer, *Recollections of the Peninsula,* pp.107-8.
10. W. Grattan, *Adventures with the Connaught Rangers,* pp.28-9. Chambers, p.211. Napier, *History,* vol.III, p.331.
11. Masséna to Reynier, Ney, Junot and Firion, 26 September 1810, in H. Bonnal, *La Vie militaire du maréchal Ney,* vol.III, pp.388-9 and in Oman, *History,* vol.III, Appendix XI and Horward, *Buçaco,* pp.77-9
12. Grattan, p.29.
13. Grattan, p.31.
14. Captain Lane's MS letter quoted in Duncan, p.277. Grattan, p.32.
15. Grattan, p.33.
16. Grattan, p.35.
17. Picton's report to Wellington can be found in *Supplementary Despatches,* vol. VI, pp.633-5. See also T. Picton, *Memoirs of Lieutenant-General Sir Thomas Picton,* vol.i, pp.320-1. Chambers, p.214.
18. Chambers, p.61 Picton's report, ibid, p.61.
19. Foy, *Vie Militaire,* p.102-3. Oman, ibid, p.374. Horward, *Buçaco,* pp.105-6.
20. Extract from a *Memorandum of the Battle of Buçaco* by Colonel Walker in Horward, *Buçaco,* p.108. *Supplementary Despatches,* vol.VI, pp.636-7. Picton's report, ibid.
21. *Supplementary Despatches,* ibid. Douglas' report is quoted in Chambers, p.76.
22. A. Leith Hay, *A Narrative of the Peninsular War,* p.164. Foy, ibid, p.104.
23. Oman, ibid, pp.377-8.
24. See Fane's report in Chambers, p.114. D. Horward in *The Battle of Buçaco* (p.117) states

that Ross' guns were only taken after a fierce hand-to-hand struggle. Napier *(History,* vol. III, p.334) claims that the artillery "drew back". As the entire British artillery at Buçaco suffered just eight casualties (Oman, ibid, Appendix XII) and as such resistance from Ross would have been quite pointless, Napier's commentary would appear to be the more accurate. However, if Simon was wounded in the act of capturing the guns (Chambers, p. 115) then the gunners may have put up some kind of fight before withdrawing.

25. G. Napier, *Passages in the Early Military Life of General Sir George T. Napier,* p.124. J. Leach, *Rough Sketches of the Life of an Old Soldier,* pp.165-7.
26. G. Napier, p.125.
27. Chambers, pp.122-7.
28. Oman, ibid, p.382.
29. M. Guingret, *Relation Historique et Militaire de la campagne de Portugal sous le maréchal Masséna,* p.67, quoted in Horward, *Battle of Buçaco,* p.123.
30. Oman, ibid, pp.384-5.
31. *Dispatches,* vol.6, p.467.
32. Marbot, pp.421-2.
33. *Dispatches,* vol.6, pp.474-5.
34. Guingret, pp.77-9, quoted in Pelet, p.189.
35. *Dispatches,* vol.6, p.571.
36. Marbot, p.430. Burghersh, pp.176-7. A. Schaumann, *On the Road with Wellington,* p.261.
37. G. Napier, pp.130-1. Pelet, p.201.
38. Burghersh, pp.179-80. Masséna's justification for leaving the invalids at Coimbra was given by Koch, (p.216): "hospitals are not like magazines or depots, he [Masséna] argued, where profit is the over-riding consideration: one could not exactly use their contents."!
39. D'Urban, p.152. J.T. Jones, MS Autobiography, p.40.

Chapter 7.
1. Oman, *History,* vol. III, pp.437-8.
2. J. Jones, p.186.
3. R. Jones, p.58. J. Jones, pp.21-3.
4. Pelet, p.225. J. Jones, pp.23-8.
5. *Dispatches,* vol.7, p.380. J. Jones, p.5.
6. *Dispatches,* vol.5, pp.590-2. Norris & Bremner, pp.61-2. J. Jones, pp.43-4. The Portuguese were supposed to provide 4,000 workmen for the Almada defences but as late as January 1811 only 200 men could be found employed on these defences. "The French will be in Alentejo before these works will be prepared," Wellington complained to Charles Stuart *(Dispatches,* vol.7, p.93) "and then there will be a breeze in Lisbon."!
7. *Dispatches,* vol.6, pp.488-90 & 492-3. J. Jones, *Memoranda,* p.34.
8. J. Jones, pp.31 & 33. MS letter of Captain Ross for 19 October 1810.
9. L. Butler, *Wellington's Operations,* vol.i, pp.315-6.
10. J. Jones, p.187. The engineers began destroying roads and bridges along the line of retreat as early as 19 September (R. Jones, p.70).
11. Mackinnon, p.71.
12. W. Gomm, *Letters and Journals of Field-Marshal Sir William Maynard Gomm,* p.185. J. Jones, p.188. *Dispatches,* vol.6, pp.494-5.
13. *Dispatches,* vol.6, pp.499-501, 504-5 & 492-3. Sidney, p.147.
14. *Dispatches,* vol.6, pp.502-3.
15. Sainte-Croix was "cut in two by a chain-shot", Marbot, p.434. Oman, *History,* vol.III, pp. 439-40.
16. *Dispatches,* vol.6, p.510. Napier, *History,* vol.III, p.361.
17. Pelet, p.137, 224-5 & 230. A. Bryant, *Years of Victory,* p.388. According to Koch (vol. VII, p.216), it was on 5 October at Leiria that Massena first received "positive" reports about the Lines from a Portuguese prisoner.

18. Pelet, p.227.
19. J. Jones, pp.39-40. Leith Hay, p.249. Pelet, p.222. Masséna to Ney, 16 October 1810, quoted in Pelet, p.232.
20. *A Soldier of the 71st* (p.54) described the manner in which the anonymous author passed the night during those first five days at the Lines: "I placed my canteen upon the ground, put my knapsack above, and sat upon it, supporting my head upon my hands; my musket between my knees, resting upon my shoulder, and my blanket over all, ready to start in a moment, at the least alarm." D'Urban, pp.157-8. *Dispatches*, vol.6, p.517.
21. Masséna to Napoleon, 22 November 1810, quoted in Foy, *Vie Militaire*, p.343. Marbot, pp.434-5. Pelet, p.234. Massena was further discouraged from attacking the Lines by the reports of French prisoners who, when being exchanged for captured British prisoners, were deliberately taken past the most heavily fortified parts of the Line, (D. Horward, *Masséna and Wellington on the Lines of Torres Vedras*, New Lights on the Peninsular War, p.128). Interestingly, Pelet (p.242) believed that a reinforcement of only 12,000 to 15,000 men would have been sufficient to attack the Lines.
22. Mackinnon, p.80. *Dispatches*, vol.6, pp.579-84.
23. *Dispatches*, vol.6, pp. 510 & 610-13. Napoleon's instructions for Soult (Mortier, V Corps) are to be found in Correspondence XX, 16,967, Napoleon to Berthier, 29 September 1810. J. Read, *War in the Peninsula*, p.161. For a detailed list of the troops occupying the Lines, see Appendix I.
24. *Dispatches*, vol.6, pp.579-84 & 555.
25. Fortescue, vol.VII, p.547.
26. Marbot, p.442. Massena to Ney, Junot, Reynier & Montbrun, 25 October 1810, quoted in Pelet, p.257. J. Barres, *Memoirs of a Napoleonic Officer*, p.147. Jock Haswell in his *The First Respectable Spy* (pp.123-6) tells the almost unbelievable tale of Colquhoun Grant of the 11th Foot, who was able to purchase considerable quantities of food from the inhabitants of the "Alto Alentejo", which is the name for the Upper, or northern, half of the province of Alentejo. Grant, somehow, smuggled both cattle and corn from the Alentejo through the French encampments in October 1810 and into the Lines!
27. *Dispatches*, vol.6, p.513.
28. Masséna to Elbé, 18 October 1810, quoted in Pelet, p.251. Napier, *History*, vol.III, p.385.
29. Marbot, p.441. D. Horward, *Wellington, Berkeley and the Royal Navy*, pp.97-8. Napier, *History*, (vol.III, pp.396-7) wrote that Beresford, who was in command of the south bank when the battery was erected, placed the artillery too far from the river-bank to be effective. This, amongst other things, led to much vitriolic, and public, correspondence between the two officers. See Beresford's *Further Strictures on those parts of Col. Napier's History of the Peninsular War* and Napier's *Justification of His Third Volume*.
30. The military criterion for daybreak was when a grey horse could be seen a mile away (J. Kincaid, *Adventures in the Rifle Brigade*, p.17). Grattan, p.49. Marbot, p.437.
31. J. Donaldson, *Recollections of the Eventful Life of a Soldier*, p.99. *A Soldier of the 71st*, pp.54-5. Napier, *History*, vol.III, p.362. Jones, MS Autobiography, pp.40-1. H. Smith, *p.37*. Sidney, pp.149-50.

Chapter 8.

1. Kincaid, *Adventures*, p.15.
2. *Dispatches*, vol.6, pp.624-5.
3. *A Soldier of the 71st*, p.56. Simmons, pp.121-3. *General Orders*, vol.2, p.230.
4. Napier, *History*, vol. III, p.393. *Dispatches*, vol.6, pp.629-30. J. Leith, *Memoirs of the Late Lieutenant-General Sir James Leith*, pp.42-4. Tomkinson, p.61.
5. *Dispatches*, vol.6, pp.632-3 & vol.7, pp.59-60. Sidney, p.151.
6. Grattan, pp.48-9. D. Richards, *The Peninsula Veterans*, p.70. Tomkinson, p.63. *Dispatches*, vol.6, pp.628-9.
7. *Dispatches*, vol.7, pp.23-4 & vol.6, p.572. Marbot, p.439.

8. Pelet, p.256. Tomkinson, p.67.
9. Tomkinson, pp.76-7.
10. D'Urban, p.169. Donaldson, p.102. R. Bremner, "The Building and Manning of the Lines of Torres Vedras", New Lights on the Peninsular War, pp. 116-8.
11. Dickson, vol.3, p.347. Ward, *Wellington's Headquarters*, p.81. *Dispatches*, vol.6, pp.520-1. R. Jones, pp.84-6. D. Gates, *The Spanish Ulcer* p.225. J. Page, *Intelligence Officer in the Peninsula*, pp.98-9.
12. L. Junot, *Memoirs*, vol.7, p.62. Tomkinson, pp.58-9. *Dispatches*, vol.6, p.554. Napier, *History*, vol.III, Appendix I, Section II. Oman, *History*, vol.III, Appendix VIII.
13. Pelet, p.323. J. Sarramon, "Marine Land Operations during the Peninsular War", *New Lights on the Peninsular War*, p.186. Marbot, p.447. The meeting of 18 February is recorded in Koch, vol.VII, pp.313-24.
14. Belmas, vol.iii, pp.470-3. *Dispatches*, vol.7, pp.175-6. Major Dickson (vol.2, p.232) described La Romana as "the soul of the Spanish cause."
15. *Dispatches*, vol.7, p.163.
16. Pelet, p.417.
17. D'Urban, p.185. Oman, *History*, vol.IV, p.83. J. Kincaid, *Random Shots from a Rifleman*, p.130. *Dispatches*, vol.7, pp.338-9.
18. Simmons, p.137. J. Cooper, *Rough Notes of Seven Campaigns*, p.53.
19. A. Pearson, *The Soldier Who Walked Away*, p.78. Picton, vol.1, pp.387-8. Donaldson, p.104. Grattan, pp.59-60. Tomkinson, pp.77-8 & 80. *Dispatches*, vol.7, pp.358-9.
20. Masséna to Berthier, 6 March 1811, quoted in Pelet, pp.411-2.
21. *Dispatches*, vol.7, p.358. Grattan, pp.57-8. Donaldson, p.106.
22. *Dispatches*, vol.7, pp.410 & 371. Masséna to Berthier, 19 March 1811, quoted in Oman, *History*, vol.IV, p.162. Marbot, p.455. The correspondence between Masséna and Ney which led to the latter's dismissal can be found in Koch, vol.VII, pp.402-12.
23. *Dispatches*, vol.7, pp.426-7. Napier, *History*, vol. III, p.491.
24. M. Thiers, *History of the Consulate & the Empire of France under Napoleon*, Vol.XII, p.216.
25. Napier, *History*, vol.III, p.520.
26. A. Bryant, *Years of Victory*, p.428. A. Craufurd, p.177.

Chapter 9.
1. *Dispatches*, vol.7, pp.455-7.
2. Oman, *History*, vol. III, Preface, vii-viii.
3. E. Longford, *Wellington – The Years of the Sword*, p.260.
4. Walker, "Masséna's Lines of March in Portugal", p.478. Donald Horward *(Battle of Buçaco, p.71)* claims that it is "safe" to assume that Masséna knew of the Boialvo road but that he chose to ignore it, preferring instead to attack Wellington. C. Raeuber ("Military Topographical Reconnaissance's in Portugal, 1810", *New Lights on the Peninsular War*, p.174) suggests that the 'Dépôt de guerre' was unwilling to send these valuable maps on a hazardous journey through guerrilla-infested Spain and Portugal.
5. Pelet, p.169. Marbot, p.418.
6. Marbot, pp.418-9.
7. Pelet, pp.135-42.
8. Marbot, p.433. Oman, *History*, vol. III, pp.456-7.
9. Leith, p.40. Oman, *History*, vol. VI, pp.65 & 68-9. Kincaid, *Adventures*, pp.13-4.
10. Koch, vol.VII, pp.19-22. Napoleon did eventually reorganise his armies in Spain to enable a concentration of forces in support of Masséna but these orders did not reach Spain until Masséna was already in retreat. See Napier, *History*, vol. III, pp.457-8 & Appendix VII, Sections 6-10.
11. Pelet, p.143.
12. *Mémoirs et Correspondance Politique et Militaire du Roi Joseph*, vol. vi, p.207. F. Firiòn, *Journal historique de la campagne de Portugal*, p.34, quoted in Horward, *Battle of Buçaco*, p.24.

Supplementary Despatches, vol.VI, pp.606-7.

13. *Dispatches,* vol.6, p.7.
14. *Supplementary Despatches, ibid.* Marbot, p.429.
15. Napier, *History,* vol.III, p.338.
16. *Dispatches,* vol.7, pp.306-7.
17. *Dispatches,* vol.6, pp.494 & 513.
18. Oman, *History,* vol. III, p.162,
19. *Dispatches,* vol.6, pp.470-6 & 535-7. *Supplementary Despatches,* vol.VI, pp.606-7. Marquis of Londonderry, *Story of the Peninsular War,* p.187.
20. D. Gates, *The Spanish Ulcer,* p.225, states that Wellington's "scorched earth" stratagem "claimed the lives of perhaps 50,000 Portuguese peasants in 1810".
21. *Dispatches,* vol.7, pp.104-5. J. Jones, p.188.
22. *Dispatches,* vol.6, pp.579-84 & 555-6.
23. Oman, *History,* vol. III, pp.456-8.
24. Letter to an unnamed correspondent, reproduced in Longford, *Wellington,* p.259.
25. *Supplementary Despatches,* vol VII, p.176. *Dispatches,* vol.8, p.118.
26. *Dispatches,* vol.8, p.580. J. Grehan, *The Forlorn Hope,* p.66.
27. J. Jones (p.107) states that by 1812 the Lines were "as perfect as they could be made". Wellington also planned to link two rivers (presumably the Arruda and the Zizandre) with a defensive canal of a depth sufficient to float ships of 300 tons. See Norris & Bremner, p.15.
28. *Dispatches,* vol.7, p.59.
29. *Dispatches,* vol.5, pp.556-9.
30. *Dispatches,* vol.9, p.170. Wellington to Bathurst, 21 July 1812, *Dispatches,* vol.9, pp.296-8.
31. *Dispatches,* vol.9, p.270.
32. Longford, *Wellington,* p.307.
33. F. Foch, *The Principles of War,* p.283.

Bibliography and Source Information

MANUSCRIPT AND UNPUBLISHED SOURCES IN THE ROYAL ENGINEERS MUSEUM & LIBRARY

The Diaries of Major J.T. Jones RE when he was Brigade Major.
The Autobiography of Major-General Sir John T. Jones RE.
Packet of letters from Captain George Ross RE to Sir H. Dalrymple 1810-11.
Commanding Engineer's Letter Books of Lt.-Col. Richard Fletcher.
Collection of Letters from Captain (later Lt. Gen.) Henry Goldfinch.
Follow the Sapper. Typescript by P.H. Kealy.
Military Engineering in the Peninsular War. A digest of references compiled by Major J.T. Hancock RE.

PRIMARY PUBLISHED SOURCES

Aitchison, J. *An Ensign in the Peninsular War – the letters of John Aitchison.* Edited by W.F.K. Thompson. (London 1981).
Anonymous *A Soldier of the Seventy-First.* Edited by C. Hibbert. (London 1975).
Barres, J.B. *Memoirs of a Napoleonic Officer.* (London 1925).
Beamish, N.L. *History of the King's German Legion.* (London 1832).
Beresford W. *Further Strictures on those parts of Col Napier's History of the Peninsular War.* (London 1831).
Burghersh, Lord. *Memoir of the Early Campaigns of the Duke of Wellington in Portugal and Spain. By an officer employed in his army.* (London 1820).
Burgoyne, J. *Life and Correspondence of Field Marshal Sir John Burgoyne.* Edited by George Wrottesley (London 1873).
Castlereagh, R. *Correspondence, Despatches and other papers of Viscount Castlereagh.* (London 1850-3).
Colville, J. *The Portrait of a General – a chronicle of the Napoleonic Wars.* (Salisbury 1980). Cooper, J.S. *Rough Notes of Seven Campaigns in Portugal, Spain, France and America During the Years 1809-1815.* (Carlisle 1914; reprinted Staplehurst, 1996).
Costello, E. *The Peninsular and Waterloo Campaigns.* (London 1967).
Creevey, T. *The Creevey Papers. A selection from the correspondence & diaries of the late Thomas Creevey.* Edited by H. Maxwell. Vol. I (London 1904).
Croker, J.W. *The Croker Papers – correspondence and diaries of the late … Secretary to the Admiralty from 1809 to 1830.* (London 1885).
Dickson, A. *The Dickson Manuscripts, being diaries, letters, maps, account books, with various other papers.* Edited by Major J.H. Leslie. (London 1908).
Donaldson, J. *Recollections of the Eventful Life of a Soldier, by the late Joseph Donaldson, Sergeant in*

the Ninety Fourth Scots Brigade. (Edinburgh 1845).

Du Casse, *Mémoirs et Correspondance Politique et Militaire du Roi Joseph.* (Paris 1855). D'Urban, B. *The Peninsular Journal of Major-General Sir Benjamin D'Urban, 1808-17.* (London 1930; reprinted by Greenhill Books, London, 1990).

Eliot, W.G. *A Treatise on the Defence of Portugal, with a military map of the country, etc.* (London 1811).

Ford, R. *A Handbook for Travellers in Spain.* (London 1845).

— *Gatherings from Spain.* (London 1906).

Foy, M.S. *History of the War in the Peninsula, under Napoleon: to which is prefixed a view of the political and military state of the four belligerent powers.* (London 1827).

— *Vie Militaire du général Foy.* Edited by M. Girod de 1'Ain. (Paris 1900).

Gleig, G.R. *The Hussar: the story of Norbert Landsheilt, Sergeant in the York Hussars and the 20th Light Dragoons.* (London 1837).

Gomm, W.M. *The Letters and Journals of Field-Marshal Sir William Maynard Gomm.* (London 1881).

Grattan, W. *Adventures with the Connaught Rangers, 1809-1814.* (London 1902; reprinted by Greenhill Books, London 1989).

Halliday, A. *Observations on the Present State of the Portuguese Army, as organised by Lieutenant-General Sir William Carr Beresford.* (London 1811).

Jones, J.T. *Account of the War in Spain, Portugal, and the South of France.* (London 1821).

— *Journal of Sieges carried on by the Army under the Duke of Wellington, in Spain, during the years 1811 to 1814; with notes and additions.* (London 1846).

— *Memoranda Relative to the Lines thrown up to cover Lisbon in 1810* (London 1829).

Jones, R. *An Engineer Officer under Wellington in the Peninsula.* Edited by H.V. Shore. (Cambridge 1986).

Junot, L. *Memoirs of Madame Junot, Duchess of Abrantes.* (London 1832).

Kincaid, J. *Adventures in the Rifle Brigade.* (London 1829; reprinted Staplehurst, 1991).

— *Random Shots from a Rifleman.* (London 1835; reprinted Staplehurst, 1998).

Koch, F. *Memoirs de Masséna.* (Paris 1850).

Leach, J. *Rough Sketches of the Life of an Old Soldier.* (London 1831).

Leith, J. *Memoirs of the Late Lieutenant-General Sir James Leith.* (London 1818).

Leith Hay, A. *A Narrative of the Peninsular War.* (London 1834).

Londonderry, Marquis of. *Story of the Peninsular War.* (London 1857).

Mackinnon, H. *A Journal of the Campaign in Portugal and Spain, etc.* (Bath 1812).

Mayne, R. & Lille, J. *A Narrative of the Campaigns of the Loyal Lusitanian Legion.* (London 1812).

Marbot, J.B. *The Memoirs of The Baron de Marbot.* Translated by A.J. Butler. (London 1893).

Napier, G.T. *Passages in the Early Military Life of General Sir George T. Napier.* (London 1886).

Napier, W.F.P. *History of the War in the Peninsula and the South of France from the year 1807 to the year 1814.* (London 1835).

— *The Life and Opinions of General Sir Charles James Napier,* Vol. I. (London 1857). Neves Costa, J.M. das. *Memória Militar respective ao Torreno ao Norte de Lisboa, Maio 1809, acrescentada com observacões e notas do mesmo autor em 1814,* (Lisbon, 1888).

Page, J. *Intelligence Officer in the Peninsula. Letters and Diaries of Major The Hon. Edward Charles Cocks 1786-1812.* (Tunbridge Wells 1986).

Pearson, A. *The Soldier Who Walked Away – autobiography of Andrew Pearson: a Peninsular veteran.* Edited by A.H. Haley. (Liverpool 1988).

Pelet, J.J. *The French Campaign in Portugal, 1810-11.* Annotated and translated by Donald Horward. (Minneapolis 1973).

Picton, T. *Memoirs of Lieutenant General Sir Thomas Picton.* Edited by H.B. Robinson. (London 1836).

Proceedings upon the Inquiry Relative to the ARMISTACE and CONVENTION etc. made and concluded in Portugal. (London 1809).

Rocca, M. de. *Memoirs of the War of the French in Spain.* (London 1815).

Schaumann, A. *On the Road with Wellington – the diary of a war commissary in the Peninsular Campaigns.* Edited and translated by A.N. Ludovici. (London 1924).

Simmons, G. *A British Rifleman – the journals of Major George Simmons during the Peninsular War and the campaign of Waterloo.* (London 1899).

Sherer, M. *Recollections of the Peninsula.* (London 1824: reprinted Staplehurst, 1996). Smith, H. *The Autobiography of Lieutenant General Sir Harry Smith.* Edited by G.C. Moore Smith. (London 1901).

Stanhope, P.H. *Notes of Conversations with the Duke of Wellington, 1831-1851.* (London 1888).

Thiebault, Baron. *The Memoirs of Baron Thiebault.* Translated & condensed by A.J. Butler. (London 1896).

Tomkinson, W. *The Diary of a Cavalry Officer in the Peninsular and Waterloo Campaigns, 1809-1815.* (London 1894).

Warre, W. *Letters from the Peninsula, 1808-12.* Edited by E. Warre. (London 1909). Wellington, A. *The Dispatches of Field Marshal the Duke of Wellington, during His Various Campaigns etc.* Edited by J. Gurwood. (London 1837-39).

— *Supplementary Despatches, Correspondence and Memoranda of Field Marshal Arthur, Duke of Wellington.* Edited by his son. (London 1857-72).

— *General Orders of the Duke of Wellington in Portugal, Spain and France from 1809 to 1814.* Compiled by J. Gurwood. (London 1839).

Wilkie, F. *Peninsular Sketches by Actors on the Scene.* (London 1845).

SECONDARY SOURCES

Aldington, R. *Wellington.* (London 1946).

Atteridge, A. *The Bravest of the Brave, Michel Ney, Marshal of France, 1769-1815.* (New York 1912).

Berkeley, A.D. (ed.). *New Lights on the Peninsular War.* Selected Papers from the International Congress on the Iberian Peninsula. (Lisbon 1991).

Birmingham, D. *A Concise History of Portugal.* (Cambridge 1993).

Bryant, A. *Years of Victory, 1802-1812.* (London 1944).

— *The Age of Elegance.* (London 1954).

Butler, L. *Wellington's Operations in the Peninsula.* (London 1904).

Chad, G.W. *Conversations of the Duke of Wellington with George William Chad.* (Cambridge 1956).

Chambers, G. *Wellington's Battlefields Illustrated: Busaco 1810.* (London 1910).

Chandler, D.G. *On the Napoleonic Wars.* (London 1994).

— "The Lines of Torres Vedras 1810-11". *History Today,* February 1978.

— *The Campaigns of Napoleon.* (New York 1966).

Connolly, T. *The history of the Corps of Royal Sappers and Miners.* (London 1855).

Craufurd, A. *General Craufurd and his Light Division.* (London 1891).

Craufurd-Hoyle, J. "Bussaco and Masséna". *Age of Napoleon* magazine, No.31.

Cusick, R. "The Eyes of the Army", *The Waterloo Journal,* Vol. 20, No.3 & Vol. 21, No.1

Duncan, F. *History of the Royal Regiment of Artillery.* Vol. II. (London 1879).

Fletcher, I. (ed). *The Peninsular War. Aspects of the Struggle for the Iberian Peninsula.* (Staplehurst 1998).

Foch, F. *The Principles of War.* Translated by Hilaire Belloc. (London 1921).

Fortescue, J. *A History of the British Army.* Vols. 6-10. (London 1935).

Francis, D. *Portugal 1715-1808.* (London 1986).

Gates, D. *The Spanish Ulcer: A History of the Peninsular War.* (London 1986).

Glover, M. *Wellington, as Military Commander.* (London 1969).

— *Wellington's Peninsular Victories.* (London 1963).

Grant & Temperley. *Europe in the 19th & 20th Centuries.* (London 1952).

Grehan, J. *The Forlorn Hope. The Battle for the Spanish Frontier 1811-12.* (London 1990).

— "The French Invasion of Portugal" "The Lines Before Lisbon". *Napoleonic Notes & Queries* magazine, No.8.

— *Age of Napoleon* magazine, Nos.19 & 20.

Griffith, P. *Wellington Commander. The Iron Duke's Generalship.* (Chichester 1985).

Guedalla, P. *The Duke.* (London 1931).

Hart, L, *The Strategy of the Indirect Approach.* (London 1941).

Haswell, J. *The First Respectable Spy. The Life and Times of Coluhoun Grant, Wellington's Head of Intelligence.* (London 1969).

Huges, Q. "Wellington and fortifications". *FORT* magazine, Vol. Fourteen, 1986.

Horward, D. D. *The Battle of Bussaco: Masséna vs. Wellington.* (Florida 1965).

— *Napoleon and Iberia. The twin sieges of Ciudad Rodrigo and Almeida, 1810.* (London 1994).

— "Wellington's Peninsular Strategy, Portugal, and the Lines of Torres Vedras". *Portuguese Studies Review* 2 (1993).

— "Andre Masséna, Prince D'Essling". *The Journal of the International Napoleonic Society,* vol. I, No. I, (1997).

— "Wellington, Berkeley and the Royal Navy: Seapower and the defence of Portugal (1808-12)". *British Historical Society of Portugal 18th Annual Report.* (Lisbon 1991).

James, L. *The Iron Duke. A military biography of Wellington.* (London 1992).

Livermore, H. *A History of Portugal.* (Cambridge 1947).

Longford, E. *Wellington – The Years of the Sword.* (London 1969).

Marshall-Cornwall, J. *Marshal Masséna.* (London 1965).

— "The Battlefield of Bussaco". *The Geographical Magazine,* July 1961.

— "The Lines of Torres Vedras". *Royal Engineers Journal,* 1961.

Nafziger, G.F. *The Armies of Spain and Portugal 1808-14.* (West Chester 1992).

Norris, A. & Bremner, R. *The Lines of Torres Vedras.* (Lisbon 1980).

Oman, Carola. *Sir John Moore.* (London 1953).

Oman, Sir Charles. *A History of the Peninsular War.* (Oxford 1902-30; reprinted by Greenhill Books, London, 1995-7).

— *Wellington's Army, 1809-14.* (London 1913).

Porter, W. *History of the Royal Corps of Engineers.* (London 1889).

Read, J. *War in the Peninsula.* (London 1977).

Richards, D.S. *The Peninsular Veterans.* (London 1975).

Robertson, I. *Portugal.* (London 1988).

Sidney, E. *Life of Lord Hill.* (London 1845).

Silva, A.A.E. *The Battle of Buçaco.* Translated by E. Leal. (Undated, Portugal).

Southey, R. *History of the Peninsular War.* (London 1823).

Thiers, M.A. *The History of the Consulate & the Empire of France under Napoleon.* Vols. 9-12. (London 1850-56).

Vetch, R. H. "The Fyers Family". RE *Journal for 1910,* Jan to June.

Vicente, A.P. "Masséna in Portugal". *British Historical Society of Portugal 17th Annual Report and Review.* (Lisbon 1990).

Walker, W. "Masséna's Lines of March in Portugal and French Routes in Northern Spain". *English Historical Review,* July 1901.

Ward, S.P.G. *Wellington's Headquarters.* (Oxford 1957).

— *Wellington.* (London 1963).

Weller, J. *Wellington in the Peninsula, 1808-14.* (London 1962).

— "Wellington's Peninsula Engineers". *Royal Engineers Journal,* 1963.

Yonge, C.D. *The Life of Arthur, Duke of Wellington.* (London 1891).

Index